P9-APQ-473

ROGET'S THESAURUS

1993 Edition

The Right Word
for
The Right Time

P.S.I. & Associates, Inc.
13322 S.W. 128th St.
Miami, FL 33186
(305) 255-7959

INFORMATION

Synonyms...

> Are those words which appear under the alphabetical listing. All have the same meaning.

Antonyms...

> Are those words which appear under the alphabetical listing in parentheses. All have the opposite or different meanings.

Parts of Speech...

> Abbreviations:
>
> n - noun
> v - verb
> adv - adverb
> adj - adjective

ISBN #1-55993-225-2

28488

A

abate-*v* decrease, diminish, lessen, wane, ebb, decline, descend, subside, melt, die away, subtract, decay, (advance, gain strength, grow, add, enlarge, increase, augment)

abdicate-*v* resign, give up, vacate, retire, renunciate, abjuration, renounce, disclaim, anarchy, relaxation, loosening, remission, (authorize, influence, despotism, command)

abduct-*v* take, catch, hook, nab, bag, clutch, sequester, distress, capture, extortion, rapacity, receive, evict, (unclench, release, replevin, return, give, restore, render)

abide-*v* persist, remain, stay, endure, maintain, keep, continue, sustain, uphold, carry on, keep one's course, (desist, cease, discontinue, halt, pause, rest)

ability-*n* ableness, cogent, competency, validity, skill, adroitness, craft, proficiency, knack, (bungle, fumble, botch, incompetent, raw, green, disability, impotent)

ablaze-*adj* afire, burning, fiery, shining, bright, heat, caloric, temperature, warmth, spark, fever, bonfire, (cool, cold, icy, dark, obscure, gloomy, somber, lightless)

able-*adj* ability, competent, efficient, enablement, capable, competent, dexterous, proficient, (incompetent, unskilled, awkward, clumsy, helpless, exhaust)

abnormal-*adj* unconventional, oddity, rarity, freak, bizarre, aberration, irregular, individuality, idiosyncrasy, (normal, conform, regular, usual, typical)

aboard-*adv* inhabit, dwell, reside, stay, lodge, presence, occupancy, attendance, inhabit, moored, roost, (absent, void, vacuum, away, gone, missing, lost, elsewhere)

abode-*n* dwelling, lodging, domicile, residence, address, home, fatherland, quarters, roost, camp, household, native land, inhabit, bivouac, native, cottage, hermitage

abolish-*v* destruction, dissolution, annihilation, nullify, annul, put an end to, tumble, topple, smash, destroy, break, undo, (produce, do, make, construct, form, fabricate)

about-*adv* reference, refer, analogy, pertaining, related, connect, associate, near, close, nigh, approximate, around, (disconnected, independent, no relation, irrelevant, remote, far, out of the way)

above-*adv* superior, exceed, transcend, out-do, pass, surpass, top, beat, over, eclipse, precede, ultra, supreme, aloft, overhead, elevated, lofty, upper, (below, underlie, down, ebb, inferior, less, smaller)

abroad-*adv* remote, removed, afar, distant, away, off, yonder, farther, further, beyond, apart, asunder, (earshot, close, near, nigh, bordering, contiguous, adjoining, adjacent, proximate, home, intimate, beside, here)

abrupt-*adj* instantly, sudden, moment, flash, burst, hasty, instantaneously, presto, (eternity, ever, perpetual, flowing, everlasting, continued, evergreen, immortal)

absence-*n* alibi, emptiness, vacuum, void, exemption, hiatus, truant, absent, vacate, withdraw, gone, missing, lost, wanting, omitted, empty, devoid, (presence, occupancy, attendance, fill, pervade, permeate)

absolve-*v* forgive, pardon, amnesty, conciliation, excuse, exonerate, release, forget, acquit, discharge, free, liberate, immune, clear, (revenge,

vengeance, avenge, vendetta, vindictive)

absorb-*v* combine, mix, join, union, unify, synthesize, incorporate, fusion, blending, embody, amalgamate, blend, merge, fuse, consolidate, import, (disperse, disembody, disintegrate, break up, unravel, evict)

abstract-*adj* sole, single, lone, solitary, desolate, by itself, epitome, analysis, digest, brief, summary, draft, note, excerpt, synopsis, textbook, prospectus, (accompanied, appendage, coexistence)

abuse-*v* hurt, ill-treat, molest, persecute, harm, injure, victimize, maul, maltreat, do violence, misuse, desecrate, (good, value, virtue, benefit, profit, do a good turn, do no harm, be good)

academic-*adj* teaching, instruction, education, discipline, lesson, curriculum, course of study, school, academy, scholastic, collegiate, educational, (misinform, render unintelligible, uncertain, conceal)

accelerate-*v* sharpen, quicken, excite, urge, stimulate, foment, speed up, spurt, rush, dash, bolt, dart, swiftly, hurry, (slow, languor, drawl, creeping, delay, move slowly, creep, crawl, lag, linger, dawdle, apply the brake, reduce the speed)

accept-v assent, admit, agree, concur, avow, own, acknowledge, ratify, approve, consent, comply, concede, confirm, allow, grant, give in, embrace an offer, satisfy, receive, take, (denial, contradiction, refuse, give, donate, bestow, cede, deliver, endow, invest, award, bequest, contribute, hand, pass)

access-n approach, path, route, near, pursue, approximate, impending, method, manner, procedure, track, (recession, withdrawal, deadlock, retirement, departure, recede, remove)

accessory-n addition, add, annexation, tack to, append, also, too, complement, addendum, supplement, adjunct, accompany, associated, with, auxiliary, partner, colleague

accident-n occurrence, misfortune, act of God, mishap, mischance, disaster, calamity, contingency, fortune, haphazard, casualty, tragedy, adversity, (well, alert, satisfactory, remedy, utility, happiness)

accomodate-v fit, suit, conform, adjust, adapt, oblige, furnish, supply,

unison, harmony, concord, concert, congruity, keeping, fitness, aptness, relevancy, adaptation, (discord, dissidence, conflict)

accompaniment-n adjunct, accessory, appendage, concomitant, attribute, context, concomitance, affix, augment, garnish, sauce, complement, (remainder, residue, remnant, rest, relic, leavings)

accomplice-n confederate, ally, abettor, accessory, assistant, colleague, recruit, adjunct, help, partner, mate, collaborator, friend, confidant, (opponent, antagonist, adversary, wrangler)

accomplish-v fulfill, do, achieve, effect, execute, perform, attain, feat, acquirement, fulfillment, performance, realization, achievement, (destruction, waste, dissolution, downfall, ruin, fall, crash)

accord-v tally, harmonize, concur, grant, bestow, acquiesce, conformity, uniformity, agreement, constancy, level, smooth, dress, (diversified, varied, irregular, uneven, rough)

account-n score, record, recital, narration, description, answerable, explicable, liable, responsible, amenable, money matters, finance,

bill, budget, tally,
(unaccountable)

accretion-*n* concretion,
adhesion, increment,
growth, accumulation,
increase, enlargement,
extension, development,
augment, (decrease,
lessening, subtraction,
reduction, shrinking, ebb)

accrue-*v* bring in, yield,
result, arise, annexation,
increase, supplement,
insertion, affix, additive,
extra, plus, further, also,
(deduction, retrenchment,
amputation, curtailment,
abrasion, deduct)

accumulate-*v* collect,
gather, hoard, increase,
assemble, amass,
collection, compilation,
levy, gathering, muster,
assembly, (dispersion,
divergence, scattering,
dissipation, spread)

accuracy-*n* preciseness,
precision, verity,
correctness, just, proper,
true, correct, exact, fact,
truth, gospel, authenticity,
veracity, honest, sober,
(error, fallacy, inexactness,
report, mistake, fault)

accustom-*v* inure, season,
familiarize, habituate,
common, general, natural,
ordinary, track, practice,
rut, groove, precedent,
(newness to, leave off,
cast off, break off, violate,
infringe)

ache-*v* smart, shoot, twinge,
hurt, pain, discomfort,

suffering, twitch,
headache, spasm, cramp,
crick, thrill, sharp, gnawing,
torment, (pleasure,
physical, sensual,
sensuous, comfort, luxury)

achievement-*n*
performance, fulfillment,
execution,
accomplishment, exploit,
feat, trace, vestige,
courage, bravery, valor,
boldness, spirit, defiance,
(cowardice, timid,
baseness, fear, faint heart)

acknowledge-*v* grant,
concede, confess, admit,
own, assent, disclose,
answer, response, reply,
retort, repartee, discover,
conclusive, satisfy,
(inquiry, search, pursuit,
review, scrutiny, analysis)

acquaint-*v* familiarize,
notify, apprise, inform, tell,
communicate, intimation,
represent, round robin,
present, case, estimate,
specification, report,
(conceal, hiding, secret,
screen, disguise,
masquerade)

acquittal-*n* exculpation,
clearance, clearing,
exoneration, discharge,
absolution, quietus,
reprieve, pardon, absolve,
release, liberate, let off,
(condemnation, accuse,
conviction, restraint)

acrid-*adj* acrimonious, tart,
pungent, bitter, severe,
caustic, biting, keen,
sharpness, roughness,

mustard, pepper, brine, stinging, unsavory, virulence, spleen, asperity, (condiment)

act-*n* ordinance, decree, deed, exploit, statute, law, edict, scene, perform, do, operate, behave, play, feign, simulate, action, doing, (inaction, passiveness, idle, misbehave, lax)

advocate-*v* recommend, counsel, suggest, prescribe, to advise, to support, advise, instruction, charge, enforce, enjoin, (intendant, husband, moderator, speaker, proctor)

aeronaut-*n* pilot, flyer, navigator, aviator, airman, aviatrix, scout, balloonist, Icarus, seaman, skipper, marine, (wayfarer, voyager, passenger, tourist, explorer, straggler, rambler)

aesthetic-*n* artistic, refined, cultured, cultivated, appealing, sensibility, physical, feeling, sensation, impression, cultivate, tudor, (opium, insensible, paralyze, blunt, callous, dull)

afar-*adv* aloof, abroad, away, distant, distance, horizon, reach, spread, remote, mundane, away, yonder, farther, apart, (nearness, proximity, adjacency, breadth, span, close, handy, home)

affair-*n* event, business, occurrence, matter, concern, question, eventuality, incident, transaction, proceeding, phenomenon, advent, (impending, destined, loom, threaten, await)

affectation-*n* insincerity, pretension, airs, modishness, charlatanism, quackery, artificiality, (modesty, diffidence, timidity, shyness, humility, demureness)

affection-*n* bent, quality, malady, ailment, fondness, tenderness, devotion, nature, spirit, tone, temper, habit, soul, turn, bosom, breast, heart, (experience, response, impression, emotion)

affirmation-*n* ratification, corroboration, allegation, confirmation, assertion, profession, avowal, emphasis, positiveness, dogmatism, (negation, uncertainty, refutation, disclamation)

afraid-*adj* apprehensive, fearful, timorous, alarmed, cowardly, terrified, uncertainty, demure, suspense, caprice, levity, dilly dally, boggle, (determination, resolve, conclude)

agency-*n* causality, method, impelling force, force, function, office, exercise, maintenance, work, swing, action, official, acting, operant, (inaction, powerlessness)

agent-*n* servant, proxy, doer, actor, operator, perpetrator, executor, representative, go-between, mediate, deputy, consignee, trustee, nominee, (deputy, substitute, vice, proxy, minister)

aggravation-*n* heightening, intensification, vexation, annoyance, acridity, irritation, render worse, acerbate, worsen, (relief, alleviation, mitigation, assuagement)

aggression-*n* inroad, encroachment, invasion, attack, assault, charge, offense, incursion, invasion, against, impugn, assume, harry, invade, (defense, guard, resistance, safeguard)

agile-*adj* quick, lithe, active, nimble, spry, brisk, activity, liveliness, spirit, dash, energy, smartness, alacrity, industry, movement, bustle, stir, fuss, (inactivity, inertness, dullness, languor, sleep, sound)

agitation-*n* jar, jolt, shake, trepidation, shock, flutter, perturbation, disconcertion, confusion, turmoil, turbulence, tumult, stir, ripple, jog, dance, flutter, (order, rest, stability)

agony-*n* anguish, pain, suffering, torment, torture, smart, twitch, spasm, headache, cramp, discomfort, throb, piercing, rack, (pleasure, sensual, comfort, luxury, enjoy, at ease, cozy, snug)

agreement-*n* understanding, accord, keeping, unison, reconcilement, union, harmony, consonance, (disagreement, dissent, inequality, disharmony, unconformity, discord)

agriculture-*n* agrarian, rural, farming, husbandry, cultivation, tillage, gardening, florist, field, meadow, flower, plantation, (taming, breeding, aviary, fishery, trainer)

aid-*v* assistance, help, succor, promotion, cooperation, furtherance, advocacy, defense, patronage, countenance, alleviation, support, lift, advance, relief, rescue, (hindrance, opposition, neglect)

ailment-*n* affection, illness, disorder, disease, malady, sickness, infirmity, complaint, attack, seizure, stroke, canker, virus, plague, pestilence, (health, soundness, vigor, perfect, robust, bloom, recover)

alarm-*n* fear, dread, scare, fright, panic, warning, signal, summons, excite, agitate, arouse, startle, affright, terrify, appall, caution, prediction, omen, beacon, give notice, beware, sentinel, watchman

allay-v ease, assuage, lessen, mitigate, slacken, pacification, accommodation, arrangement, adjustment, terms, compromise, armistice, suspension of hostilities, (warfare, fighting, crusade)

allegiance-n duty, homage, obedience, loyalty, observance, compliance, submission, passiveness, devotion, obey, control, follow, service, (insubordination, violation, non compliance)

alliance-n connection, affinity, compact, league, cooperation, concurrence, complicity, collusion, union, concur, (opposition, antagonism, counter action, cross-fire, clashing)

allot-v divide, share, assign, distribute, apportion, appropriation, portion, contingent, lot, measure, dole, pittance, ration, ratio, quota, allowance

allow-v admit, concede, grant, tolerate, let, suffer, permit, permission, leave, concession, grace, dispensation, release, authorization, warranty, (inhibition, disallowance, interdict, embargo)

allowance-n salary, grant, stipend, concession, pay, contribution, reward, remittance, discount, apportion, allot, consign, dispensation, division, deal, cast, share, portion, administer

allude-v connote, imply, infer, suggest, declaratory, intelligible, literal, synonymous, implied, explicit, latent, expressive, understand, interpret, (nonsense, jargon, gibberish, jabber, mere words)

allure-v tempt, attract, draw, desire, wish, fancy, fantasy, want, need, exigency, leaning, bent, partiality, propensity, willingness, liking, love, fondness, relish, (neutral, indifferent, cold, frigid)

alms-n charity, gratuity, grant, dole, giving, bestowal, donation, presentation, delivery, consignment, dispensation, investment, award, (receiving, acquisition, acceptance, admission)

alongside-adv beside, abreast, side by side, broadside on, neck and neck, on a level, parallel, nearness, proximity, adjacency, (distance, remoteness, elongation, offing, background)

aloof-adj distant, remote, reserved, unneighborly, secluded, away, afar, beyond, further, abroad,

(near, nigh, close, adjoining, handy, intimate)

alternate-*v* periodically, recurrence, succession, taking of turns, changeable, inconsistency, instability, mobility, unstable, (stability, unchangeable, consistent)

altitude-*n* tallness, height, loftiness, perpendicular, distance, elevation, giant, eminence, pitch, loftiness, prominence, (low, flat, level, squat, prostrate)

amateur-*n* novice, dilettante, volunteer, nonprofessional, unaffected, bad taste, dowdy, shabby, ill bred, untamed, (refined, professional, tasteful, pure, dainty)

amatory-*adj* erotic, ardent, amorous, loving, fondness, liking, regard, cherish, hug, prize, adore, suitor, admirer, sweetheart, (hatred, coolness, grudge, bitterness)

ambiguous-*adj* obscure, vague, undefined, equivocal, uncertainty, doubt, hesitation, suspense, dubious, indecisive, confused, (certainty, surety, reliable, positive)

ambition-*n* resolve, design, aspiration, longing, zeal, pretentious, bold, desirous, zealous, soaring, aspiring, intent, purpose, (speculation, venture,

chance, risk)

ambush-*n* ambuscade, trap, pitfall, lurking place, screen, cover, recess, shade, curtain, blind, cloak, cloud, (reveal, lift up, remove, acknowledge, expose, bear)

amenable-*adj* liable, responsible, yielding, accountable, answerable, duty, morality, conscience, decalogue, (fault, nonobservance, nonperformance)

amend-*v* improve, correct, rectify, change, mend, promote, cultivate, advance, forward, enhance, foster, bolster, brighten, (wreck, decay, decline, erosion, blight)

amiable-*adj* kindly, affable, agreeable, pleasant, courtesy, respect, behavior, politeness, gentility, polish, presence, (rude, insult, ill breeding, discourtesy)

ample-*adj* roomy, spacious, large, abundant, considerable, greatness, magnitude, size, immensity, enormity, might, strength, fullness, (smallness, little, diminutive, paltry)

amusement-*n* pleasure, sport, solace, pastime, entertainment, diversion, distraction, relaxation, solace, fun, frolic, merriment, (tedious, weariness, nausea)

analogy-*n* resembling, like, associated, related, correspondent, parallel, similar, semblance, affinity, agreement, look like, (diversity, disparity, difference, novelty)

analysis-*n* decomposition, inquiry, consideration, study, disintegration, break-up, investigation, dissection, resolution, dissolve, (combination, mixture, union, incorporation)

analyst-*n* recorder, historian, chronicler, compiler, notary, clerk, registrar, secretary, scribe, biographer, time keeper, almanac, calendar, journal

ancestry-*n* line, lineage, family tree, family, race, descent, parent, father, dad, pedigree, tribe, clan, descent, parental, forefathers, maternity, mother

anchor-*n* stay, grapnel, safeguard, protection, hold, kedge, killick, link, connective, hyphen, bracket, bridge, (separation, parting, segregation, divorce, break)

anchorage-*n* harbor, safety, roadstead, mooring, refuge, lodgement, establishment, settlement, place, station, (displace, dislodge, exile, remove, unload)

ancient-*adj* aged, hoary,

antique, archaic, old, venerable, antiquated, maturity, decline, decay, primitive, classic, (newness, novelty, youth, modernism)

anecdote-*n* story, tale, sketch, account, narrative, description, statement, report, summary, brief, relate, recite, recount, sum up, tell, give, graphic, epic

angel-*n* divine messenger, ministering spirits, invisible helpers, good man, worthy, model, paragon, hero, demigod, innocent, saint, (bad man, evil doer, sinner, wicked)

anger-*n* enrage, inflame, arouse, irritate, annoy, exasperate, provoke, offend, infuriate, resentment, displeasure, wrath, indignation, (favorite, pet, idol, fondness, love, dear)

angle-*n* guise, aspect, phase, crook, fork, obliquity, cusp, bend, notch, ankle, measurement, elevation, distance, triangle, square, diamond

animate-*v* actuate, excite, cheer, enliven, encourage, inspire, motion, action, intention, inducement, draw, inspire, (dissuade, reluctance, detour, hold, repel)

annex-*v* add, attach, join, affix, junction, union, unite, lump, fix, bind, fasten,

stitch, buckle, button, knit,
lock, (disjoined,
disconnect, disengage,
divorce, cut, adrift)

annihilate-v exterminate,
eradicate, destroy, end,
wreck, demolish,
extinction, blow, doom,
ravage, sacrifice, abolish,
perish, (evolve, bring forth,
birth, produce, perform)

announce-v report, declare,
predict, foretell, tell, inform,
proclaim, assert, notice,
communicate, acquaint,
(conceal, hide, mystify,
masquerade, cunning)

annoy-v trouble, bother,
vex, harass, molest,
disturb, irritate, tantalize,
worry, badness, hurtful,
inflict, harm, injure,
oppress, persecute,
(produce, profit, benefit,
goodness, merit)

annul-v nullification,
diffuseness, cancellation,
counter order, invalidation,
retraction, repeal,
abolishment, rescission,
abrogation, (commission,
delegate, consign, assign)

anoint-v rub, lubricate,
salve, oil, divinity, wisdom,
goodness, justice, truth,
unity, eternity,
preservation, (scourge,
halter, stake, truncheon,
stocks)

anonymous-adj
unacknowledged,
unknown, unnamed,
misnomer, alias,
pseudonym, nickname,

(nomination, designation,
title, head, namesake)

answer-n reply, response,
acknowledgment, rebuttal,
retort, return, respond,
say, rebut, acknowledge,
echo, replication,
(question, inquiry, request,
search)

antagonism-n animosity,
antipathy, hostility,
opposition, enmity,
counteraction, polarity,
clashing, collision,
resistance, (concurrence,
cooperation, agreement)

antecede-v preexist,
precede, go before,
precedence, first, head,
lead, introduce, prefix,
prelude, preface, former,
before, (sequence, after,
succeed, follow, suffix)

anticipate-v expect, await,
forestall, be early, surmise,
predict, preparation,
provide, disposition,
forecast, cultivate,
(disqualify, unfitted,
shiftless, unprepared)

antidote-n emetic, remedy,
counter poison, help,
antiseptic, corrective,
sedative, recipe,
prescription, (poison, virus,
venom, scourge)

antipathy-n repugnance,
clashing, opposition,
abhorrence, detestation,
dislike, incompatibility,
reluctance, backward,
disgust, (desire, wish,
want, need, longing)

apathetic-adj insensible,

indifferent, cold, unfeeling, impassive, insensibility, no desire, disregard, no interest, (sensible, morale, softness, warm, tender)

ape-n simian, monkey, mimic, mock, simulate, imitate, copying, simulation, semblance, mirror, reflect, repeat, echo, match, follow, counterfeit

apparatus-n machinery, outfit, equipment, contrivance, instrument, engineer, mechanism, organ, appliance, gear, tackle, implement, utensil

apparent-adj perceptible, obvious, seeming, clear, patent, manifest, visible, appearing, conspicuous, distinct, evidence, (invisible, dim, mysterious, confused)

appearance-n sight, show, phenomenon, prospect, representation, display, stage setting, exposure, (vanishing, fading, evanescence, departure, occultation, withdrawal)

appease-v satisfy, allay, pacify, placate, quiet, soothe, mollify, pleasure, moderate, soften, tranquilize, swag, lull, compose, (violent, sharp, quicken, excite, incite)

append-v subjoin, add, affix, attach, annex, supplement, subjoin, reinforce, augment, accrue, introduce, insert,

more, include, (subtraction, amputate, abscind, pare)

appetite-n passion, craving, want, hunger, longing, desire, wish, need, exigency, inclination, greed, covetous, ravenous, (anorexia, apathy, listless, lackadaisical)

applause-n acclamation, praise, plaudit, acclaim, clapping, approbation, commendation, cheer, good word, blessing, approval, (dislike, reprehend, chide, admonish)

applicable-adj convenient, pertinent, suitable, appropriate, relevant, adequate, service, available, ready, tangible, advantageous, (useless inefficacy, worthless)

appoint-v nominate, ordain, assign, establish, prescribe, commission, delegate, consign, authorize, accredit, engage, hire, (annulment, nullification, conceal, cancel)

apportionment-n allotment, assignment, consignment, partition, allocation, division, distribution, disperse, spread, intersperse, (crowd, muster, levy, gather, flood)

appraise-v rate, judge, estimate, assess, value, survey, reckon, measure, standard, rule, compass, gage, gauge, yard, meter, coordinates, ordinate, latitude

apprehend-v arrest, seize, imprison, dread, distrust, perceive, see, understand, known, ascertain, recognize, realize, (ignorant, unexplored, bewilderment)

approach-v drawing near, advance, access, advent, admission, convergence, pursuit, drift, gain upon, converge, (avoidance, recession, go away)

approbation-n sanction, approval, advocacy, favor, renown, kudos, popularity, compliment, commendation,eulogy, homage, (detraction, disrepute, disapprobation)

appropriate-adj becoming, fit, suitable, timely, proper, adapted, agreeable, expedient, advisable, convenient, worthwhile, applicable, (undesirable, unfit, clumsy, awkward)

apt-adj clever, quick, dexterous, skillful, influence, important, rampant, dominant, regnant, predominant, support, (powerless, uninfluential, irrelevant, inertness)

arbitrar-adj overbearing, imperious, harsh, tyrannical, dictatorial, peremptory, domineering, despotic, austere, (lenient, mild, gentle, tolerant, forbearing)

argument-n data, case, discussion, debate, controversy, wangling, contention, dispute, examine, pros and cons, (deceptive, sophistical, irrelevant, evasive)

aristocrat-n patrician, lord, noble, nobleman, empire, monarchy, royalty, (democracy, demagogy, republic, magistrate, socialism, anarchy, relaxation, toleration, freedom)

arrangement-n provision, preparation, array, assortment, allotment, distribution, analysis, organize, sort, distribute, (disorder, disarrangement, disturb, confuse)

arrive-v advent, coming, debarkation, landing, reception, welcome, goal, destination, harbor, haven, port, (egress, departure, embarkation, exit, leaving)

arrogant-adj airs, swagger, haughtiness, pretension, ostentation, insolence, take, demand, usurp, appropriate, seize, assume, dignity, pride, self-respect

arsenal-n armory, depot, magazine, storehouse, arms, weapons, armament, partisan, battery, gunnery, missile, shrapnel

artful-adj adroit, tricky, crafty designing, sly, shrewd, dexterous, falsity,

deception, untruth, lying,
misrepresentation, perjury,
forgery, (frankness,
truthfulness, sincerity)
artificial-*adj* false, sham,
unnatural, affected,
counterfeit, imitation,
deception, untruth,
delusion, collusion,
treachery, trick, cheat,
(truthfulness, veracity,
frankness, honesty)
artistic-*adj* talented,
beautiful, graceful,
accomplished, cultural,
exquisite, aesthetic, skillful,
clever, ability, ingenuity,
capacity, (unskillful,
stupidity, indiscretion)
ask-*v* implore, beseech,
inquire, interrogate, beg,
entreat, request, question,
search, research, pursuit,
review, scrutiny, sifting,
(answer, respond, reply,
rebut, retort)
askew-*adj* oblique, crooked,
awry, distorted, inclination,
slope, slant, leaning,
beveled, tilt, bias, twist,
swag, oblique, descend,
decline
ass-*n* dolt, booby, donkey,
fool, idiot, wiseacre,
simpleton, ninny, oaf, lout,
loon, addle, innocent,
babbler, (sage, wise man,
mastermind, thinker,
authority)
assassin-*n* cutthroat, killer,
murderer, slayer,
homicide, manslaughter,
slay, butcher, victimize,
massacre, strangle, stifle,

(alive, breathe, respire)
assert-*v* allege, claim,
avow, maintain, state,
affirm, belief, credence,
credit, assurance, faith,
trust, confidence,
dependence, (misbelief,
discredit, infidelity, dissent,
retraction)
astringent-*adj* styptic, sour,
tart, austere, binding,
contraction, reduction,
lessening, shrinking,
collapse, decrease, (large,
expand, widen, enlarge,
grow)
astute-*adj* acute, bright,
shrewd, quick, intelligent,
capacity, comprehension,
intellect, sagacity,
judgment, cunning, brains,
(imbecility, dull,
incompetence, idiocy)
athletic-*adj* acrobatic,
strong, robust, powerful,
gymnastic, strength,
energy, vigor, force, main,
spring, elasticity, tone,
(weakness, debility,
relaxation, languor)
atonement-*n*
indemnification, expiation,
redemption, conciliation,
propitiation, recompense,
compromise, (impenitence,
obduracy, callousness)
attack-*v* encroachment,
onset, onslaught,
encounter, assault, charge,
aggression, thrust, kick,
punch, assail, invade,
(defense, protection,
guard, shield)
attention-*n* alertness, heed,

observance, intentness, scrutiny, study, mindfulness, thought, consideration, reflection, (inattention, neglect, oversight, disregard)

audacity-*n* overconfidence, gall, impudence, temerity, insolence, rashness, imprudence, indiscretion, presumption, (caution, discretion, calculation, deliberation)

auspicious-*adj* fortunate, favorable, propitious, promising, expedient, occasion, opportunity, suitable, proper, (unsuitable, improper, lose, waste)

authority-*n* authorization, power, warrant, right, dominion, dictation, command, influence, facts, evidence, collateral, (laxity, obedience, servant, submission)

auxiliary-*adj* assistant, collaborator, adjuvant, helping, aiding, ancillary, support, lift, favor, relief, rescue, ministry, aid, (prevention, stoppage, enemy, opponent)

avail-*v* benefit, profit, serve, succeed, suffice, usefulness, adequacy, conduce, gainful, advantageous, valuable, (inadequacy, unskillful, lost, seek)

averse-*adj* reluctant, loath, opposed, counter, unwillingness, renitency, reluctance, indifference, backward, slowness, (willing, mind, heart, incline, eager)

await-*v* contemplate, impend, anticipate, expectation, approach, future, coming, heritage, posterity, close, next, eventual, (past, gone, former, ancient, antiquity)

award-*v* adjudication, compensation, bestowal, conferment, decision, giving, donation, presentation, accordance, delivery, endowment, (receiving, acquisition, acceptance, admission)

awkward-*adj* unskillful, ungainly, clumsy, ungraceful, incompetency, inability, inexperience, fumble, boggle, blunder, flounder, stumble, (skill, expert, craft, competence)

B

babble-*v* chatter, prattle, rave, gibber, murmur, gurgle, gossip, empty sound, nonsense, jargon, gibberish, jabber, bombast, (meaning, expression, bearing, substantial)

backsliding-*adv* apostasy, retrogression, lapse, countermovement, regression, retreat, withdrawal, retirement, recession, reflection, (progression, advance, ongoing, headway)

backward-*adv* delayed, dull, stagnant, tardy, loath, disinclined, reluctant, remiss, retrograde, unwillingness, reluctance, (willingness, punctual, inclination, leaning)

bad-*adj* sinful, imperfect, rancid, unsuitable, wicked, tainted, hurtful, virulence, injurious, deleterious, noxious, aggrieve, oppress, (good, excellence, merit, virtue, worth)

baffle-*v* outwit, confound, check, balk, frustrate, foil, nonplus, restrict, restraint, blockade, hindrance, obstacle, drawback, (assistance, help, support, lift, advance)

bag-*n* container, pouch, sack, protrude, sag, capture, entrap, catch, receptacle, enclosure, receiver, compartment, sac, pocket, sheath, satchel

bait-*n* worry, badger, lure, trap, decoy, harass, deception, falseness, untruth, fraud, deceit, misrepresentation, delusion, juggling, (veracity, truthfulness, sincerity)

balance-*n* evenness, scales, equilibrium, steadiness, parallel, match, compare, contrast, identification, collate, confront, (crooked, uneven, unbalanced)

balk-*v* shy, stop, back, thwart, disappoint, foil, frustrate, hindrance, deception, falseness, untruth, fraud, deceit, trick, cheat, (true, frank, open, candor, sincerity)

ball-*n* hop, dance, party, shot, sphere, globe, projectile, roundness, cylinder, drum, rotund, spheroid

balm-*n* ointment, balsam moderation, gentleness, calmness, relaxation, mitigation, lullaby, sedative, (violence, vehemence, might, turbulence)

banish-*v* expatriate, exile, dismiss, expel, eject, exclude, punish, emission, evacuation, drainage, reject, discard, cut, (admit, introduce, inject, insertion, absorb)

bare-*adj* simple, mere, nude, naked, undraped, empty, destitute, unfurnished, disclose, uncover, reveal, expose, (cover, screen, shake, full, furnish)

bark-*n* skin, rind, shell, cortex, howl, yelp, yap, bay, cry, growl, yip, roar, bellow, grunt, snort, squeak, purr, mew, croak, moo

barren-*adj* arid, sterile, unfertile, unprofitable, fruitless, worthless, impotence, waste, desert, unproductive, inoperative,

(fertility, multiplication, productive, generate)

barter-v trade, exchange, bargaining, swap, traffic, marketing, interchange, reciprocation, shuffle, retaliate, (substitution, supplanting, alternative)

base-n groundwork, footing, foundation, foothold, substratum, basic, lowest, fundamental, platform, dishonesty, disgrace, shabbiness, (integrity, rectitude, honesty, faith)

bashful-adj sheepish, modest, timid, diffident, shy, constrained, humility, difference, reserve, nervous, (conceit, confidence, approbation, applause)

bear-v yield, hold, sustain, suffer, feel, tolerate, carry, transport, convey, transfer, deportation, carriage, conveyance, delegate, consign

beat-v defeat, conquer, pulsate, throb, hit, strike, bruise, batter, overcome, accent, rhythm, pulse, track, course, (break down, collapse, fail, lose ground)

beauty-n loveliness, grace, elegance, symmetry, comeliness, fairness, attractiveness, (ugliness, deformity, inelegance, distortion)

becoming-adj proper, fit, attractive, seemly, ornamental, decorous,

beam, bloom, grace, (unfit, clumsy, awkward, objectionable)

beg-v plead, petition, ask alms, implore, beseech, crave, request, motion, overture, appeal, (depreciation, protest, receive, mediation)

beginning-n start, onset, commencement, introduction, prelude, prologue, debut, outbreak, outset, source, rudiment, genesis, cause, introductory, prefatory, initiative, inaugural, (end, rear, sequel)

belief-n faith, assurance, credence, trust, hope, dependence, conviction, persuasion, conclusion, dogma, theory, principle, (doubt, unbelief, uncertainty)

belligerent-adj disputatious, pugnacious, quarrelsome, warlike, fighting, hostilities, mobilize, armed, combative, (pacify, composed, reconcile)

benefactor-n protector, savior, patron, guardian, guardian angel, altruist, supporter, (evildoer, opponent)

benefit-n avail, behalf, gain, profit, advantage, aid, assist, serve, improve, helpful, valuable, useful, utility, (useless, inadequacy, lose, waste)

benevolence-n charity, love, kindness,

unselfishness,
philanthropy, humanity,
tenderness, amiability,
mercy, (malevolence)

bereavement-n destitution,
loss, deprivation, affliction,
death, decease, release,
departure, perish, expire,
(alive, respire, living, lively)

besiege-v circumscribe,
storm, surround, hedge,
beleaguer, attack, request,
ask, beg, crave, prey,
petition, invite,
(depreciation, intercession,
protest, receive)

betray-v deceive, divulge,
ensnare, trick, reveal, let
slip, disclosure, discover,
breathe, break, split,
acknowledge,
(concealment, cover,
screen, mask, shade)

bewilder-v stagger, daze,
dazzle, perplex, confuse,
mystify, confound, puzzle,
wonder, marvel, astonish,
amaze, (expectance,
common, ordinary)

bewitch-v hypnotize,
charm, fascinate, enchant,
inveigle, incentive,
provocation, induce,
inspire, stimulate,
(discouragement, damper,
dissuade)

bias-n prejudice, tendency,
inclination, warp, slope,
prepossession, proneness,
bent, turn, tone, conduce,
dispose

bid-v invite, ask, proffer,
direct, order, enjoin,
instruct, summon, call,

offer, presentation, tender,
motion, present, move,
(refusal, rejection, decline,
repulse)

bigot-n fanatic, dogmatist,
iconoclast, formalist,
Pharisee, misconception,
bias, warp, twist, partial,
narrow, (result, conclusion,
judge, deduce, derive)

bind-v restrain, secure,
tighten, force, fasten, join,
union, junction, associate,
closeness, attach, affix,
link, fetter, (sunder, divide,
sever, cut, cleave)

bisection-n divergence,
bifurcation, branching, half,
separation, split,
(duplication, iteration)

biting-adj nipping, keen,
pungent, piquant, sharp,
telling, forceful, irritate,
pinch, prick, gripe,
painfulness, trouble,
(pleasurable, agreeable,
flatter, enchantment)

blacken-v defame, blot,
malign, besmirch, smudge,
detract, defamation,
scandal, slander, liable,
criticism, decry, derogate,
(flattery, humor, smooth)

blemish-n deformity, taint,
disfigurement, failing,
defacement, defect,
imperfection, mar, sully,
damage, deform, tarnish,
(improvement, ornament,
perfection)

blend-v compound,
combine, mix, fuse,
amalgamate, cross,
merge, interbreed, union,

synthesis, unite, consolidate, (analysis, dissection, decompose, resolve)

blessing-*n* approbation, boon, Godsend, benefit, benediction, approval, sanction, advocacy, esteem, (dislike, censure, object, disapprove)

blight-*n* rot, corruption, decay, impairment, foil, blast, thwart, deterioration, recession, decrease, degenerate, (improvement, mend, elevation, build)

blind-*adj* sightless, unseeing, inattentive, shade, screen, artifice, ruse, pretext, ambush, subterfuge, (luminary, light, flame, see, sight, candle)

bloat-*v* puff up, swell, expand, dilate, distend, increase, extend, spread, obesity, inflation, larger, (reduction, lessening, shrinking, collapse)

block-*n* street, terrace, row, lump, mass, hinder, impede, check, obstruct, prevent, preclude, hindrance, stricture, (support, lift, advance, favor, rescue)

bloom-*n* prosper, blossom, flower, glow, flourish, thrive, be in health, prosperity, welfare, affluence, luck, (adversity, failure, mishap, rot, disaster)

bodily-*adj* material, physical, corporeal,

substantial, entirely, completely, wholly, en masse, (immaterial, spiritual, unearthly)

bogus-*adj* sham, fake, false, counterfeit, spurious, fraudulent, pretended, deception, untruth, deceit, trick, cheat, (veracity, truth, sincerity, honesty)

bold-*adj* daring, intrepid, courageous, fearless, forward, dauntless, project, prominence, protrude, (depress, hollow, concave, vaulted)

border-*n* boundary, brim, rim, margin, frontier, edge, verge, brink, flange, side, lip, threshold, portal, fringe, (enclosure, wrapper, barrier)

bore-*v* pierce, drill, cloy, annoy, diameter, caliber, dullard, pest, hole, puncture, perforation, passage, canal, (close, blockade, plug, stop)

bottomless-*adj* unending, abysmal, unfathomable, depth, depression, shaft, well, crater, deepen, buried, (shallowness, shoals, superficial)

bound-*adj* spring, vault, jump, confine, circumscribe, limit, restrain, swiftness, spurt, rush, dash, race, lively, gallop, (slowness, creeping, loiterer, retire)

bounty-*n* subsidy, grant, generosity, liberality, munificence, benevolence,

giving, donation,
consignment, charity,
(receiving, acquire,
assignee)

braid-v plait, interweave,
interlace, intertwine,
joining, union, unite, bind,
attach, fix, splice, truss,
tether, (disjoin, disconnect,
disengage, separate)

branch-n wing, arm,
member, ramification,
offshoot, limb, bough, twig,
fork, divide, bifurcate,
diverge, radiate

brand-n stamp, stain, sort,
kind, grade, stigma,
firebrand, burning,
cauterization, ignite,
(cooling, refresh, congeal,
starve)

bravado-n boasting, bluster,
vaunting, braggadocio,
flourish, bombast, brag,
resonance, exult, crow

breadth-n broadness, width,
expanse, amplitude,
spaciousness, tread, span,
reach, bore, caliber,
thickness

break-v fracture, shatter,
sever, rend, violate, tame,
transgress, infringe,
subdue, interruption,
interval, gap, (adjoin,
touch, contact, adhere,
coincide)

breathe-v inhale, respire,
live, exist, divulge, utter,
whisper, disclose, puff,
blow, dust, blast, breeze,
gale, blowing, fanning

brevity-n briefness,
shortness, succinctness,

terseness, conciseness,
little, curtail, abridge, curt,
compact, stubby, (long,
length, span, elongate)

bribe-n graft, price,
allurement, seduction,
hush-money, recompense,
fee, corrupt, suborn, tempt,
tip

bright-adj vivid, intense,
deep, intelligent, apt,
clever, lustrous, radiant,
luminous, flashing,
glistening, glowing, brilliant

brisk-adj alert, lively, swift,
quick, nimble, velocity, fly,
gallop, vanish, brief, quick,
sudden, short, spasmodic,
cursory, (long, eternity,
persistence)

bristling-adj sullen, angry,
perverse, thorny, spiny,
spiked, sharpness, barbed,
horned, nib, tooth, (dull,
bluntness, obtuse, bluff)

brittleness-n frailness,
fragility, delicateness,
splintery, crack, snap, split,
splinter, crumble,
(toughness, strength,
tenacious, resisting)

broadcast-v diffuse, scatter,
disseminate, utter, spread,
disperse, sow, dispense,
disband, dispel,
(assemblage, collection,
levy, gathering)

broken-v shattered, divided,
disconnected, docile,
infirm, gentle,
domesticated, weakness,
languor, fragility, (strength,
power, energy, vigor)

bubble-n sparkle, gurgle,

buckle-n twist, bend, warp, fastening, fastener, clasp, link, junction, union, unite, bond, bridge, braid, hook, girdle, (disjoin, disconnect, divorce, cut)

bulk-n amount, volume, measure, largeness, mass, expanse, greater part, whole, integrity, collectiveness, lump, (division, segment, fragment, piece)

bulletin-n statement, report, journal, news, information, word, advice, dispatch, publicity, notice, (secret, mystery, riddle, conundrum)

bully-n brawler, tyrant, roisterer, swaggerer, threaten, bluster, domineer, browbeat, combatant, litigant, competitor, rival, (submissive, surrender, resignation)

buoyant-adj light, floating, resilient, springy, sanguine, foamy, rise, hover, spire, soar, tower, swim, surge, (descent, fall, drop, downfall, tumble)

bureaucracy-n officialism, red-tape, authority, influence, power, command, empire, sway, (laxity, loose, freedom, tolerate)

effervescent, foam, boil, nothingness, zero, never, unsubstantial, burp, (substantial, article, something, substance)

burglar-n bandit, robber, housebreaker, thief, filcher, swindler, forger, coiner, fence, smuggler, wrecker, pirate

burlesque-n buffoonery, farce, take-off, parody, comedy, drollery, ridiculous, ludicrous, preposterous, monstrosity, (formality, prudery, demureness, modesty)

burn-v sear, parch, char, destroy, blaze, flame, hot, swelter, boil, torrid, tropical, sultry, stifling, stuffy, suffocating, oppressive, (cold, cool, chill, frigid, inclement)

burrow-n tunnel, mine, dig, excavate, penetrate, rooted, inhabit, domesticate, moored, anchored, established, lodged, (displacement, banishment, removal, dislocate)

bushy-adj shaggy, hairy, clumpy, dense, jungle, prairie, grass, hedge, rush, week, foliage, growth, woody

business-n employment, occupation, undertaking, pursuit, avocations, financial activities, affair, concern, case, interest, (inaction, inactivity, leisure)

busy-adj occupied, active, engrossed, employed, engaged, industrious, diligent, officious, flurry, rustle, stir, perturbation, (idle, dawdle, mope, inactivity, relaxation)

buttress-n abutment, prop, truss, brace, support, aid, block, anvil, shore, jamb, beam, rafter, (suspend, hand, fast to, pensile, hanging)

buy-v procure, purchase, acquire, invest, shop, market, buyer, vendee, patron, customer, client, pay, market, (sell, sale, dispose of, mortgage, auction)

bygone-adj old, former, departed, antiquated, obsolete, gone by, past, yore, away, latter, look back, ancestry, lapse

C

cab-n carriage, hansom, taxicab, hackney, hack, vehicle, conveyance, van, wagon, cart, coach, caravan, car

cabinet-n closet, room, repository, case, ministry, council, committee, chamber, board, bench

cage-n confine, restrain incarcerate, imprison, enclosure, receptacle, reservatory, compartment, hole, nook, stall

cajole-v coax, wheedle, deceive, delude, flatter, praise, soothe, humor, exaggerate, charm, (scandal, defamation, slander, derogate)

calamity-n catastrophe, disaster, affliction,

casualty, adversity, failure, mishap, accident, trial, tribulation, reverse, (welfare, well being, luck, success)

calculate-v estimate, count, reckon, compute, numerate, numbering, enumeration, summation, poll, recite

calendar-n register, list, almanac, schedule, chronicle, clock, watch, hour glass

caliber-n bore, diameter, gauge, capacity, ability, power, force, dimension, bulk, magnitude, big, great, considerable, (smallness, dwarf, pygmy, minute)

call-v muster, assemble convene, convoke, elect, appoint, summon, invite, shout, yell, designate, signal, invitation, offer, visit, urge, impulse

calling-n vocation, outcry, profession, notice, business, occupation, employment, pursuit, undertake

callous-adj stiff, unfeeling, hardened, obdurate, insensibility, unfeeling, senseless, thick-skinned, dull, numb, dead, (sensible, moral, cultivate, impress)

calm-adj placid, serene, impassive, peaceful, composed, tranquil, quiet, rest, still, silence, (motion, volatile, restless, mobility, shift)

camouflage-*n* screen, cloak, disguise, concealment

camp-*n* shack, encampment, quarters, tent, locate, encamp, lodge, abode, dwelling, lodging, domicile, nest, (settler, squatter, indigent)

cancel-*v* abolish, repeal, delete, revoke, overrule, abrogation, annulment, stop, disclaim, dismiss, discard, (initiate, commission, start, delegate, consign)

candid-*adj* unaffected, frank, artless, sincere, blunt, outspoken, veracity, sincerity, candor, honesty, fidelity, truthful, (falsify, deception, untruth, lying)

cannibal-*n* anthropophagite, savage, man-eater, brute, ruffian, terrorist, desperado, bully, dangerous, (benefactor, good savior, saint)

canon-*n* law, charge, code, rule, precept, courage, bravery, valor, boldness, gallantry, rashness, confidence, (cowardice, timidity, cower, week-minded)

canopy-*n* tester, awning, overhanging, shelter, dome, vault, sky, cover, tent, umbrella, parasol, sun-shade, envelope

canvas-*n* tent, sailcloth, tarpaulin, painting, picture, covering, gather way, spread sail

canvass-*v* solicit, seek, examine, discuss, request, address, overture, asking, begging, invite, beseech, plead, (depreciate, mediation, protest, intercessory)

cap-*n* headpiece, headdress, skullcap, barrette, fez, completion, achieve, fulfillment, execution, finish, attain, reach, (shortcoming, incomplete)

capital-*n* admirable, first-class, excellent, primary, principal, resources, assets, riches, opulence

caprice-*n* humor, notion, fancy, quip, conceit, whim, (permanence, stability)

captivate-*v* delight, charm, fascinate, enchant, pleasant, pleasurable, agreeable, enrapture, indulge, beatify, (painful, infliction, annoyance, grievance)

capture-*v* apprehend, seize, catch, arrest, secure, taking, hook, nab, bag, receive, accept, distraint, (return, release, replevin, restore)

career-*n* progress, course, path, passage, success, occupation, business, employment, pursuit, undertake, serve

careless-*adj* nonchalant, heedless, easy-going, negligent, thoughtless, reckless, impulsive, indiscreet

caress-*n* fondle, hug, pet, embrace, clasp, cling-to, endearment, kiss, smack, hug, cuddle, gallivant, ogle, sweet upon, (moodiness, sullen, sulky, ill-tempered)

caricature-*n* ridicule, parody, satirize, take-off, repetition, duplication, copy, simulate, mimic, forgery

carnage-*n* bloodshed, massacre, butchery, killing, homicide, murder, assassination

carry-*v* bear, convey, uphold, sustain, support, purchase, stand, foundation, buttress, stanchion, main stay

cart-*n* wagon, pushcart, dray, tumbrel, vehicle, transport, displace, displant, unload, empty, transfer, vacate, (lodgement, stow, installation, localize)

carve-*v* quarter, slice, dissect, mold, hew, cut, disjunction, separation, parting, divorce, detach, divide, split, (join, unite, close, together)

castrate-*v* neuter, spay, geld, emasculate, purify, cleanliness, lavation, clear, purgative, (impurity, contamination)

casual-*adj* random, accidental, occasional, incidental, contingent, external, conditional, fortuitous

casualty-*n* misfortune, disaster, calamity, mishap, accident, event, adventure, crisis, emergency, contingency, consequence, (loom, await, impend)

cause-*v* birth, beginning, origin, prime, principle, producer, generator, creator, determinant, motive, root, basis, foundation

caustic-*adj* pungent, biting, burning, acrimonious, corroding, mordant, repulsive, discourteous, blunt, gruff, harsh, austere, (courtesy, politeness, compliment)

caution-*n* discretion, heed, circumspection, wariness, forethought, vigilance, watchfulness, admonition

cave-*n* grotto, den, cavern, lair, hole, abode, dwelling, domicile, lodging, nest, arbor, cell, retreat, roost

cavity-*n* opening, hole, dent, depression, hollow, excavation, dip, scoop, excavate, tunnel, burrow, (projection, bulge, swell, nob)

cease-*v* discontinue, halt, end, stop, terminate, refrain, closure, desist, pause, rest, interrupt, suspend, cut, (start, continue, initiate, sustain, uphold)

cede-*v* surrender, give up, concede, yield, relinquish, submission, resignation, homage, succumb, submit, (combatant, belligerent, competitor)

celebration-*n* observance, commemoration, jubilation, ovation, triumph, inauguration, honor, installation, coronation

celestial-*adj* holy, unearthly, divine, beatific, Elysian, heavenly, solar, empyreal, starry, otherworldly

celibacy-*n* misogyny, purity, singleness, bachelorhood, virginity, maidenhood, spinster, unmarried, (marriage, wedlock, union, mate)

censure-*n* faultfinding, hypercritical, carping, condemnatory, disesteem, dislike, disapprove, object to, frown, (approval, sanction, esteem, praise)

ceremonial-*adj* ritualistic, formal, pompous, solemn, display, show, parade, ostentatious, showy, grand, flashing

certainty-*n* sureness, certitude, assuredness, safety, inevitable, fact, infallibility, dogmatic, (unbelief, uncertainty)

cessation-*n* discontinuance, interruption, respite, intermission, interval, recess, impediment, halt, lull, suspension, truce

chafe-*v* vex, fret, gall, annoy, rub, warm, pain, suffering, twitch, soreness, crick, sharp, piercing,

gnawing, (pleasure, sensual, comfort, luxury)

chaff-*v* refuse, husk, persiflage, raillery, ridicule, deride, travesty, mock, sarcastic, ironical, banter, rally

chagrin-*n* vexation, mortification, painfulness, anxiety, irritation, worry, ordeal, trouble, fret, (happiness, enjoyment, comfort, ease)

chance-*n* luck, fortune, unforeseen occurrence, fate, lot, destiny, fortuity, risk, gamble, uncertainty, jeopardy, happen, come, arrive, befall, turn up, (attribution, intention)

channel-*n* duct, waterway, conduit, canyon, chasm, aqueduct, canal, moat, ditch, water gate

chant-*n* melody, song, psalm, canticle, hymn, vespers, mass, prayer, service, vigils

chapter-*n* part, section, division, passage, branch, portion, segment, parcel, piece, detachment, verse, clause, (totality, collectiveness, completeness, bulk)

char-*v* parch, sear, burn, carbonize, scorch, boil, heat, fusion, inflame, roast, toast, cauterize, incinerate, (refrigerate, cool, fan, refresh)

charitable-*adj* unselfish, generous, liberal, kind, altruistic, donor, eleemosynary, gratis

charlatan-*n* fraud, cheat, impostor, impersonator, quack, deceiver, hypocrite, pretender, humbug

charm-*n* fascination, attractiveness, amulet, talisman, incantation, lure, draw, seduce, conjure, hypnotize

chasm-*n* pit, abyss, gap, fissure, cleft, hole, opening, orifice, passage, channel, gully, mine, gallery, (closure, blockade, shut, obstruct)

chaste-*adj* unaffected, classic, virtuous, undefiled, simple, virginal, symmetry, finish, uniform, balanced, equal, regular, (distortion, warped, irregular)

cheat-*v* swindle, defraud, trick, beguile, dupe, delude, deceive, deception, falseness, fraud, delusion, treachery, (truthful, veracity, frankness, honesty)

cheer-*n* yell, shout, festivity, hospitality, enliven, inspirit, approval, sanction, esteem, praise, applaud, joyous

cheerless-*adj* dismal, somber, gloomy, depressing, sad, dreary, despondent

cherish-*v* prize, treasure, nurture, revere, love, fondness, liking, affection, feeling, tenderness, (hate, alienation, coolness)

chew-*v* grind, eat, crunch, masticate, gulp, gluttony, feed, devour, swallow, take, dispatch, munch, gnaw, (discharge, secretion, ejection)

chief-*n* first, principal, foremost, supreme, main, head, leader, commander, important, paramount, significant, (insignificant, trivial, nothing, trash)

childish-*adj* simple-minded, infantile, silly, weak, credulous, puerile, youthful, young, shallow, foolish, (wisdom, intellect, cunning, mature)

chivalrous-*adj* knightly, brave, courteous, gallant, war, tenure, courage, honor, generosity

choke-*v* strangle, suffocate, congest, clog, stifle, obstruction, blockage, closure, bolt, seal, clinch, (opening, yawning)

chronic-*adj* unceasing, survive, lasting, inveterate, constant, eternity, perpetuity, persistent, standing, survival, (transient, passing, fleeting, flying)

chronicle-*n* registry, annals, archives, account, epoch, almanac, calendar, journal, diary, pendulum, (anticipation, disregard, neglect)

cipher-*n* cryptogram, code, monogram, cryptograph, naught, zero, numeration, pagination, recension, summation, (catalog, inventory, schedule, index)

circle-*n* globe, ring, orb, disk, circlet, encircle, circumnavigate, gird, circumscribe, surround, compass, inclose

circulate-*v* spread, report, pass, change hands, propagate, revolve, rotation, revolution, gyration, whir, whirl

circumference-*n* periphery, perimeter, circuit, girth, outline, perimeter, ambit, circuit, lines, contour, profile, zone, belt, (verge, brink, brow, side)

circumscription-*n* bound, limit, confinement, case, restriction, enclosure, restraint, envelope, (perimeter, zone, belt, girth, band)

circumstance-*n* situation, condition, environment, surroundings, position, time, place, occurrence, event, quandary, fix, predicament, dilemma

circumvent-*v* thwart, elude, frustrate, outwit, baffle, prevent, preclusion, interruption, hindrance, (assist, help, promotion, patronage)

civilize-*v* polish, refine, cultivate, humanize, breeding, good, polite, conform, admissible, (comical, ridiculous, absurdity, ludicrous)

claim-*v* requirement, plea, assert, contend, require, deserve, title, pretense,

prerogative, imposition, requisition

claimant-*n* accuser, heir, prosecutor, pretender, petitioner, solicitor, applicant, suitor, beggar, hunter

clamor-*n* outcry, uproar, racket, tumult, din, contention, agitation, cry, shout, roar, scream, cheer, hoot, holler

clamp-*n* fastener, clasp, brace, band, joining, union, connection, unite, attach, affix, (disjunction, disconnection, disunion, division)

clan-*n* faction, breed, brotherhood, set, sort, family, association, paternity, parent, father, sire, lineage, pedigree

clash-*v* conflict, collide, dispute, contend, impact, collision, concussion, shock, disagreement, discord, dissidence, (concert, conformity, uniformity)

class-*n* category, division, section, grouping, caste, clique, coterie, order, sort, manner, nature, type, gender, designation

classification-*n* grouping, sorting, systematization, order, allocation, designate, group, tabulate, index, file, systematize, arrange

cleanness-*n* pureness, purity, clearness, neatness,

immaculateness, purgation, purification, (impurity, dirty, unclean, decay, corruption)

clear-_adj_ bright, unclouded, distinct, intelligible, open, patent, transparent, simpleness, purification, single, sheer, neat

cleft-_adj_ fissure, break, gap, crack, crevice, dissection, forking, branching, divide, split, cloven, halve, (double, renewal, twin)

clever-_adj_ dexterous, adroit, talented, able, gifted, intelligence, capacity, sagacity, discernment, (shallow, imbecility, incapacity)

climax-_n_ zenith, pinnacle, acme, culmination, crest, supremacy, majority, excel, match, culminate, (minority, deficiency, smallness)

clinch-_v_ confirm, close, end, fasten, secure, clench, rivet, clamp, grapple, combination, mixture, junction, union, (analysis, dissection, decompose)

clique-_n_ coterie, set, group, circle, crowd, party, faction, side, crew, ban, horde, posse, family, clan

clog-_n_ hamper, impede, encumber, obstruct, investment, covering, attire, shoe, pump, boot, sandal, slipper, galoche

club-_n_ stick, cudgel, resort, fraternity, association, rendezvous, party, faction,

side, crew, band, horde

clumsy-_adj_ awkward, stupid, unwieldy, bungling, incompetent, unskilled, unfitness, inexpedient, undesirable, inadvisable, (opportunism, graceful, expedient)

clutch-_v_ seize, clench, collar, grip, keep, retain, grasp, hold, secure, retentive, inalienable, (release, abandon, dereliction, dispensation)

coagulate-_v_ thicken, clot, congeal, curdle, density, solidity, constipation, cohesion, cake, crystallize, (sponginess, rarefactive, expansion)

coarse-_adj_ homespun, rough, uncouth, unpolished, crude, rude, vulgar, discord, burr, jangle, creaking, gruff, (refined, cultivated, tact, delicate, good taste, finesse, discriminate)

coax-_v_ entice, cajole, persuade, wheedle, motive, intention, inducement, move, draw, inspire, (dissuade, against, warn, indispose)

coerce-_v_ make, impel, force, compel, coaction, duress, enforcement, conscription, drive, constrain, (compelling, coactive)

cogent-_adj_ forcible, strong, potent, convincing, power, might, force, energy, capable, valid, adequate,

almighty, (powerless,
incapable, disabled)

cogitate-*v* muse, ponder,
consider, meditate,
thought, reflection,
consideration, speculation,
consultation, (vacancy,
fatuity, dismiss,
thoughtlessness
unoccupied)

cognizant-*adj* conscious,
sensible, observant,
aware, knowledge, insight,
familiarity, leaning,
reading, doctrine,
(ignorance, blindness,
glimmering)

coherence-*n* adherence,
aggregation, accretion,
congruity, connection,
consistency, harmony,
conformity, viscidity

cold-*adj* chilliness, chill,
coolness, iciness, gelidity,
frigid, biting, piercing,
nipping, raw, wintry,
anguish, arctic

colleague-*n* ally, partner,
associate, companion,
mate, helper, hand, friend,
cooperator, pal,
accomplice, (opponent,
antagonist, adversary)

collect-*v* amass, compile,
demand, exact, meet,
throng, flock, assemble,
ligation, gather,
compilation, conclave,
(dispersion, disjunction,
divergency)

collide-*v* crash, meet,
bump, conflict, clash,
impulse, impetus,
momentum, push, thrust,

shove, throw, explode,
(recoil, rebound, revulsion,
retract)

colloquial-*adj*
conversational, informal,
chatty, metaphor, figure of
speech, phrase, analogy,
irony, figurativeness,
personification

colonize-*v* establish, settle,
found, people, place,
situate, locate, localize,
make a place for,
plantation, camp,
(displaced, misplaced,
exile, removal)

combination-*n* aggregation,
union, mixture, composite,
coadunation, synthesis,
inosculation, (disjunction,
decomposition)

command-*v* regulation,
order, ordinance, act,
bidding, direction,
injunction, commandment,
ruling, instructions,
dispatch, message,
(lowness, debasement,
depression)

commence-*v* begin, start,
enter upon, outset,
inception, genesis, birth,
originate, conceive,
source, dawn,
embarkation, initiate, (end,
close, terminate, conclude)

commend-*v* recommend,
praise, acclaim, approve,
approbation, applause,
clap, esteem, sanction,
admiration, appreciate,
(dislike, insinuation,
ostracism)

comment-*n* observation,

remark, criticism, annotation, interpretation, argument, controversy, debate, reasoning, (mystify, evasion, intuition, instinct)

commission-n warrant, charge, instruction, authorization, mandate, brevet, permit, delegation, consignment, nomination, charter, installation, investiture, accession, (annulment, prohibition)

commit-v perpetrate, consign, intrust, perform, action, doing, performance, exercise, citation, execute, achieve, (inaction, abstinence, passive)

common-adj conventional, usual, prevalent, current, customary, regular, vulgar, ill-bred, general, universal, (special, designate, realize, determine)

commotion-n disturbance, tumult, turmoil, disorder, agitation, stir, tremor, shake, ripple, jog, jolt, jar, (oscillation, vibration, liberation)

communion-n intercourse, converse, partnership, association, talk, participation, possession, partaking, (possessor, holder, occupant)

compact-n deal, contract, understanding, bargain, engagement, agreement, stipulation, covenant, terse, condensed, thick,

constricted, compressed, dense, (contention, disagreement)

companion-n partner, chum, colleague, associate, accompany, coexist, attend, synchronize, (alone, isolate, disjoin, one, sole, solitary)

company-n association, partnership, group, crowd, cast, syndicate, firm, companionship, assemblage, (dispersion, disjunction, divergence)

compartment-n niche, part, enclosure, division, portion, item, segment, fragment, (collectiveness, completeness, bulk, mass)

compassion-n condolence, sympathy, tenderness, mercy, pity, commiseration, fellow-feeling, yearning, forbearance, (inclemency, severity, malevolence)

compatible-adj harmonious, congruous, suitable, consistent, agreeable, concert, conformity, uniformity, (discord, dissidence, variance, unfitness)

compel-v constrain, force, coerce, impel, drive, compulsion, make, press, coactive, oblige, necessitate

compendium-n epitome, bulletin, review, brief, analysis, recapitulation, summary, excerpt, note,

abstract, digest,
(dissertation, theme,
discourse)
compensation-*n*
repayment, payment,
requital, pay,
remuneration, reward,
honorarium, solatium,
mediocrity, generality,
compromise
competence-*n* proficiency,
ability, capability,
sufficiency, means, rich,
luxuriant, affluent, wealthy,
abundant, (insufficient,
meager, shortcoming,
small, scarce)
competitor-*n* contestant,
rival, entrant, aspirant,
claimant, antagonist,
adversary, opposition,
disputant, enemy, (helper,
adjunct, friend, ally,
confidant)
compile-*v* arrange, amass,
collect, make, write,
assemblage, group,
cluster, clump,
accumulation, heap, pile,
(unassembled, dispersed,
sparse)
completion-*n* attainment,
achievement, execution,
fulfillment, performance,
accomplishment,
conclusion
complex-*adj* complicated,
intricate, involved,
confused, confusion,
disarray, uproar, riot,
rumpus, jumble, huddle,
(orderly, regular, neat, tidy)
complexity-*n*
entanglement, intricacy,

complication, perplexity,
compositeness
compliance-*n* assent,
agree, acquiesce, submit,
obey, conformity, normal,
typical, formal, (abnormal,
unusual, eccentric)
complicity-*n* connivance,
conspiracy, collusion,
confederacy, cooperate,
concur, combine,
understand, unite,
(opposition, antagonism,
counteract, against)
component-*n* integral part,
constituent, ingredient,
member, subdivision,
radical, intrinsic, inherent,
immanent, subsistent,
essential, inwrought,
innate, inbred,
(extraneousness, whole)
compose-*v* make up, form,
construct, fashion,
constitute, assuage, calm,
improvise, create,
reception, (exclusion,
omission, reject)
comprehend-*v* conceive,
grasp, understand,
comprise, aware,
cognizant, conscious,
acquainted, (shallow,
unknown, superficial, half-
learned)
compress-*v* condense,
reduce, abridge, thicken,
squeeze, compact,
contract, reduction,
lessening, shrinking,
(extension, spread,
obesity)
comprise-*v* embrace,
embody, contain,

comprehend, include, admission, inclusion, enclose, receive

compromise-*n* settlement, arrangement, adjustment, agreement, composition, commute, compound, arrange, imperil, hazard,

compute-*v* reckon, count, estimate, evaluate, record, note, memorandum, archive, scroll, register, (obliterate, cancel, scratch, erase, strike out)

concavity-*n* hollow, dip, depression, cavity, antrum, trough, furrow, depression, dip, hollow, (rejection, swelling, bulge, protrusion)

concealment-*n* masquerade, secretion, latency, cover, disguise, mask, camouflage, screen, veil, shroud, shelter, secrecy, privacy, secret

concede-*v* assent, yield, acknowledge, surrender, cede, confess, grant, admittance, ratification, acquiesce, (dissent, disagreement, discontent)

conceit-*n* egoism, epigram, quip, whim, fancy, pride, vanity, complacency, glorification, airs, self-satisfied, (modesty, humility, blushing, reserve, constraint)

conceive-*v* visualize, fancy, devise, realize, grasp, comprehend, form, produce, become pregnant

concentrate-*v* gather, collect, converge, focus

center, fix, assemble, core, nucleus, heart, centralize

concession-*n* permission, acknowledgement, admission, reduction, allowance, grant, gift

conciliate-*v* propitiate, reconcile, satisfy, disarm, placate, mollify, reason, call, inducement, consideration, (dissuade, remonstrate, warn, against, repel)

conciseness-*n* succinctness, brevity, terseness, abridgment, laconicism, condensation

conclude-*v* arrange, finish, settle, terminate, infer, end, deduce, resolve

conclusive-*adj* unanswerable, convincing, indisputable, final, concluding, deduce

concoct-*v* make, hatch, invent, contrive, prepare, falsehood, untruth, lying, perjury, misrepresentation, forgery, (veracity, sincerity, candor, truthful)

concord-*n* accord, symphony, agreement, harmony, consonance, unison, correspondence, amity, congruence, unanimity, alliance

concrete-*adj* solid, definite, substantial, hard, exact, specific, adherence, together, aggregation, consolidation, tenacious, (non-adhesion, loose, relaxation)

condescend-*v* descend,

deign, vouchsafe, stoop,
humility, meek,
submission, resignation,
(dignified, stately, proud)
condiment-n seasoning,
sauce, flavoring, relish,
salt, mustard, pepper,
spice, relish
condition-n stipulation,
modification, proviso,
situation, plight, fitness,
assumption, postulate
condolence-n pity,
sympathy, commiseration,
compassion, consolation,
comfort
conduct-v deportment,
guise, behavior, carriage,
comportment, demeanor,
operate, work, manage,
govern, regulate, supervise
confederate-n associate,
ally, accomplice,
companion, transient,
passing, evanescent,
fleeting, flying
confer-v deliberate, consult,
discuss, converse, bestow,
advise, consul, suggestion,
prompt, recommend
confere-n consultation,
interview, meeting, parley
confess-v acknowledge,
admit, divulge, reveal,
disclose, assent, accept,
accede, concur, (dissent,
demur, disagree, protest)
confident-adj certainty,
trust, self-reliance, spirit,
assurance, expectant,
sure, hopeful, optimistic,
self-sufficient, candid,
open, unsuspecting,
gullible

confine-v restrain, imprison,
incarcerate, cage, bound,
enclosure, limit, inclose,
surround, imprisoned,
buried
confirm-v endorse, uphold,
corroborate, substantiate,
warrant, vouch, certificate,
facts, record, docket,
(disprove, other side,
oppose)
confiscate-v sequestrate,
seize, appropriate, taking,
capture, appropriation,
catch, nab, (return, restore,
redeem)
conflict-n battle, combat,
encounter, discord,
dissension, antagonism,
opposition, counteract,
antagonize, (cooperate,
concur, combine)
conformity-n agreement,
accord, harmony,
resemblance, congruity,
compliance, observance,
acquiescence, concession,
submission, consent
confound-v confuse,
jumble, overthrow, perplex,
bewilder, wonder, marvel,
astonish, admire, (expect,
foreseen, common)
confront-v brave, defy,
front, resist, fore, face,
outpost, pioneer, advance,
(rear, guard, stern, behind)
confuse-v muddle, disturb,
disconcert, fluster,
bewilder, mistake,
deranged, mislay, disorder,
unsettle, (arrange,
preparation)
confutation-n disproval,

disproof, refutation, refutal,
invalidation, retort, answer,
(demonstrate, prove,
establish)

congeal-v thicken, set,
condense, coagulate,
stiffen, harden, density,
solidness, mass, cake,
(thin, fine, tenuous, rarefy)

congenial-adj sympathetic,
harmonious, adapted,
compatible, agreement,
accord, adapt, fitness,
harmonize, (disagree,
hostile, repugnant,
incompatible)

congratulation-n best
wishes, felicitation,
compliment, gratulation,
condolence

congregation-n
aggregation, gathering,
fold, flock, brethren,
assemblage, collection,
muster, (dispersed,
broadcast, sprinkle)

congress-n parliament,
convention, legislature,
assembly, council,
committee, court,
chamber, board, staff

conjecture-n speculation,
inference, surmise,
supposition, assumption,
postulation, condition

conjugate-v coupled,
mated, united, bijugate,
paronymous, verbal, literal,
derivation, root,
(corruption, slang, cant)

connect-v attach, unite,
link, associate, correlate,
relation, reference,
correlation, similarity,
(disconnection, remote,
irrelevant)

conquer-v vanquish,
subdue, defeat, overcome,
prevail, success, advance,
conquest, victory, (fail,
repulse, rebuff, defeat,
overthrow, slip)

conscious-adj
understanding, aware,
keen, sensible, cognizant,
senses, observation,
intuition, judgment,
(imbecility, brutality,
without reason)

conscription-n
impressment, compulsory
enlistment, draft, compel,
force, make, drive, coerce

consecrate-v hallow,
devote, dedicate, apply,
utilization, work, yield,
manipulate, (disuse,
abstain, spare, neglect)

consent-v compliance,
assent, acquiescence,
concurrence, agreement,
concession, permission,
permit, accession,
acknowledgment, (dissent,
refusal)

consequence-n
proceeding, outcome,
result, decision,
termination, settlement,
prominence, self-
importance

consequential-adj
sequential, deducible,
derivable, inferable,
secondary, supercilious

consider-v regard, notice,
heed, believe, adjudge,
deliberate, reflect, ponder,

(vacancy, thoughtless, absent)

considerable-*adj* extraordinary, intense, notable, weighty, big, massive, substantial

consideration-*n* regard, observation, notice, kindliness, consequence, inducement, deference, esteem, perquisite

consign-*v* delegate, assign, commit, authorize, send, deliver, dispatch, ship, allotment, assignment, charge, task, apportionment

consistent-*adj* compatible, harmonious, conformable, homogeneous, accordant, agreement, accommodate, conventional, (abnormity, infringement, irregular)

consolation-*n* comfort, solace, assuagement, sympathy, encouragement, relief, softening, alleviation, restorative, (aggravated, exasperation, embitter)

consolidate-*v* incorporate, federate, merge, solidify, compact, coherence, adhere, holdfast, tenacity, (looseness, relaxation, freedom, disjunction)

consonance-*n* accordance, tunefulness, concord, harmony, accord

conspicuous-*adj* prominent, famous, renowned, eminent, notable, obvious, glaring, salient, (invisible, concealment, obscure)

conspirator-*n* plotter, accomplice, confederate, traitor, combine, scheme, concur, intrigue, plot

constant-*adj* incessant, unflagging, continual, steadfast, stanch, loyal, agree, uniform, level, smooth, (diversify, varied, uneven)

constitution-*n* structure, construction, state, condition, code, law, charter, temperament, disposition, nature

constraint-*n* necessity, coercion, repression, unnaturalness, bind, contract, squeeze

construction-*n* formation, structure, build, explanation, translation, erection, creation

consultation-*n* interview, deliberation, conference

consume-*v* annihilate, burn, demolish, devour, use up, exhaust, drain, expend, destruction, ruin, downfall, (fabricate, produce, achievement)

consummate-*v* unmitigated, sheer, perfect, finished, profound, intense, complete, fill, replenish, (deficiency, wanting, defective)

contact-*n* meeting, union, conjunction, adhesion, contiguity, proximity, apposition, abutment, touch, adhere, attach, append, adjoin, (interval, distance)

contagion-*n* pestilence, epidemic, transmission, virus, communication, poisonousness, toxicity

contagious-*adj* communicable, catching, infectious

contain-*v* comprise, embody, include, incorporate, hold, portion, segment, fragment, parcel

container-*n* vessel, utensil, vase, jar, bag, bottle

contaminate-*v* pollute, taint, corrupt, foul, defile, uncleanliness, impurity, decay, filth, dregs, (clean, launder, wipe, mop, disinfect)

contemplate-*v* consider, design, ponder, purpose, reflect, muse, view, sight, glimpse, behold, discover, (blindness, undiscerning)

contempt-*n* scorn, disdain, detestation, abhorrence, despise, disrepute, insignificant, immaterial, trivial, (important, prominence, concern, superior)

contemptuous-*adj* derision, mockery, sneer, spurn, abhor, underestimate (respect, reverence)

contend-*v* hold, maintain, allege, strive, struggle, debate, dispute, reasoning, argument, proposition, (chicane, mystification, quibble)

contention-*n* altercation, struggle, strife, feud, contest, litigation,

disagreement, debate, dispute, belligerency

contents-*n* constituents, ingredients, cargo, filling,

contingency-*n* prospect, likelihood, situation, case, predicament, incidental, casual, provisional, conditional, accidental

continual-*adj* incessant, repeated, constant, unceasing, perpetuity

continuance-*n* pursuance, maintenance, extension, permanence, duration, perpetuation, stay

contortion-*n* deformation, twist, distortion, crookedness, warp, irregular, unsymmetrical, misshapen, ill-proportioned, stumpy, (symmetrical, shapely, regular, uniform)

contour-*n* form, outline, shape, figure, circumference, parameter, zone, belt

contraband-*n* forbidden, illegal, smuggled, illicit, deception, deceit, juggle, cheat, hoax, decoy, waylay

contract-*n* arrangement, bargain, compact, promise, guarantee, promissory, pledged, (release, absolute, unconditional)

contradict-*v* deny, dissent, refute, disprove, gainsay, (identical, equivalent, the same)

contrariety-*n* antagonism, opposition, repugnance, clashing, disagreement, antipathy, discrepancy, inconsistency, contrast

contrary-*adj* opposed, adverse, opposite, antagonistic, hostile, perverse

contrast-*v* dissimilarity, unlikeness, disparity, antithesis, foil

contribute-*v* conduce, tend, advance, subscribe, donate, giving, consignment, charity, generosity, (acquisition, acceptance, admission)

contrivance-*n* gear, device, apparatus, scheme, trick, stratagem

control-*v* dominion, power, sway, direction, regulation, might, force, energy, pressure, strength, ability, (disability, helplessness)

controversy-*n* dispute, argument, debate, quarrel, altercation, contention, reasoning, discussion, comment, (evasion, quibble, pervert, mystify)

conundrum-*n* puzzle, riddle, enigma, secret, maze, profound, labyrinth, paradox, (information, intelligence, advice, report)

convalesce-*v* recover, rally, improve, revive, restoration, renovation, resume, cure, heal, remedy, (relapse, retrogradation, return)

convenient-*adj* serviceable, suitable, opportune, advantageous, adaptable, expedient, eligible, seemly,

becoming, (unfit, undesirable)

conventional-*adj* habitual, customary, formal, usual, common, general, familiar, regular, vernacular, (infraction, disuse, violate, infringe)

convergence-*n* confluence, concentration, concourse, focalization, meeting, assemblage

conversion-*n* transmutation, change, metamorphosis, growth, regeneration, assimilation

convey-*v* transport, carry, bear, grant, cede, will, transfer, deportation, carriage, delegate, consign

convict-*v* find guilty, doom, prisoner, captive, criminal, rascal, scoundrel, villain, ruffian, jail-bird, (good man, hero, angel, saint)

conviction-*n* view, opinion, sentence, penalty, belief, credence, faith, assume, esteem, (unbelieving, doubtful, misgiving)

convince-*v* satisfy, assure, convert, persuade, belief, faith, confidence, reliance, certainty, (doubtful, fallible, suspicious)

convoy-*v* escort, attend, conduct, guard, watch, support, accompany, custody, safety, security, surety, (insecurity, jeopardy, risk, hazard)

convulse-*v* stir, shake, disturb, rend, wring, pain, suffering, aching, spasm, piercing, sharp, (pleasure, sensual, comfort, luxury)

cool-*adj* wary, unfriendly, self-possessed, chilly, lukewarm, easygoing, placid, compose, calm, freeze, chill, harden

cooperation-*n* combination, joint operation, union, participation, concert, collaboration

coordinate-*n* organize, adjust, harmonize, arrange, preparation, assortment, allotment, catalog, tabulate, (dislocate, disarrange, break up)

copious-*adj* plentiful, full, abundant, profuse, ample, sufficiency, adequacy, enough, fullness, (incompetence, deficiency, poverty)

copy-*n* counterpart, effigy, facsimile, likeness, similitude, semblance, imitation, model, representation, study

cord-*n* string, twine, rope, bond, tie, fastening, shackle, rein, rivet, padlock, anchor

cordial-*adj* hearty, friendly, genial, warm, sincere, pleasure, sensual, comfort, luxury, enjoy, (torment, anguish, agony)

core-*n* nucleus, kernel, heart, gist, pith, substance, center, middle, axis, concentric

corner-*n* niche, nook, monopolize, control, spot, point, premises, place, pigeon hole, compartment

corpse-*n* carcass, dead body, skeleton, remains, cadaver, carrion, bones, relic, mummy, fossil

corpulence-*n* fleshiness, portliness, obesity, fatness, bulk, greatness, expanse, large, big, ample, (small, pygmy, minute, undersized)

correct-*v* reprove, punish, chastise, remedy, mend, discipline, rectify, repair, set right, strict, accurate, true, perfect, unerring

correlation-*n* reciprocity, interdependence, mutuality, correspondence, comparison, relative, cognate, (irrelative, irrespective, arbitrary)

correspondence-*n* letters, writings, epistle, news, dispatch, bulletin, accordance, agreement

corrigible-*adj* tractable, amenable, submissive, docile, improvement, better, increase, ripen, mature, (worse, deteriorate, degenerate)

corrode-*v* rust, decay, wear, waste, deteriorate, (improve, elaborate, promote, cultivate, advance)

corrupt-*adj* base, dishonest, tainted, rotten, spoiled, profligate, dissolute, immoral, infect, taint, pervert, debase

cosmic-*adj* otherworldly,

heavenly, terrestrial, universal

cost-*n* expense, charge, outlay, disbursement, expenditure, expensive, dear, high-priced, (discount, reduction, allowance, rebate)

council-*n* committee, court, chapter, chamber, board, directorate, syndicate, cabinet, staff, parliament, (precept, direction, charge)

count-*v* estimate, consider, figure, reckon, compute, enumerate, numbering, calculation, recite

countenance-*n* expression, aspect, visage, features, patronage, favor, front, foreground, advance, (behind, rear, stern, rum)

counterfeit-*v* fictitious, bogus, spurious, fake, imitation, false, copy, duplication, mirror, reproduce, (original, unlimited)

countersign-*v* watchword, authentication, seal, password, identification, secondary evidence, confirmation, corroboration, (unattested, unauthenticated)

countless-*adj* innumerable, incalculable, numberless, illimitable, infinite, immense, immeasurable, exhaustless

country-*n* nation, state, power, home, territory, district, rural regions, field, meadow, garden

couple-*n* join, pair, yoke, link, tie, mate, firm, fast, taut, taught, secure, set, intervolved, (sunder, divide, disjoin, dissect, cut up, carve)

courage-*n* bravery, valor, fearlessness, heart, resoluteness, daring, spirit, boldness, dash, gallantry, heroism, mettle, nerve, grit, fortitude, resolution

courier-*n* messenger, runner, traveler, envoy, emissary, reporter, informer, correspondent, crier

course-*n* procedure, path, behavior, succession, channel, drift, trend, progress, flight, routine, (await, loom, predestine, doom)

court-*n* palace, castle, staff, retinue, train, bar, session, bench, make love, woo, cajole, invite, solicit, praise, (forbearance, refraining, avoidance, evasion, elusion)

courtesy-*n* politeness, refinement, cultivation, gentility, urbanity, culture, elegance, civility, polish, (discourtesy, repulsive, disrespect, impudent)

courtship-*n* suit, courting, wooing, flirtation, endearment, caress, fondling, embrace, salute, kiss, amorous, (glum, morose, frumpish, surly)

cove-*n* inlet, bay, harbor, lagoon, gulf, concavity,

depression, dip, hollow, indentation, cavity, dent, pit, basin, (convexity, prominence, projection, swelling)

covenant-n agreement, pact, compact, bargain, agree, stipulate, undertake, observe, comply, perform, (fail, neglect, omit, elude, evade, ignore, infringe)

covering-n screen, shield, shelter, protection, carapace, concealment, seclusion, hide, mystification, (uncover, inform, enlighten, open)

covet-v want, crave, envy, long for, desire, wish, greedy, hunger, hanker, solicitude, anxiety, yearning, aspiration, (cold, frigid, lukewarm, careless, listless)

cowardice-n graveness, pusillanimity, timidity, timorousness, baseness, effeminacy, abject fear, faintheartedness

coy-adj demure, retiring, shrinking, shy, tremble, shake, shudder, nervous, restless, despondent, (hope, trust, aggressive, outspoken, forward)

crabbed-adj tempered, surly, cross, perverse, peevish, illegible, intricate, squeezed

crack-v burst, break split, seam, rut, cleft, rip, fissure, sunder, divide, separate, disjoin, isolate, abscind,

(attach, fix, join, unite, connect, hold, bind)

craft-n handicraft, trade, artfulness, trickery, deceit, vessel, boat, expertness, art, skill, dexterity, adroitness, competence, (quackery, folly, stupidity, indiscretion)

cram-v crowd, jam, stuff, choke, guzzle, gorge, assemble, muster, group, cluster, pack, bunch, (disperse, disjunction, scatter, sow, spread)

cramp-n hamper, restrain, handicap, paralyze, cripple, incapacitate, contract, reduce, diminish, (expand, extend, augment, develop, swell)

crass-adj stupid, raw, elude, gross, ignorant, incomprehension, simplicity, shallow, superficial, green, (instructed, learned, educated, enlightened)

crave-v yearn for, long for, beseech, ask, beg, pray, desire, petition, ravening, hungry, famished, desirous

crawl-v grovel, fawn, cower, drag, lag, lumber, creep, saunter, plod, trudge, moderate, slow, (speed, scuttle, gallop, rush, velocity)

crazy-adj mad, lunatic, sick, crack-brained, shaky, fanaticism, oddity, eccentricity, twist, insane, crazed, frantic, raving, (sanity, soundness, rationality, lucidity)

creator-*n* originator, maker, author, producer, god, supreme being

creature-*n* lower animal, beast, individual, mortal, dependent, slave, being, thing, something, matter, substantial, (nonentity, shadow, phantom, nothing, naught)

credence-*n* reliance, trust, assurance, acceptance, acknowledgment, credit, faith, dependence, (uncertain, doubtful, incredulous)

credibility-*n* belief, believable, trustworthiness, honesty, faith, trust, confidence, reliance, repute, honor, merit, esteem, prestige

creed-*n* dogma, faith, doctrine, belief, firm, implicit, persuasion, articles, canons, catechism, (doubt, distrust, disputable, unworthy)

crest-*n* culmination, tip, height, top, plume, seal, device, ridge, summit, vertex, apex, zenith, pinnacle, (base, bottom, nadir, foot, fundamental)

crew-*n* mob, company, gang, throng, sailors, squad, crowd, horde, body, tribe, party, clan, brotherhood, (adrift, stray, dishelvelled, streaming, scatter)

cringe-*v* flinch, shrink, wince, fawn, grovel, submit, yield, non-resistance, obedience, surrender, succumb, parasite, bow, stoop, servile, supple, (bully, dictate)

cripple-*n* disable, hurt, incapacitate, enfeeble, helpless, prostration, paralysis, palsy, apoplexy, exhaustion, (potent, capable, virtue, qualification)

crisis-*n* emergency, trial, extremity, exigency, crux, full of incident, eventful, stirring, bustling, (loom, await, eventually, forthcoming)

critical-*adj* disparaging, faultfinding, judicious, analytical, crucial, turning point, reprove, flay, censure, examine, analyze, judge

crooked-*adj* deceptive, fraudulent, sneaking, warped, awry, twisted, askew, distorted, (symmetrical, shapely, finished, beautiful)

cross-*n* intersection, traversing, decussation, hybridization, passage, entwine, weave, twist, wreathe, dovetail

crouch-*v* bend, stoop, fawn, cower, cringe, low, neap, debased, underlie, slouch, wallow, grovel, depress, (tower, pillar, dome, height, elevate)

crown-*n* diadem, coronet, crest, top, reward, garland,

prize, accredit, empower, commission, represent, (dismiss, cancel, revocation, repeal)

crucial-*adj* decisive, final, determining, supreme, demonstrate, prove, establish, show, verify, (refute, disprove, expose, rebut)

crude-*adj* unfinished, vulgar, raw, rude, uncouth, unprepared, unwrought, incomplete

cruel-*adj* savage, inhuman, unkind, barbarous, brutal, merciless, ruthless

crumble-*v* perish, break up, fall to pieces, decay, degenerate, deteriorate

crush-*v* press, squeeze, suppress, overwhelm, disconcert, shame, bruise

crust-*n* coating, coat, hull, shell, rind, cover, canopy, bandage, veneer, inunction, incrustation , conceal, (uncover, expose)

cry-*v* clamor, shout, outcry, ejaculation, utterance, vociferation, call, shriek, howl, scream, screech, sob, weeping, lamentation, plaint, whimper

cue-*n* password, catchword, hint, intimation, inform, acquaint, communicate, present, specification, (disguise, screen, mystify, seclusion)

culprit-*n* offender, victim, criminal, felon, evildoer, rough, rowdy, ruffian, bully, hangman, incendiary,

criminal, (model, paragon, hero, demigod, innocent, benefactor)

cultivate-*v* develop, work, foster, till, advance, farm, georgic, geoponic, gardening, husbandry, agriculture

cultivation-*n* refinement, breeding, civilization, learning, education, tillage, agriculture, husbandry, improvement

cunning-*adj* subtlety, deceit, craftiness, chicanery, circumvention, guile, knavery, maneuvering, skill, dexterity

cup-*n* glass, mug, goblet, hollow, excavation, chalice tumbler, tankard, jug

curb-*n* restrain, control, check, repress, slacken, retard, confine, duress, custody, restrict, (liberate, free, unfetter, untie, loosen, relax)

curiosity-*adj* research, inquisitiveness, thirst for knowledge, inquiring mind, interest, (uninterested, indifferent, impassive)

current-*adj* common, instant, prevalent, circulating, flow, stream, draft, existing, present, actual, present time, (any time, sometime)

curse-*n* denounce, damn, swear, blaspheme, bane, imprecation, anathema, hurtful, sting, painful, bane, scourge, (remedy, help, redress, sedative)

curt-*adj* blunt, brusque, rude, abrupt, brief, short, succinct, concise, brevity, abbreviate, compress, compact, (lengthy, endlong, interminable)

curtail-*n* lessen, reduce, abridge, abbreviate, cut, retrench, mutilate, amputate, abscind, thin, prune, (add, annex, reinforce, supplement)

curtain-*n* veil, screen, hanging, blind, drapery, conceal, hide, masquerade, hiding place, reserve, (mention, acquaint, informant, outpouring)

custody-*n* imprisonment, care, bondage, charge, protection, keeping, confinement, durance, duress, arrest, (liberate, free, redemption, acquittal)

custom-*n* rule, fashion, precedent, practice, patronage, trade, usage, regular, usual, habitual, normal

cut-*v* divide, split, sever, shape, reap, gather, separate, part, detach, divorce, rupture, (attach, fix, firm, fast, join, unite)

D

dabble-*v* trifle, potter, moisten, paddle, splash, dilute, immerse, wash, sprinkle, drench

dagger-*n* stiletto, knife,

poniard, sword, weapon, armament, saber, resentment, displeasure, animosity, wrath

dainty-*adj* exquisite, pretty, delicate, particular, meticulous, delicious, appetizing, tasty, attractive, lovely, (annoying, nuisance, infestation, molestation)

dally-*v* philander, flirt, dawdle, prolong, idle, protract, delay, suspend, waive, retard, postpone, procrastinate, (prompt, immediate, haste, sudden)

damage-*n* injure, impair, harm, mutilate, hurt, deteriorate, wane, degenerate, decay, injury, loss, (fructify, ripen, mature, promote)

damp-*adj* humid, moist, foggy, watery, moisture, wet, dank, infiltrate, muggy, drench, dewy, (dry, arid, drought)

dance-*v* prance, glide, move, flutter, perform, party, ball, cotillion, hop, jump, oscillate, agitate, pulsate, effervescence

danger-*n* jeopardy, hazard, peril, risk, insecurity, precariousness, venture, instability, exposure, (safe, secure, impregnability, invulnerability)

dangle-*v* wave, hang, swing, be suspended, droop, sling, pendulum, depend, pensive, loose, flowing, (support, aid, prop, stand, anvil, stay)

dare-v challenge, venture, brave, face, defiance, threat, defy, bluster, (agree, accord, sympathize)

darkness-n blackness, murk, swarthiness, obscurity, duskiness, gloominess, dimness, dinginess, lightless, opacity, tenebrous

dart-n throw, hurl, direct, spurt, shoot, scud, propel, project, fling, cast, pitch, chuck, toss, (pull, haul, draw, lug, rake, drag, tow, trail, train)

dash-v break, crush, shatter, depress, discourage, frustrate, imbue, blend, speed, rush, sprint, mark, stroke, line, trace, hint, tinge, grain

daunt-v frighten, alarm, cow, discourage, fear, timid, anxiety, solicitude, care, apprehension, (courage, bravery, valor, spirit)

daze-v bewilder, dazzle, stupefy, blind, spark, flash, blaze, scintillation, shine, glow, glitter, twinkle, brighten, (dark, obscurity, gloom, dusk, extinction)

dazzle-v impress, confound, bedazzle, awe, refraction, distortion, illusion, false light

dead-adj lifeless, deceased, defunct, departed, late, inanimate, extinct, fatal, mortal, destructive, murderous

deal-v allot, distribute, dispense, inflict, give, deliver, administer, arrange, allotment, sort, classify, (derangement, disorder, disorganize)

dearness-n expensiveness, high price, costliness, overcharge, extravagance, sumptuous, valuable, (cheapness, dislike, hate, loathe)

debar-v hinder, forbid, check, obstruct, exclude, deny, prohibit, bar, stile, barrier, restraint, prevent, impediment, obstacle, (aid, assistance, promote, reinforce)

debase-v deprave, degrade, depreciate, lower, dishonor, disgrace, deterioration, degradation, corruption, adulteration

debate-v discussion, argument, controversy, contention, conversation, oral communication, reasoning, comment, (answer, response, reply, replication)

debt-n liability, debit, obligation, claim, due, deferred payment, deficit, insolvency, (credit, trustworthiness, reliability)

decay-v putrefy, crumble, rot, wither, fall to pieces, decompose, pare, reduce, attenuate, scrape, render smaller, (expand, spread, extend, overgrown)

decease-v demise, dying,

departure, passing, death, dissolution, release, rest, extinction, bereavement, (respiration, vitality, animation, subsist)

deceit-*n* falsehood, sham, fraud, treachery, trickery, double dealing, perversion, hollowness, quackery, prevarication, (truthful, veracious, scrupulous)

decent-*adj* ordinary, clean, virtuous, passable, modest, pure, indifferent, middling, mediocre, average, tolerable, (unparalleled, superhuman)

decide-*v* resolve, settle, determine, choose, decree, arbitrate, fix upon, judge, result, conclusion, valuation, (misjudge, bias, warped, partiality)

decipher-*v* translate, decode, discover, explain, make out, interpret, definition, explanation, solution, answer, (misrepresent, misinterpret, distort)

decision-*n* resolve, decree, verdict, firmness, will, purpose, judgment, result, conclusion, deduction

declaration-*n* proclamation, avowal, announcement, bulletin, assertion, notice, profess, acknowledge

decline-*v* waste, age, die, decay, refuse, repel, shun, spurn, slope, declivity, descent

decomposition-*n*

dissolution, break-up, disjunction, disintegration, cariosity, putrefaction, putridity (cleanliness, combination)

decoration-*n* embellishment, trimming, adornment, ribbon, laurel, medal, ornament, wreath, festoon, (simplicity, plain, homely, unaffected, chaste)

decoy-*n* lure, inveigle, entice, entrap, ensnare, deception, falseness, untruth, fraud, deceit, guile

decrease-*v* diminution, lessening, mitigation, reduction, abatement, shrinkage, contraction, shorten, abbreviate, (increase, augmentation, addition, accumulation)

decree-*n* ordinance, edict, mandate, verdict, decision, regulation, command

decrement-*n* diminution, decrease, deduction, attenuation, abatement, waste, loss, (addition, adjunct)

decry-*v* disparage, slander, belittle, underestimate, censure, degrade, depreciation, undervaluing, modesty, (overestimating, exaggeration, vanity)

dedicate-*v* devote, offer, consecrate, inscribe, mark, name, figure, repute, enthrone, celebrate, glorify, (disrepute, discredit, disgrace, stain)

deduction-*n* curtailment,

subtraction, removal, .
excision, abstraction,
consequence, implication,
derivation, corollary,
discount, allowance,
(addition, attach, join,
interpose, append)

deed-_n_ feat, exploit, action,
performance, document,
evidence, confirmation,
warrant, credential,
admission, (vindication,
counter-protest, oppose,
rebut, countervail)

deep-_adj_ bottomless,
profound, unfathomable,
abstruse, astute,
designing, cunning,
concavity, submerged,
(shallow, superficial)

deface-_v_ mutilate, distort,
injure, disfigure, mar,
blemish, deteriorate,
shapeless, formless,
deform, (conformation,
formation, build, trim,
fashion)

defame-_v_ slander, abuse,
disparage, revile, taint,
smirch, sully, disrepute,
discredit, shame, disgrace,
(regard, respect, dignity,
splendor)

defeat-_v_ vanquish, subdue,
conquer, refute, rebut,
silence, overcome, failure,
abortion, inefficacy,
ineffectual, (success,
advancement, good
fortune, prosperity)

defect-_n_ flaw, fault, lack,
deficiency, imperfection,
weakness, shortcoming,
error, failing, blemish,

deficient, unsound

defense-_n_ security, guard,
protection, preservation,
resistance, vindication,
support, advocacy, plea,
espousal, fortification,
entrenchment, palisade,
(attack, aggression,
encroachment, offense,
onslaught, assail)

defensible-_adj_ impregnable,
invulnerable, supportable,
maintainable, excusable,
justifiable

defer-_v_ retard, postpone,
delay, procrastinate,
adjourn, yield, comply, give
in, capitulate

defiance-_n_ challenge,
threat, provocation,
opposition, disobedience,
insurgency, rebellion,
insubordination, revolt,
(obedience, submission)

deficient-_adj_ lacking, short,
wanting, insufficient,
inadequate, shortcoming,
inferior, minority, small,
subordinate, (superior,
supreme, great,
advantageous)

define-_v_ construe, expound,
explain, bound, limit,
circumscribe, description,
meaning, distinct

definite-_adj_ clear, plain,
positive, specific,
particular, limited, precise,
concrete, certain, surety,
(doubtful, uncertain,
vague, fallibility)

deflect-_v_ curve, bend, turn,
swerve, diverge, deviation,
stray, introvert, divert,

digress, departure, (set, undeviating, straight, directly)

deformity-*n* misproportion, disfigurement, ugliness, crookedness, malformation, distortion, (symmetrical, shapely, beautiful, parallel, uniform)

defraud-*v* swindle, hoax, trick, dupe, cheat, deceive, untruth, fraud, guile, misrepresentation, chicane, (truthful, frankness, sincerity, honesty)

defray-*v* settle, meet, liquidate, discharge, pay, acknowledgment, release, receipt, repayment, satisfaction, reimbursement, (non-payment, default, repudiation)

defy-*v* face, confront, brave, oppose, challenge, threaten, dare, defiance, disobey

degrade-*v* shame, disgrace, humiliate, dishonor, fall, abasement, deteriorate, despicable, unbecoming, scandalous, (dignity, stateliness, splendor, noble)

degree-*n* gradation, grade, step, extent, measure, point, amount, mark, rate, standard, height, range, scope, intensity, strength, (quantity, instantaneity)

deify-*v* idolize, venerate, canonize, immortalize,

exalt, repute, distinction, dedication, consecration, enthronement, celebration, (dishonor, shameful, stain, disgrace)

deity-*n* omnipotence, god, omniscience, providence, supreme being, creator, almighty, hold, preserve, atone, redeem

dejection-*n* despondency, melancholy, depression, pessimism, despair, sorrow, sadness, grief, dolefulness, distress, weariness, (cheerfulness, happy, geniality, gaiety)

delay-*v* retard, obstruct, linger, defer, impede, postpone, procrastinate, put off, adjourn, late, tardy, belated, (immediately, briefly, shortly, quickly, presently)

delectable-*adj* pleasant, delightful, tasty, delicious, pleasurable, savory, relish, delicacy, appetizing, zestful, (acrid, repulsive, nasty, sickening, nauseous)

delegate-*v* substitute, envoy, agent, proxy, assign, consign, entrust, authorize, empower, commission, assignment, deputation, (annulment, nullification, cancel)

delete-*v* cancel, expunge, erase, obliterate, efface, (record, note, register, endorse, memo)

deliberate-*v* meditate, reflect, reason, ponder,

well-considered, gradual, voluntary, leisurely

deliberation-*n* coolness, caution, prudence, deliberateness, slowness, discretion, prudence, calculation, foresight, (impetuous, levity, imprudence, presumption, audacity)

delicacy-*n* daintiness, luxury, elegance, tidbit, discrimination, tact, culture, sensitiveness, frailty, infirmity, savoury, palatable, ambrosia

delicious-*adj* delectable, dainty, pleasing, luscious, palatable, tasty, relish, good, ambrosia, zest, appetizing, sweet, nectarous, (offensive, repulsive, nasty, nauseous)

delight-*n* please, gratify, charm, enchant, enjoy, pleasure, fruition, satisfaction, happiness, rapture, ecstasy, (annoyance, irritation, worry, plague)

delineate-*v* block, depict, sketch, portray, set forth, illustrate, represent, imitate, sculpture, engrave, design, draft, trace, (distort, exaggerate, daub)

delinquent-*adj* derelict, remiss, neglectful, rough, rowdy, ruffian, bully, incendiary, thief, murderer, criminal, (model, paragon, hero, innocent, benefactor)

delirious-*adj* crazed, raving, mad, insane, light-headed, lunacy, eccentricity, maniacal, reasonless, demented, (sanity, soundness, rationality, sobriety, lucidity)

deliverance-*n* liberation, release, rescue, reprieve, extrication, emancipation, redemption, salvation, (restraint, retention)

delude-*v* dupe, bluff, trick, fool, hoodwink, deceive, false impression, deception, hallucination, fault, blunder, (fact, reality, accuracy, delicacy, rigor)

deluge-*v* downpour, flood, inundation, rainstorm, supersaturate, excessive, superabundant, overflowing, (insufficient, meager, paltry, empty)

delusion-*n* illusion, magic, fallacy, misconception, hallucination, conjuring, infatuation, oddity, (sane, rational, reasonable)

demand-*v* order, impose, ask, exact, question, require, claim, requisition, request, market, ultimatum

demolish-*v* devastate, ruin, overthrow, wreck, crush, explode, invalidate, defeat, (establish, prove, make good, verify)

demonic-*adj* devilish, hellish, possessed, fiendish, vampire, ghoul, fiend, supernatural, **weird**, unearthly, haunted

demonstration-*n* verification, proof,

substantiation, conclusiveness, testimony, exhibition, mass-meeting, (confutation, refute)

demoralize-v incapacitate, unnerve, undermine, corrupt, deprave, pervert, render-powerless, disqualify, (powerful, puissant, potent, capable)

demur-adj protest, cavil, object, wrangle, scruple, remonstrance, disbelieve, dissent, unwilling, hesitate, (determination, resolve, vigor, resoluteness)

demure-adj precise, priggish, solemn, sad, sedate, shy, bashful, retiring, modesty, reserve, constraint, blushing, (vain, pretentious, conceit, selfishness)

den-n sanctum, cave, lair, study, retreat, cell, abode, dwelling, lodging, domicile, residence, habitation

denial-n repudiation, negation, contradiction, disallowance, disbelief, disavowal, protest, recusancy, (affirmance, declaration, oath, assurance)

denomination-n persuasion, designation, name, side, specification, kind, sect, class, division, category, province, domain

denote-v betoken, signify, represent, express, imply, convey, designate, specify, indication, feature, type, characteristic

denounce-v arraign, charge, censure, rebuke, blame, curse, damn, accuse, reprehend, chide, admonish, disapprove, (approval, approbation, advocacy, esteem)

density-n solidness, body, compactness, thickness, impenetrability, impermeability, coherence, ignorance, crassness, ineptitude, opacity, dullness, obtuseness, (intelligence, rarity)

dent-n depression, hollow, indentation, cavity, concavity, dip, cavernous, excavate, burrow, tunnel, (convex, project, swelling, bilge, bulge, protrusion)

denunciation-n defiance, condemnation, curse, arraignment, imprecation

deny-v differ, protest, contradict, reject, doubt, discredit, dissent, discontent, disagreement, non-conformity, (assent, acquiescence, admission, unanimity)

department-n jurisdiction, bureau, office, division, part, function, capacity, sphere, orb, field, line, walk, routine

departure-n embarkation, start, exit, leaving, egress, parting, withdraw, adieu, farewell, removal, (return, remigration, arrive)

depend-v trust, credit, rely, hang, be contingent, uncertain, casual, doubtful, dubious, vague, hesitant, (positive, absolute, definite, decisive, without question)

depict-*v* delineate, portray, represent, picture, describe, mimic, illustrative, imitate, figurative, (distort, exaggerate, misrepresent)

deplore-*v* bewail, lament, regret, mourn, complain, grievous, sad, pitiable, repine, (content, satisfaction, ease, cheerfulness)

deport-*v* banish, transport, exile, remove, send, transit, displace, drift, bring, fetch, transpose

deposit-*v* installment, pledge, payment, alluvium, place, situate, locate, settlement, establish, (displace, eject, removal, unload)

deposition-*n* sworn evidence, affidavit, allegation, dethronement, expulsion, archive, docket, certificate, (efface, obliterate, erase, cancel)

depository-*n* warehouse, storehouse, vault, store, repository, conservatory, closet, reservoir, cistern

depression-*n* sinking, cavity, hollow, dip, diminution, humiliation, abasement, subversion, melancholy, dispiritedness, gloom, despondency, sadness, (cheerfulness, elevation)

deprive-*v* bereave, strip, dispossess, despoil, rob, clutch, capture, distress, divestment, extortion, eviction, (restitution, replevin, redemption, atonement)

depth-*n* profoundness, extent, profundity, intensity, completeness, abundance, (shallowness, veneer, superficiality)

deputy-*n* substitute, proxy, surrogate, delegate, agent, representative, alternate

derangement-*n* discomposure, disorder, confusion, embarrassment, mess, tangle, inversion, mania, insanity, madness, (sanity, arrangement)

dereliction-*n* abandonment, relinquishment, neglect, omission, desertion, failure, fault, evasion, (duty, respect, homage)

deride-*v* disdain, scorn, jeer, mock, ridicule, irruption, snigger, satirize, parody, travesty

derive-*v* secure, get, gain, account for, deduce, infer, etymologize, trace, estimation, valuation, appreciation, assessment, (discover, find, determine, evolve)

derogatory-*adj* scandalous, unbefitting, ignoble, discreditable, disrepute, degrade, dishonor, expel, disgrace, (distinct, repute, dignity, rank, standing)

descend-v dismount, slide, go down, tumble, detail, special, particular, specific, proper

descent-n drop, plunge, fall, declination, comedown, gravitate, decline, sink, spring, issue, (ascent, ascension, rising, originate, upgrowth)

description-n statement, account, record, report, summary, outline, depiction, representation

desert-n waste, wilderness, forsake, abandon, leave, run away, worth, due, recompense, meed

deserter-n fugitive, truant, runaway, apostate, changeful, reactionary, apostatize, (arbitrary, dogmatic, positive, uninfluenced)

design-v arrangement, make-up, depiction, drawing, aim, intent, project, pattern, model

designate-v show, specify, indicate, name, call, particularize, individualize, special, proper, detail, definite, (general, prevail, generic, collective, broad)

desire-v inclination, fancy, wish, whim, propensity, fondness, need, want, exigency, urgency, hunger, necessity, passion, (dislike, indifference, satiety)

desist-v halt, discontinue, stop, quit, cease, abstain, interrupt, pause, rest, suspend, (continue, persistence, sustain)

desolate-adj uninhabited, deserted, waste, forlorn, miserable, forsaken, lonely, seclusion, solitude, isolation, (sociality, visit, welcome, hospitality)

despair-n dejection, misery, despondency, wretchedness, anguish, hopelessness, desperate, relinquish, (hope, trust, confidence, reliance, faith)

desperate-adj wild, frantic, frenzied, raging, reckless, despairing, incurable, impossible, impervious, impassible, (practical, feasible, compatible)

despise-v scorn, condemn, disdain, disregard, hate, disgust, contempt, derisive, withering, pitiful, despicable

despond-v lament, mourn, despair, falter, sink, melancholy, sad, dejected, depressed, heaviness, dismal, demure, gravity, (cheerful, geniality, gaiety, liveliness)

destination-n port, goal, halting place, point, mark, end, close, termination, conclusion, finale, consummation, (beginning, commencement, opening, outset)

destiny-n fortune, fate, lot, fatalism, prospect, decree, expectation, impending, future, (eventuality, incident, proceeding)

destitute-*adj* poor, penniless, lacking, bereft, needy, deficiency, inadequate, emptiness, poorness, depletion, (sufficient, adequate, enough, luxury)

destruction-*n* demolition, ruination, dissolution, devastation, cataclysm, perdition, extermination, annihilation, extirpation, (preservation, production)

desultory-*adj* disconnected, digressive, rambling, fitful, aimless, erratic, broken, spasmodic

detach-*v* disconnect, sever, unfasten, loosen, separation, segregation, portion, division, squad, detail, (unite, join, together, connect)

detail-*n* item, particular, feature, party, patrol, description, account, statement, report, summary, specification, delineation, representation

detain-*v* withhold, delay, retard, secure, retention, retain, detain, keep, custody, tenacity, grasp, gripe

detect-*v* discern, reveal, expose, unearth, perceive, discover, find, determine, evolve, fix upon, determine, (result, conclusion, upshot, deduction)

deter-*v* discourage, hinder, restrain, hold back, dissuade, deprecation, dampen, deport, against, remonstrate, disincline, (induce, entice, allure, bewitch)

deterioration-*n* impairment, detriment, injury, harm, debasement, damage, loss, degeneration, vitiation, dilapidation, disrepair (improvement, betterment, amendment)

determination-*n* firmness, resolution, resolve, judgment, decree, result, conclusion, evaluate, assess, estimate, (misjudge, positive, intolerant, impracticable)

determine-*v* impel, insure, influence, ascertain, conclude, define, decree, designate, specify

detest-*v* loathe, abhor, abominate, despise, dislike, disgust, disagreeable, disincline, repel, sicken, nauseous, (desire, wish, fancy, fantasy, want, need, inclined)

detraction-*n* derogation, disparagement, scandal, defamation, calumny, contempt, disapprobation, (approbation, flattery)

develop-*v* promote, build, evolve, grow, enlarge, produce, perform, flower, generate, impregnate, prolific, induce, (destruction, dissolution, ruin, annihilate, abolish)

development-*n* consequence, outgrowth,

growth, expansion,
evolution, effect,
eventuality, resulting from,
emanate, (cause, origin,
source, element, principle)

deviation-*n* divagation,
digression, aberration,
variation, alteration,
diversion, declination,
swerve, warp, drift,
(continuance, direction,
straightness)

device-*n* stratagem, trick,
design, contrivance,
appliance, emblem, type,
figure, representation,
characteristic, diagnostic

devious-*adj* circuitous,
erring, rambling, indirect,
diversion, digression,
refraction, departure,
aberration, (course,
aligned, direct, straight)

devise-*v* create, contrive,
scheme, originate, will,
bequeath, plan, scheme,
design, project,
suggestion, resolution

devoid-*adj* destitute, void,
lacking, wanting, absent,
not present, empty, truant,
vacant, elsewhere,
inexistent, (present, fill,
pervade, permeate,
occupy, moored)

devote-*v* destine, preordain,
addict, consecrate,
dedicate, apply, utilize,
resolve, determination,
desperation, vigor, (fickle,
levity, weakness, waver,
hesitate)

devotee-*n* zealot, fanatic,
fan, enthusiast, believer,

religionist, inclination,
desire, magnet, attraction,
aspirant, solicitant,
(reluctance, lackadaisical,
half-hearted)

devotion-*n* loyalty, passion,
fidelity, worship, homage,
yearning, gallantry,
benevolence, attachment,
rapture, adoration, (hate,
detest, abominate, abhor)

devour-*v* consume,
annihilate, swallow,
masticate, rumination,
gulp, eat, edible,
succulent, potable,
bibulous, (eject, emission,
egestion, evacuation)

devout-*adj* sincere,
reverent, pious, religious,
holy, beatification,
regeneration, conversion,
veneration, (irreverence,
hypocrisy, bigot, impiety,
sacrilege, blasphemy)

diabolic-*adj* impious,
infernal, devilish, satanic,
fiendish, hurtful, injurious,
deleterious, malignity,
malevolence, (goodness,
excellence, beneficial,
proficient)

dialect-*n* tongue, speech,
brogue, cant, idiom,
vernacular, colloquialism,
slang, expression,
provincialism

dictate-*v* suggest,
prescribe, direct, order,
charge, compose, draw up,
advice, council, instruction,
enforce, recommend

dictatorial-*adj* domineering,
overbearing, autocratic,

peremptory, superiority, insolence, arrogance, overbearance, (servile, obsequious, supple, cringe)

die-v fade, expire, perish, depart, to be killed, mold, seal, punch, matrix, death, dissolution, departure, (life, vitality, respire, vivification, animation)

dietetic-adj alimental, dietary, nutritious, treatment, help, remedy, medicine, antiseptic, corrective, restorative, sedative, (bane, curse, rust, leaven, poison)

difference-n unlikeness, dissimilarity, variety, diversity, heterogeneity, dissonance, disparity, contradiction, contrast, incongruousness, dispute, contend, bicker, (identity, similarity)

differentiate-v separate, discriminate, adapt, distinguish, set apart, sever, estimate, refinement, diagnosis, (uncertain, unmeasured, overlook)

difficulty-n arduousness, impracticability, hardness, impossibility, tough, scrape, entanglement, (smooth, facilitate, ease, unclog)

diffuseness-n verbosity, amplification, wordiness, verbiage, loquacity, looseness, exuberance

digest-v classify, settle, arrange, summarize, assimilate, transform, endure, think out, reflect, cogitate, consider, (vacant, unoccupied, inconsiderate)

dignity-n honor, nobility, distinction, stateliness, august, lofty, majestic, haughtiness, vainglory, supercilious, (humble, disgrace, service, submissive)

digress-v diverge, swerve, ramble, wander, deviate, stray, straggle, sidle, rove, dodge, meander, veer, (straight, aligned, undeviating, course)

dilapidated-adj crumbling, decayed, ruined, worn out, deterioration, debasement, recession, retrogradation, (improvement, melioration, betterment, amendment)

dilemma-n perplexity, mess, difficulty, strait, difficulty, impractical, embarrassment, impossibility, tough, hard, (manageable, wieldy, submissive, yielding)

dilute-v thin, reduce, weaken, water, declension, delicacy, invalidation, decrepitude, asthenia, fragile, unsubstantial, (strength, power, energy, stamina)

dim-adj obscure, dull, hazy, vague, cloudy, faint, blackness, darkness, obscurity, gloom, pale, fade, lack luster, (shine, glow, glitter, shimmer)

dimension-*n* extent, area, measurement, expanse, size, proportions, amplitude, mass, capacity, enormity, (intangible, impalpable, inappreciable, infinitesimal)

diminish-*v* curtail, abase, reduce, decrease, weaken, small, slight, little

dip-*v* slope, declivity, decline, inclination, slant, lean, include, distort, oblique, depression, hollow, indentation, cavity, (convexity, prominence, projection, swell)

diplomacy-*n* tact, skill, negotiation, address, politics, chicanery, maneuver, concealment, guile, strategy, (artlessness, simplicity, innocence, candor)

dire-*adj* dreadful, shocking, horrible, calamitous, deplorable, fearful, ominous, bad, annoyance, molestation, abuse, (valuable, advantageous, profitable, edifying)

dirty-*adj* soiled, sullied, filthy, stormy, murky, threatening, leaden, contamination, unclean, impure, defilement, (clean, pure, lavation, disinfection)

disagreement-*n* difference, dissonance, discrepancy, inequality, variance, dissent, controversy, inaptitude, impropriety, unsuitability, opposition

disappearance-*n* vanishing, evanescence, dissolution, fading, occultation, eclipse, exit, departure, dissolve, (appearance, visible, show, manifest)

disappointment-*n* frustration, chagrin, bafflement, discontent, failure, disconcerted, miscalculation, (expectation, breathless, anticipation, contemplation)

disapprobation-*n* disapproval, displeasure, disfavor, denunciation, condemnation, rebuke, admonition, reprimand, castigation, objurgation, reprobation

disaster-*n* affliction, cataclysm, calamity, adversity, accident, blow, failure, misfortune, catastrophe, downfall, (prosper, welfare, affluence, success)

disbelieve-*v* discredit, doubt, challenge, lack faith, infidelity, misbelief, dissent, incredulous, suspicious, septic, (credulity, gullible, simple, confident, believing)

discard-*v* abolish, reject, repudiate, cancel, nullify, oversight, absent, abstracted, perplex, bewilder, trash, (observe, scrutinize, study, revise)

discern-*v* appreciate, comprehend, perceive, experience, detect, distinguish, discriminate

discharge-v release, exude, absolve, abolish, discard, perform, settle, transact, dismiss, oust, disband

disciple-n follower, pupil, adherent, student, scholar, apprentice, beginner, recruit, novice, neophyte, apostle, (teacher, trainer, instructor, institutor, master)

discipline-n orderliness, subordination, control, obedience, correction, chastisement, development

disclosure-n divulgence, vent, utterance, exposure, revelation, admission, declaration, confession, avowal, (concealment, ambush)

discomfort-n suffering, discontent, soreness, painfulness, disquiet, displeasure, annoyance, irritation, chagrin, (happiness, cheerfulness, refreshment, enchantment)

disconcert-v upset, abash, trouble, frustrate, bewilder, perplex, balk, disrepute, discredit, tarnish, degrade, beggar, stigmatize, (dignity, stateliness, solemnity, grandeur)

disconnection-n separation, interruption, cleavage, break, dissociation, irrelation, deviation, sunder, divide, dissect, anatomize, sever, (join, unite, associate, suture, stitch)

disconsolate-adj sorrowful, melancholy, hopeless, forlorn, desolate, dejection, depression, prostration, (liveliness, life, vivacity, jocularity, mirth)

discontent-n uneasiness, dissatisfaction, regret, disappointment, soreness, mortification, repining, (content, serenity, gratification, happiness)

discontinuity-n disunion, fracture, disconnection, cessation, disruption, (continuity, succession, sequence)

discord-n dissidence, clash, dissension, disagreement, difference, variance, division, schism, faction, (concord, harmony, agreement)

discount-v concession, abatement, allowance, qualification, poundage, rebate, depreciation

discourage-v depress, deter, dishearten, daunt, divert, dissuade, deport, remonstrate, warn, disincline, (stimulate, excite, inspirit, persuade)

discourtesy-n incivility, rudeness, impoliteness, tactlessness, rusticity, unmannerly, disrespect, impudence, barbarism, (courtesy, politeness, gentility, refinement)

discovery-n ascertainment, detection, exposure, finding, revelation, contrivance, unearthing, invention, device, design, (concealment, veil, cover, camouflage, screen)

discredit-v shame, debase, disbelieve, disgrace, disrepute, dishonor, tarnish, defile, pollute, humiliate, reproach, (distinguish, elevate, dedicate, ascent, exaltation)

discretion-n prudence, option, volition, freedom, wariness, caution, wary, judicious, choice, elect, preference, choose, (indifference, indecision, neutrality)

discrimination-n distinction, differentiation, diagnosis, estimation, discernment, acuteness, clearness, acumen, insight

discuss-v examine, analyze, reason, argue, debate, consider, study, controversy, inquire, question, investigate, (answer, retort, discover, rationale)

disengage-v disentangle, disconnect, sever, free, extricate, clear, liberate, release, emancipation, dismissal, (confine, duress, restraint, repress)

disfigure-v deface, impair, mutilate, mangle, mar, ugly, deformity, inelegance, blemish, squalor, eyesore, gaunt, (beauty, elegance, grace, form, gloss)

disgrace-n dishonor, shame, degrade, discredit, humiliate, corrupt, recreant, venal, insidious, perfidious, arrant, (upright, honest, equitable, impartial)

disguise-n camouflage, mask, concealment, blind, cloak, pretense, hide, mystify, secrecy, reserve, cover, screen, (enlighten, acquaint, knowledge, publicity)

disgust-v repugnance, loathing, aversion, repletion, dislike, gall, abomination, sicken, repel, (desire, passion, crave, care for, affect)

dishonest-adj fraudulent, false, crooked, dishonorable, deceptive, untruth, guile, misrepresentation, distortion, (veracity, honesty, frankness, truthful, true)

disinfect-v purify, cleanse, fumigate, sanitize, ventilate, immaculate, clear, clarify, deodorize, refine, (dirt, filth, soot, contaminate)

disjunction-n disunion, disconnection, parting, partition, break, disengagement

dislike-v disinclination, displeasure, disfavor, reluctance, repugnance, abomination, antipathy, abhorrence, hatred

dislocate-v disarrange,

displace, disjoin, disunite,
derange, separate,
disjunctive, asunder,
distinct, unconnected

dismal-*adj* gloomy, somber,
depressing, funereal,
sorrowful, mournful,
annoyance, grievance,
nuisance, vexation,
(gratify, delight, gladden,
captivate)

dismantle-*v* destroy,
undress, strip, disrobe,
worthless, inadequate,
waste, cripple, lame,
useless, (utility,
usefulness, conducive,
remunerative)

dismiss-*v* send away,
banish, discharge, let go,
disband, eject, relinquish,
abandon, dispense,
riddance, (retain, keep,
detain, custody, tenacity)

disobedience-*n* unruliness,
insubordination, mutiny,
intractableness, revolt,
recalcitrance,
obstinacy, noncompliance,
contumacy

disorder-*n* disarrangement,
confusion, untidiness,
disarray, derangement,
anomaly, disunion,
anarchy, chaos, clutter,
disorganization

disown-*v* repudiate, deny,
renounce, disclaim, reject,
retract, dispute, ignore,
rebut, disavow, protest,
(affirmation, declare,
positive, emphatic,
definitive)

disparage-*v* belittle, decry,

discredit, underrate,
abuse, scoff at,
underestimate, depreciate,
modesty, minimize,
(oversensitive, exaggerate,
vanity, magnify)

dispatch-*v* dismiss, slay,
alacrity, expedition,
promptness, urgency,
precipitation

dispense-*v* allot, portion,
distribute, bestow,
administer, apportion,
disperse, diffuse, shed,
spread, dissemination,
(assemble, collect, gather,
muster, compilation)

dispersion-*n* distribution,
scattering, propagation,
dissipation, dissemination,
allocation, apportionment

displacement-*n* transfer,
dislocation, replacement,
disturbance, eject,
expulsion, dismissal,
deposition

displease-*v* vex, disturb,
annoy, offend, maltreat,
sicken, repel, disenchant,
disagreeable, distasteful,
(pleasant, agreeable,
amuse, delectable)

disposition-*n* emotion,
temperament, passion,
predisposition, tendency,
inclination, propensity

disprove-*v* refute, rebut,
defeat, confute, negative,
expose, invalidation,
conviction, clincher,
(categorical, decisive,
crucial)

dispute-*v* clash, wrangle,
bicker, confute, argue,

debate, challenge, quarrel, discord

disqualify-v incapacitate, disfranchise, unfit, disable, helpless, exhaust, invalid, inefficiency, collapse, (attribute, quality, qualify, potent)

disregard-v affront, slight, insult, overlook, underrate, belittle, inconsiderate, escape one's attention, (attention, consideration, reflection, regard)

disrepute-n dishonor, discredit, disfavor, disesteem, derogation, abasement, degradation, ignominy, disgrace

dissatisfy-v offend, vex, provoke, annoy, anger, displease, chafe, anxiety, concern, grief, bitterness, tribulation, (happiness, felicity, comfort, delight)

dissemble-v feign, hide, disguise, mask, simulate, deception, untruth, guile, misrepresentation, pretense, sham, (veracity, truthfulness, frankness, sincerity)

dissent-v nonagreement, nonconsent, difference, variance, discordance, schism, disaffection, secession

dissertation-n treatise, theme, thesis, essay, discourse, investigation, commentary, lecture, sermon

dissimilarity-n unlikeness, divergence, variation,

difference, novelty, originality, diversity, disparity, (similarity, resemblance, similitude, semblance)

dissolve-v end, destroy, abolish, disintegrate, vanish, evaporate, fade, liquefy, decompose, disappear, (visible, perceptible, perceivable, discernible)

distance-n remoteness, span, space, interval, coldness, frigidity, reservation, aloofness, out skirts, (nearness, proximity, propinquity)

distasteful-adj unsavory, unpalatable, bitter, disagreeable, uninviting, unsatisfactory, painful, irritating, grievance, (pleasure, attraction, loveliness)

distinct-adj apart, explicit, separate, characterize, clear-cut, distinguishable, disconnected, disjoined, divide, sever, (attach, entangle, twine, cohere, incorporate)

distinguished-adj renowned, famous, celebrated, noted, illustrious, eminent, superior, supreme, majority, (inferior, smaller, subordinative, deficient)

distortion-n deformation, contortion, twisting, perversion, irregular, misrepresentation, misunderstanding, exaggeration, (interpret, decipher, understand, explanatory)

distress-*n* sorrow, agony, affliction, anguish, grief, misery, misfortune, pain, concern, unhappiness, infelicity, (enjoyment, gratification, fruition, relish)

district-*n* tract, section, neighborhood, division, commune, county, state, region, sphere, ground, circuit, territory, (space, expanse, range, latitude)

distrust-*n* qualm, doubt, suspicion, apprehension, disbelief, mistrust, discredit, infidelity, dissent, doubtful, (believe, credit, faithful, dependence)

disturb-*v* upset, muddle, shake, stir, misplace, worry, trouble, disquiet, tumult, disorder, perturbation, derangement, agitation

disuse-*n* desuetude, non-use, abandonment, neglect, relinquishment, discontinuance

divergence-*n* ramification, furcation, branching, divarication, separation, detachment, dispersion, deviation, disagreement

diversion-*n* recreation, pastime, variation, break, sport, festivity, gala, rejoicing, (weariness, irksome, monotonous)

divert-*v* delight, deflect, entertain, switch, turn inequality, multiformity,

divergence, variation, dissimilitude

divestment-*n* unstrapping, unclothing, excoriation, desquamation, excavation, uncover, strip, bare, denude, dishabille, (invest, cover, vesture, array)

divide-*v* assign, separate, distribute, allot, sunder, cleave, part, detach, sever, dissect, mangle, disconnect, (pin, nail, secure, set, firm, fast, close)

divine-*adj* superhuman, godlike, celestial, holy, religious, perfection, indefectibility, paragon, summit, (imperfect, inadequate, deficient, fault)

dizzy-*adj* vertiginous, giddy, light-headed, confused, absent, abstracted, inattentive, muddle, disregard, (attentive, observant, reflective, regardful)

docile-*adj* submissive, gentle, tractable, obedient, aptitude, edification, willing, inclined, geniality, volunteering, (unwilling, disinclination, volition)

doctrine-*n* maxim, theory, creed, dogma, principle, record, note, register, testimonial, commemorate, (obliterate, cancel, delete, erase)

domestic-*adj* broken, tame, inland, home, family, inhabitant, resident, dweller, occupier, native

doom-*n* judgment, sentence, fate, fortune, ruin, lot, destiny, future, impend, destined, threaten, loom, forthcoming, (eventual, proceed, circumstance, casualty)

door-*n* gate, entrance, portal, obstacle, outlet, inlet, barrier, beginning, inception, introduction, source, (end, close, termination, conclusion)

doubt-*v* question, mistrust, disbelieve, distrust, incredulity, disbelief, skepticism, agnosticism, suspicion

downfall-*n* overthrow, fall, misfortune, wreck, crash, destruction, breaking up, disorganization, desolation, (productive, flowering, erection, perform)

downright-*adj* plainly, bluntly, completely, absolutely, utterly, simply, innocence, candor, sincere, honestly, (cunning, craftiness, artificial, maneuvering)

downy-*adj* lanate, woolly, flocculent, soft, fluffy, pliable, mollify, mellow, relax, mash, knead, yielding, (hard, rigid, inflexible, stiff, starched)

draft-*n* sketch, drawing, breeze, air, select, enlist, impress, conscript, commandeer

drag-*v* creep, trail, lag, crawl, elapse, pull, tug, traction, rake, tow, wrench, jerk, haul, (propel, project, throw, fling, cast, pitch, toss)

drain-*v* flow out, leak, discharge, empty, exhaust, egestion, evacuation, vomit, emission, effusion, expulsion, (reception, admission, importation, ingestion)

draw-*v* lure, attract, fabricate, describe, sketch, portray, drag, pull, haul, design, picture, draft, (misrepresent, distort, exaggerate, caricature, daub)

dreadful-*adj* horrible, frightful, tremendous, shocking, formidable, depressing, dejected, heaviness, sadness, (cheerful, genial, gay, good humor)

dream-*n* vision, reverie, fantasy, fancy, shadow, inattentive, absent, bemused, preoccupied, engrossed

dreary-*adj* somber, gloomy, depressing, monotonous, humdrum, dull, solitude, seclusion, isolation, lonely, (happy, content, coexist)

dregs-*n* settlings, lees, sediment, residue, trash, refuse, riffraff, common, low, beggarly, uncivilized, (aristocrat, noble, gentlemen, distinctive)

dress-*n* attire, clothe, drape, deck, berate, scold, adorn, embellish, garments, raiment, apparel, vesture, garb

drink-v sip, quaff, tipple, carouse, imbibe, absorb, toast, pledge, libation, potation, draft, gulp, swallow, (eject, emission, emit, evacuate)

drive-v impel, oblige, force, urge, steer, manage, control, ride, travel, thrust, aim, compel, enforce

driver-n coachman, whip, charioteer, teamster, chauffeur, director, manager, master, taskmaster

droop-v despond, decline, sink, wither, fade, hang, lean, drop, decay, retrograde, go down, downhill, (improve, meliorate, betterment, mend)

drop-v slide, sink, fall, discontinue, collapse, faint, discard, give up, drip, trickle, descent

drown-v suffocate, drench, submerge, overpower, overwhelm, deaden, victimize, choke, stifle

drunkenness-n inebriety, intemperance, drinking, inebriation, insobriety, intoxication, libations, bacchanalia

dryness-n aridity, aridness, drought, parched, desiccation, dehydration, evaporation

duality-n twofold, double, biform, duplicity, polarity,

two, deuce, couple, pair, twins

dubious-adj questionable, doubtful, suspicious, uncertain, hesitation, perplexity, embarrassment, dilemma, (certainty, gospel, reliable, infallible)

ductile-adj pliable, pliant, flexible, malleable, tactile, manageable, compliant, docile, tractable

duel-n affair of honor, single combat, fight, competition, rivalry, contest, opposition, satisfaction, (peace, harmony, tranquil, concord)

dullness-n stupidity, slowness, stagnation, dimness, sluggishness, apathy, obscurity, uninteresting, insipid, unimaginative

dumb-adj voiceless, silence, taciturnity, slow-witted, stupid, inarticulate, suppress, mute, (voice, sound, utter, articulate)

duplication-n doubling, iteration, renewal, facsimile, copy, imitate, mirror, reflect, reproduce, repeat, (original, unmatched, unique)

durability-n permanence, continuance, persistence, immutability, stability, unchangeable, constant, (erratic, vagrant, alternating, mobile)

duty-n respect, deference, homage, reverence, obligation, service, responsibility, task, commission, charge, trust

dwarf-*n* midget, pygmy, Lilliputian, little, urchin, elf, puppet, shrimp, runt, minute, (mammoth, elephant, hippopotamus, colossus)

dwelling-*n* domicile, abode, house, residence, habitation, housing, home, berth, throne, tenement, barn, mansion, villa, hermitage

dwindle-*v* contract, lessen, shrink, diminish, decline, decrease, abate, depreciate, deteriorate, shorten, (increase, enlarge, expand, augment, raise)

E

each-*adj* apiece, seriatim, respectively, severally, individual, special, particular, separate, (generally, generic, universal)

eager-*adj* zealous, ardent, earnest, fervent, intent, willing, voluntary, inclined, favorable, ready, forward, (unwilling, renitency, reluctance, indifference)

earliness-*n* promptitude, punctuality, readiness, quickness, haste, speed, swiftness, alacrity, prematureness, precocity, anticipation, hastiness, (lateness, tardiness, delay, deferring)

earnest-*adj* fervent, zealous, ardent, grave, eager, solemn, weighty, serious, determined, purposeful

ease-*n* enjoyment, readiness, contentment, expertness, cheerfulness, comfort, resignation, satisfaction, (discontent, grief, disappointment, mortification)

easy-*adj* unconcerned, smooth, untroubled, unconstrained, gentle, facile, simple, tractable, manageable, compliant

eat-*v* devour, consume, fare, rust, corrode, erode, masticate, consume, nourishment, subsistence, provision, (excrete, discharge, secrete, outpour)

ebb-*v* waste, decay, decline, recede, withdraw, return, reflux, recoil, regress, fall, deteriorate, resilience, (progress, advance, proceed, improve)

eccentric-*adj* irregular, peculiar, odd, deviating, erratic, unsettled, demented, possessed, maddened, moonstruck

ecclesiastical-*adj* religious, priestly, clerical, sacerdotal, scriptural, biblical, prophetic, apostolic, canonical

echo-*n* repercussion, repeat, reverberation, reproduce, resound, ring, reflex, hollow, sepulchral, chime, (dead sound, dampen, muffled, thud)

economy-*n* frugality, thriftiness, savings, prevention of waste, parsimony, retrenchment, careful, saving, sparing, (liberality, generosity, munificent, freely, bountifulness)

educate-*v* instruct, tutor, direction, guidance, preparation, discipline, practice, study, lecture, inoculation, impregnate, enlighten, inform, coach, disseminate, (bewilder, perversion, misinformation, deceive, mislead, unedifying)

effect-*n* consequence, result, outgrowth, development, derivative, (cause, origin, source, foundation, groundwork)

efficient-*adj* skillful, capable, clever, knowledgeable, adroit, masterful, accomplished, ingenuity, endowed, competent, (unskilled, blunder, inability, stupidity, failure, fumble, disqualify)

ego-*n* vanity, conceit, self-esteem, admiration, gaudery, assurance, complacency, praise, glorification, laudation, (modesty, timidity, humility, reserve, demureness, sheepish)

either-*adj* choice, option, alternative, selection,

prefer, to set apart, preference, elect, discretion, decision, (neutrality, indifference, waive, abstain, refrain, indecision, neither)

elate-*v* cheerfulness, gaiety, geniality, good humor, glee, merriment, hilarity, laughter, rejoice, liveliness, jocularity, mirth, exhilaration, joviality, vivacity, (dejected, depressed, weariness, melancholy, sadness, dismal, despondent, solemnity, sorrowful)

elect-*v* choice, option, discretion, alternative, decision, poll, ballot, vote, selection, pick, choose, cull, separate, prefer, excerpt, (neutral, indifference, waive, abstain, refrain, reject)

elementary-*adj* simple, homogeneity, sheer, neat, unsophisticated, basic, (combined, complicated, developed, complex)

elevation-*n* height, altitude, pitch, loftiness, stature, prominence, mount, tower, soar, surmount, lofty, rise, mountainous, upper, gigantic, picture, drawing, sketch, (lowness, depression, lowlands, underlie, crouch, slouch, grovel, at a low ebb)

eliminate-*v* deduction, retrenchment, removal, mutilation, amputation, curtailment, withdraw, diminish, abscind, prune, subtract, decrease, (addition, annexation, adjection, increase, supplement, inclusive, reinforce)

embark-v departure, port-of-embarcation, outset, start, removal, adieu, farewell, starting point, set out, quit, vacate, (admission, insertion, immigration, insinuation, penetrate)

embarrass-v difficulty, dilemma, perplexity, entanglement, awkwardness, quagmire, unwieldy, restriction, hindrance, impediment, restraint, (support, uplift, advance, furtherance, promotion, favor, patronage, advocacy)

embellish-v ornament, decoration, architecture, lace, fringe, border, edging, wreath festoon garland, pattern, improve, (disfigure, deformity, delete, blemish, flaw, scar)

embitter-v aggravate, render worse, exasperation, exacerbation, overestimation, exaggeration, acerbate, heightening, (relief, deliverance, refreshment, easement, softening, alleviation, mitigation, soothing)

embroil-v derange, unsettle, disturb, confuse, muddle, fumble, perturbation inversion, complicate, disorder, involve, convulse, disconsert, dissension, division, rupture, (harmony, agreement, sympathy, unison, accord, reunion, conciliation)

embryo-n beginning, commencement, opening, inception, initial, onset, genesis, birth, start, originate, conceive, initiate, groundwork, foundation, pivot, hinge, (creation, harvest, result, end, termination, conclusion, finale, consummation, death, finality, finish, close, expiration)

emergency-n critical situation, crisis, pinch, quandary, full of incident, circumstance, adventure, contingency, phenomenon,eventuality, concern (ease, feasibility, flexibility, smooth, lighten, manageable, submissive, disburden)

emigrate-v migrate, traverse, wander, travel, journey, egress, exit, evacuation, emersion, export, emerge, emanate, evacuate, (ingress, entrance, entry, influx, incursion, invasion, import, infiltration, immigration, admission)

emit-v ejection, emission, effusion, rejection, extrusion, discharge, expulsion, eviction, excrete, secrete, shed, void, effuse, spend, pour forth, (reception, admission admittance, importation, introduction, absorption, inhalation, suction, insertion)

emotion-*n* feeling, affection, suffering, endurance, tolerance, supportance, experience, response, sympathy, sensation, pathos, passion, eagerness, enthusiasm, excitation, (insensitivity, indifference, peacefulness, impassive)

empire-*n* property, realty, land, acres, ground, command, sway, rule dominion, sovereignty, government, jurisdiction, (laxity, toleration, anarchy, relaxation, deposition, abdicate, depose, dethrone)

employ-*v* occupation, function, capacity, place, post, vocation, calling, occupy, undertake, transact, task, engagement, profession, commission, subjection, dependence, subordination, bondage, servitude, (freedom, independence, play, free, franchise, liberal, dismissal)

empower-*v* permission, allow, liberty, indulge, authorize, admission, accordance, might, power,

potency, ability, able, qualify, (impotence, disability, incapacity, invalidity, incompetence, helplessness, collapse, exhaust, disqualification)

empty-*adj* void, clear, vacate, depart, eject, exit, evict, emission, expulsion, extrusion, deport, exhaust, spend, use, consume, impoverish, drain, disperse, squander, (provide, supply, fill, furnish, replenish, recruit, provide, admit, ingest, absorb, gulp)

emulate-*v* excellence, goodness, merit, virtue, worth, superiority, perfection, prime, exude, imitate, copy, simulation, follow, model after, assimilation, (originality, unparalleled, mistreat, injurious, detrimental, mischievous, nocuous)

enact-*v* perform, movement, evolution, perpetration, execution, deed, proceeding, participate, put-in-motion, achieve, rule, regulation, ordinance, statute, (unlawfulness, inactivity, idle, refrain, incomplete, non-performance, incomplete)

enamel-*n* polish, varnish, gilding, embellish, lacquer, paint, veneer, (blemish, disfigure, deform, injure, tarnish)

enchanting-*adj* elegant, beauty, grace, polish,

radiance, splendor, gorgeous, dazzling, refined, idolatrous, adoration, (repugnant, shudder, irritating, revolting, annoying, provoking, obnoxious, repulsive, offensive)

enclosure-n domain, territory, district, zone, compartment, place, spot, document, envelope, den, cell, dungeon, (liberate, free, extricate, open, spacious, boundless, uncircumscribed)

encroach-v trespass, infringe, extravagate, surpass, overstep, exceed, invalidate, unlawful, unauthorized, forfeited, improper, disfranchisement, (sanction, warranty, immunity, franchise, vested-interest, deserve, merit, substantiate)

encumber-v difficulty, impracticability, tough, dilemma, perplexity, entanglement, awkwardness, delicate, vexed, impossible, hindrance, restriction, obstruction, stumbling-block, (ease, flexibility, feasible, smooth, disencumber)

end-n terminate, close, finish, final, conclusion, expire, result, discontinue, (beginning, start, open, commence, initial, inaugurate, genesis)

endeavor-v pursuit, enterprise, pursuance, adventure, quest, exert, labor, resolution, intention, purpose, determined, ambition, aim, (indiscriminate, promiscuous, incidental, repose, without purpose)

endorse-v confirmation, corroboration, support, ratification, authentication, admission, indication, attest, document, refer, substantiate, verify, acknowledge, concur, cooperate, agree, affirm, consent, recognize, avow, (dissent, discordance, protest, contradict, disagree, conflicting, disavow, object)

endure-v durable, persistent, lasting, continuing, permanence, survive, longevity, prolongation, protraction, remain, continue, abide, lingering, eternal, everlasting, perpetual, stable, established, unchanged, subsist, (alter, change, modify, deviate, transformation, revolution, short-lived, perishable, impermanent)

enforce-v persuade, prevail, enlist, engage, animate, incite, provoke, instigate, actuate, encourage, dictate, press, compel, force, compulsory, constraint, necessitate, oblige, stringent, duress, coercion, (loss of right, discourage, encroach, breach, violate, forfeit, unsanctioned)

engage-v motive, reason, intention,inducement, attraction, enticement, allurement, fascination, influence, bribe, lure, campaign, crusade, expedition, mobilization, tactics, strategy, battle, combative, militant, appoint, commission, assign, commit, authorize, (annul, cancel, revoke, dismiss, abolish, retract, rescind, reverse, disclaim, dissolve, null)

engrave-v memory, remembrance, retention, reminiscence, recognition, keepsake, figure, emblem, motto, put an indication, label, imprint, Hallmark, inscribe, (forgotten, unremembered, obliteration, mindless, oblivious)

engulf-v dive, plunge, submerge, sink, importation, admission, ingestion, absorption, inhalation, suction, interjection, import, engorge, inhale, ingest, (ejection, emission, epulation, spew, disgorge, dislodge, expectorate, eviscerate, deport)

enjoy-v pleasure, sensual, gratification, titillation, comfort, luxury, relish, revel, bask, cordial,

palatable, fruition, satisfaction, delight, refresh, happiness, rapture, overjoyed, captivated, ecstasies, entranced, (suffer, pain, ache, displeasure, discomfort, weariness, irritation, worry, infliction, vexation, sorrow, unhappiness)

enlarge-v increase, augment, extend, develop, grow, spread, gain, intensify, enhance, magnify, exaggerate, add, expand, swell, inflate, germinate, larger, amplify, bulbous, (decrease, subtract, reduce, decrease, shrink, diminish, contract, shrivel)

enough-adj sufficient, adequate, full, abundance, copious, profuse, galore, outpouring, abound, exuberate, inexhaustible, ample, commensurate, (insufficient, inadequate, want, lack, require, deplete, empty)

enterprise-n undertaking, engagement, venture, speculate, negotiate, commerce, interchange, quest, pursue, follow, pursuit, course, (abstain, refrain, escape, retreat, reject, disengage, elude, elusive, evasive)

entertain-v observance, attention, application, diligent, recognize, mindful, regardful,

examine, scrutinize,
consider, social gathering,
joviality, hospitality,
welcome, festive,
fraternize, visit, consort,
reception, party,
(seclusion, exclusion,
privacy, reclusion,
isolation, desertion)

entrance-*n* inlet, orifice,
mouth, porch, portal,
portico, door, gate,
threshold, vestibule, origin,
source, begin, commence,
enter, debut, inaugurate,
ingress, entry, influx,
immigration, (egress, exit,
evacuation, emerge.
discharge, conclude)

entrust-*v* commission,
delegate, assign, procure,
errand, appoint, nominate,
return, install, employ,
empower, represent,
bestow, give, present,
consign, dispense, endow,
award, gift, donation,
grant, benefaction,
(acquire, receive, accept,
assign, beneficiary, admit,
cancel, repeal, dismiss,
abolish)

enunciate-*v* pronounce,
accentuate, aspirate,
deliver, vocal, phonetic,
articulate, distinct, remark,
emphatic, assert, affirm,
report, express, state,
communicate, present,
(retract, repudiate, rebut,
silence, mute, suppress,
muffle, raucous, husky)

envoy-*n* messenger,
emissary, ambassador,

marshal, crier, trumpeter,
courier, representative,
functionary, diplomat,
delegate, commissioner

equal-*adj* sameness,
symmetry, balance,
evenness, monotony,
level, equivalent, match,
capability, capacity,
quality, attribute,
endowment, virtue, gift,
qualification, susceptibility,
(helplessness, inability,
incompetence, inept,
unevenness, inequality,
partial)

eradicate-*v* extract, remove,
eliminate, extricate,
exterminate, eject,
eviscerate(insert, implant,
inject, import, introduce)

erect-*v* form, fabricate,
produce, create, construct,
manufacture, build,
organize, establish,
achieve, complete,
perform, forge, carve,
chisel, constitute, institute,
accomplish, evolve,
(destroy, destruct,
dissolve, break, disrupt,
ruin, smash, annihilate)

erratic-*adj* inconstant,
versatile, changeable,
unstable, vacillate,
fluctuate, vicissitude, alter,
shifting, unstable, vary,
fickle, restless, spasmodic,
divert, deviate, wandering,
(stable, unchangeable,
constant, immobile, sound,
stiff, solid, established,
permanent, firm, settled)

escape-*v* release,

disengage, liberate,
discharge, emancipate,
dismiss, deliverance,
absolve, extricate, acquit,
free, dismantle, untie,
violate, transgress,
derelict, neglect, evade,
(responsible, accountable,
conscientious, restrain,
hinder, coerce, repress,
custody, arrest,
incarcerate, unrestricted)

establish-v found, settle,
permanent, vested,
produce, create, construct,
form, fabricate,
manufacture, produce,
institute, evolve, develop,
generate, genesis,
contrive, build, accomplish,
(ruin, smash, crash,
destroy, abolish, suppress,
overthrow, demolish,
ravage, devastate, wreck,
consume)

et cetera-adj add, annex,
increase, increment,
supplement, affix, append,
furthermore, along with,
insert, and-so-forth,
access, include, upward,
(none, naught, deduction,
removal, abstraction,
curtailment, decrease.
abscind, decimate)

eternity-n perpetuity, ever,
immortality, everlasting,
perpetuation, forever,
endless, eternal,
ceaseless, evergreen,
imperishable, always,
lasting, continual, lingering,
permanent, (temporary,
perishable, briefly,

transient, sudden, quick,
short)

ether-n buoyancy, lightness,
volatility, levity, gossamer,
float, airy, weightless,
sublimated, inflation,
sponginess, absence of
solid, thin, tenuous, hollow,
(density, solid, compact,
thick, weight, gravity,
heaviness, pressure)

evade-v conceal, secrecy,
hide, stealth, mask,
disguise, ensconce, muffle,
whisper, suppress, veil,
evasive, deceive, forge,
distort, avoid, escape,
retreat, reject, shun,
(pursue, chase,
scrupulous, frank, open,
candid, straightforward,
outspoken, undisguised)

event-n occurrence,
incident, affair, transaction,
proceeding, phenomenon,
circumstance, adventure,
consequence, happening,
encounter, undergo,
contest, competition,
engagement, tussle,
conflict, (uneventful, idle,
without incident)

evergreen-adj continuous,
progressive, successive,
unbroken, uninterrupted,
perennial, constant, entire,
linear, lasting, persistent,
perpetual, (temporary,
transient, fleeting, short-
lived, impermanent,
spasmodic, unsuccessful)

evil-adj harm, hurt, mischief,
nuisance, ill, tragedy,
badness, bane, outrage,

wrong, injure, grievance, oppress, persecute, abuse, overburden, victimize, molest, (goodness, excellence, merit, virtue, value, worth, beneficial, right, commendable)

evoke-v request, motion, apply, canvass, address, appeal, solicit, invite, petition, beseech, plead, implore, invoke, urge, beset, ask, beg, crave, pray, (protest, effect, consequence, ignore)

exact-adj similar, semblance, parallelism, likeness, match, accurate, precise, gospel, authentic, true, accurate, actual, definite, right, correct, punctual, constant, unerring, (erroneous, untrue, false, wrong, unsubstantial, inaccurate, different, incorrect)

exalt-v raise, intensify, enhance, magnify, exaggerate, increase, enlarge, develop, spread, lift, sublimate, erect, elevate, heighten, (depress, lower, reduce, over-throw, decrease, diminish, lessen, weaken, depreciate)

examine-v scan, scrutinize, inspect, review, glance, consider, account, indicate, observe, inquire, request, investigate, seek, search, explore, ransack, rummage, (answer, respond, retort,

acknowledge, escape, unobservant, thoughtless, careless, inattentive)

example-n prototype, original, model, pattern, precedent, standard, type, copy, conform, instance, sample, illustration, specimen, rule, agreement, observance, exemplification, (original duplicate, imitation, irregularity, eccentricity, abnormal, oddity, curiosity, hybrid, unconventional, infraction)

exception-n abnormal, irregular, peculiar, unusual, unexpected, unconventional, remarkable, queer, exceptional, informal, unaccustomed, exclusive, (typical, normal, formal, orthodox, sound, rigid, positive, ordinary, common, conventional)

excite-v energy, intensify, vigor, strength, pressure, poignancy, severity, agitation, effervescence, stir, stimulate, kindle, exert, inflame, (inert, dull, inactivity, languor, passive, slow, lifeless, dormant)

exclusive-adj special, particular, specify, characteristic, individualize, custom, unusual, rare, singular, curious, odd, extraordinary, strange, remarkable, noteworthy, eccentric, peculiar, abnormal, (conventional, ordinary, conformity, symmetry, conventional, regular, usual)

excuse-v forgive, pardon, condonation, remission, absolution, amnesty, reprieve, exoneration, release, indemnity, forget, acquit, vindicate, apology, justify, warrant, advocate, defend, contend, (accuse, charge, impute, reproach, denounce, inexcusable, vicious)

exercise-n task, curriculum, study, lesson, lecture, sermon, apologue, parable, action, performance, perpetration, movement, operation, work, labor, execution, procedure, deed, act, proceeding, enact, (passiveness, nothing, inactivity, unintelligent, misinformation)

exert-v hold, grasp, grip, reach, command, use, employ, exercise, application, consume, resort, wield, handle, manipulate, avail, (abstinence, relinquish, discard, dismiss, waive, neglect)

exit-n depart, embarkation, removal, exodus, valediction, adieu, farewell, flight, egress, evacuation, emerge, emanate, export, (ingress, entrance, influx, import, invasion, admission, insertion)

exonerate-v disencumber, disengage, disentangle, extricate, unravel, untie, unload, emancipate, manage, accomplish, absolve, dispense, release, (prohibit, exclude, embargo, forbid, restrictive, difficult, hard, tough, dilemma)

expand-v increase, enlarge, extend, dilate, develop, augment, gain, ascend, exalt, intensify, enhance, magnify, add, develop, spread, increment, (contraction, consume, lessen, shrink, collapse, emaciate, atrophy, lose, reduce, decrease, limit)

expedient-adj desirable, suit, fitness, agreeable, propriety, opportunism, befit, conform, acceptable, convenient, worthwhile, applicable, useful, (impropriety, unfit, undesirable, objectionable, inconvenient, inappropriate, unsatisfactory, improper)

F

fable-n fallacy, misconception, error, laxity, mistake, blunder, misprint, delusion, hallucination, deception, mislead, deceive, erroneous, untrue, fallacious, unreal, unauthenticated, (real, actual, veritable, true,

exact, accurate, definite,
precise, defined)

face-*n* exterior, surface,
outside, skin, superficial,
frontal, confront,
encounter, clash, contend,
confront, brave, dare,
summon, meet, stand-up,
valiant, resolute, stout,
determined, (cowardly,
shy, timed, soft, spiritless,
skittish, fearful, cower,
skulk, flinch, interior, inner,
within)

factor-*n* number, symbol,
figure, cipher, formula,
function, sum, multiplicand,
multiple, dividend, prime,
director, manager,
moderator, taskmaster,
delegate, consignee,
envoy, merchant, trader,
complimentary, positive,
negative, formula

fade-*v* vacant, empty, blank,
hollow, vanish, evaporate,
dissolve, disappear,
without, dreamy, shadowy,
ethereal, immaterial,
nominal, nothing, luminary,
(substantial, exist, full,
tangible, essential,
material, reappear)

fail-*v* feeble, impotent,
relaxed, powerless, weak,
soft, fragile, flimsy,
unsubstantial, rickety,
cranky, drooping, lame,
withered, shattered,
decrepit, languid, spent,
decayed, worn, (strong
mighty, vigorous, forcible,
hard, adamantine, stout,
robust)

fair-*adj* colorless,
monochrome, pale, blanch,
hueless, pallid, dull,
muddy, sallow, dingy,
ghastly, lusterless,
moderate, ordinary,
average, indifferent,
(unparalleled, ripen,
mature, shiny, dark, tone)

faith-*n* belief, credence,
credit, assurance, trust,
confidence, certainty,
conviction, hopeful,
optimism, aspire,
expectation, confidence,
reliance, (hopelessness,
despair, despondency,
pessimism, forlorn, doubt,
misbelief, infidelity,
dissent)

fallacy-*n* false, illogical,
unsound, invalid,
deceptive, evasive,
irrelevant, vague,
unwarranted,
inconsequential,
inconsistent, fallacious,
(logical, correct,
reasonable, rational,
controversial, debatable,
relevant)

false-*adj* error, fallacy,
misconception, mistake,
fault, blunder, delusive,
deceptive, heresy, untrue,
incorrect, lie, guile, perjury,
forgery, invention,
fabrication, distortion,
evade, sham, (truthful,
scrupulous, sincere, frank,
honest, sober, exact, real,
authentic, precise, actual,
certain)

falter-*v* slow, slack, tardy,

leisurely, deliberate, gradual, languid, moderate, slouch, shuffle, totter, stagger, mince, lumber, linger, loiter, saunter, plod, trudge, dawdle, (gallop, canter, trot, hasten, run, race, whisk, fast, hurry, fly, eloquent)

familiar-*adj* aware, cognizant, acquaint, inform, versed, instructed, learned, lettered, educated, enlighten, bookish, accomplished, profound, recognized, occurrence, habitual, usual, ordinary, (unusual, unconformable, ignorant, uninformed, shallow, empty, illiterate)

family-*n* kin, relation, fraternity, paternal, maternal, ancestral, linear, patriarchal, party, alliance, linked, banded, united

fancy-*n* prefer, persuade, option, select, pick, whim, humor, drollery, pleasantry, brilliant, desire, wish, solicitous, overjoyed, entranced, enchanted, ravished, fascinated, captivated, (afflicted, worried, displeased, aching, griped, grieve, lament)

fantasy-*n* desire, wish, fancy, want, need, inclination, propensity, liking, fain, anxious, curious, craving, thirst, (indifference, neutrality,

coldness, unconcern, apathy, disdain)

far-*adv* distance, space, remote, elongation, remove, span, away, inaccessible, out-of-reach, unapproachable, asunder, apart, adrift, rift, unconnected, (close, tight, taut, firm, inseparable, near, proximity, vicinity, confines, alongside)

farce-*n* absurd, imbecility, nonsense, paradox, inconsistency, blunder, muddle, preposterous, senseless, inconsistent, ridiculous, foolish, witty, quick, nimble-witted, jocular, waggish, whimsical, playful, pleasant, sparkling, (dull, dry, commonplace, pointless, flat, stale, uninteresting)

farewell-*n* depart, goodbye, outward, exit, embark, decampment, forfeiture, loss, bereavement, deprivation, lose, bereft, (recover, regain, retrieve, inherit, arrival, advent, land, welcome)

fast-*adj* firm, close, tight, taut, secure, set, intervolved, inseparable, indissoluble, fickle, erratic, afloat, alternating, speed, hasten, scamper, run, swift, nimble, agile, expeditious, galloping, quick, (gradual, slow, leisurely, tardy, gentle, easy, deliberate, relax, stagger, plod, trudge,vary, vacillate)

fat-*n* large, big, great, considerable, bulky, voluminous, ample, massive, capacious, comprehensive, spacious, might, towering, corpulent, stout, portly, full, plump, whopping, thundering, fleshy, burly, vast, (little, small, dwarf, pygmy, midget, minute, diminutive, microscopic, petty, wee, undersized, short, infinitesimal)

fathom-*n* length, line, bar, rule, furlong, examine, study, consider, calculate, dip, dive, delve, probe, sound, conclusion, ascertain, deduce, derive, gather, collect, (answer, response, reply, rebut, retort, rejoin, explain, discover)

fault-*n* interruption, disjunction, anacoluthon, break, fracture, flaw, crack, cut, gap, mistake, blunder, oversight, misprint, botchery, error, fallacy, fail, unsuccessful, unfortunate, (success, fortunate, triumphant, definite, precise, continuous, consecutive, progressive, unbroken, entire)

feather-*n* plumage, plume, crest, tuft, fringe, toupee, nap, pile, floss, fur, down, light, subtle, airy, weightless, ethereal, uncompressed, volatile, buoyant, floating, (gravity, heaviness, pressure, ponderous, smooth, polish, level, glossy, silken)

feature-*n* principle, characteristic, fixed, incurable, ineradicable, fixed, invariable, form, figure, shape, conformation, construction, cut, set, build, lineament, posture, attitude, (disfigure, deface, mutilate, derange, shapeless, unfashioned, intrinsic, subjective)

fence-*n* forgery, perjury, false, untruth, misrepresentation, lying, invention, fabrication, subreption, enclosure, refuge, sanctuary, retreat, shelter, screen, hiding place, (truthful, true, veracious, pure, sincere, candor, honesty, fidelity)

fertile-*adj* productive, prolific, teeming, fruitful, luxuriant, pregnant, generate, propagate, sufficient, ample, abundant, enough, adequate, copious, commensurate, satisfactory, valid, tangible, (deficient, inadequate, imperfect, scantiness, scarce, poverty, famine)

fetch-*v* bring, worth, rate, value, appraisement, cost, figure, demand, fare, (reduce, discount, abatement)

feverish-*adj* haste, urgency,

acceleration, spurt, rush, forced, march, dash, flutter, flurry, hurried, impetuous, excite, affect, touch, move, (leisurely, slow, deliberate, quiet, calm, undisturbed, ease)

fidelity-n veracity, truthfulness, frankness, sincerity, candor, honesty, scrupulous, frank, open, trustworthy, unaffected, honorable, faithful, loyal, (violate, lawless, transgressive, elusive, evasive, false, deceitful, fraudulent, dishonest, unfaithful)

field-n spacious, roomy, expansive, capacious, ample, wide, vast, uncircumscribed, boundless, arena, zone, meridian, territorial, parochial, provincial, patch, plot, region, realm, domain, tract, court, (niche, nook, compartment, precinct)

fight-v contention, strife, contest, struggle, belligerency, controversy, war, litigation, sparring, competition, rivalry, opposition, combative, contending, embattled, militant, (tranquil, pacific, peaceable, untroubled, harmony, quiet, neutrality, conciliatory, composing, amnesty, arrangement)

file-v arrange, distribute, sort, prepare, dispose, organize, analyze, classify,

digest, divide, catalog, tabulate, index, systematize, methodize, regulate, register, consecutive, continuous, progressive, successive, linear, (broken, interrupted, unconnected, gap, litter, scatter, disarrange, disorganize)

fill-v complete, entire, replenish, totally, brimming, plenary, occupy, inhabit, moored, domiciled, populous, attend, dwell, reside, lodge, nestle, roost, permeate, (absent, away, gone, missing, lost, omitted, nonexistent, empty, void, vacant, devoid)

final-adj end, close, terminate, dissonance, conclude, finale, period, term, consummation, finish, expire, last, complete, accomplished, culmination, result, exhaust, (beginning, commencement, opening, outset, inception introduction, inauguration, embarkation, initial, first, incipient, leading)

find-v discover, detect, hunt, determine, evolve, decision, deduction, gain, acquire, obtain, purchase, remunerative, lucrative, (lose, mislay, forfeit, deprived)

fine-adj thin, narrow, slender, close, taper, slim, scant, spare, delicate, incapacious, contracted, lean, emaciated, meager, gaunt, lanky, weedy, flimsy, slight, (thick, broad, dense, widen, ample, extend, spread)

finesse-*n* clever, talent, ability, ingenuity, capacity, endowed, skillful, dexterous, adroit, expert, apt, handy, quick, deft, ready, gain, smart, ready, proficient, masterful, thorough, accomplished, able, ingenious, (bungling, awkward, clumsy, unskillful, slovenly, gawky, inept, incompetent, stupid, unfit)

fire-*n* heat, warmth, hot, torrid, smoking, burning, alight, afire, ablaze, unquenched, smoldering, flow, sweat, sultry, hellish, inferno, (heavenly, celestial, cold, cool, frigid, fresh, keen, bleak, shivering, bitter, chill, inclement, biting, icy, glacial, frosty, freezing)

first-*adj* initial, beginning, commence, opening, outset, inception, introduction, inaugurate, manifest, apparent, entrance, inlet, dawn, genesis, birth, origin, start, front, (end, last, consummation, finish, terminate, conclude, expire, definitive)

fish-*n* chase, hunt, sport, pursuit, prosecution, quest, scramble, inquire,

investigate, unearth, ferret out, seek, search, track, trail, feel out, (answer, respond, reply, acknowledge, discover, explain, refrain, spare, abstain, unsought, avoid, neutral, evasive)

fit-*v* conform, consistent, adapt, adjust, graduate, assimilate, match, suit, harmony, unison, appropriate, deft, apply, meet, dovetail, (unfit, unsuited, inconsistent, mismatch, intrusive, uneven)

fix-*v* join, unite, attach, affix, fasten, bind, secure, clinch, twist, tie, string, strap, sew, lace, stitch, tack, knit, button, buckle, hitch, lash, truss, bandage, braid, (sunder, divide, disjoin, sever, abscind, cut, saw, snip, nip, cleave, split, chip, crack, carve)

flat-*adj* inert, dull, torpor, languor, quiescence, inaction, sloth, obstinacy, passive, sluggish, slack, tame, slow, blunt, lifeless, uninfluential, latent, dormant, low, neap, debase, nether, crouched, subjacent, squat, prostrate, (high, elevated, eminent, exalted, lofty, tall, gigantic, towering, soaring)

fleece-*v* tegument, skin, pellicle, fell, fur, leather, hide, pelt, cover, theft, steal, thievery, robbery, depredation, plunder, pillage, black-mail, burglary, buccaneer, strip, abduct, confiscate, sequester

fling-v propel, project, throw, cast, pitch, chuck, toss, jerk, heave, hurl, flirt, fillip, dart, lance, tilt, sling, send, discharge, shoot, bolt, (draw, pull, haul, lug, drag, tug, tow, trail, wrench, jerk, tactile)

float-v navigate, sail, nautical, naval, coasting, afloat, transport, tender, whaler, slaver, coaster, yacht, launch, buoyant, ascend, rise, (descent, drop, fall, gravitate, sink, droop, settle, decline, dismount)

flock-n crowd, horde, body, tribe, crew, gang, band, party, company, troop, army, regiment, assemble, dense, muster, together, collect, convene, congregate, accumulate, (disperse, adrift, stray, disheveled, dissemination, dissipation, scatter, disband, disembody, dispel)

floor-n ground, base, foundation, substructure, pavement, deck, footing, basis, bottom, nadir, foot, fundamental, horizontal, level, even, plan, flat, smooth, succeed, flushed, victorious, unbeaten, (unsuccessful, highest, top, crest, apex, zenith, upper most)

flourish-v prosperity, welfare, well-being, affluence, success, wealth, thriving, fortunate, lucky, flushed, felicitous, effective, flower, (abortive, addle, fruitless, bootless, inefficient, inefficacious, lame, insufficient, unavailing, useless, swamp)

flow-v elapse, lapse, run, proceed, advance, pass, roll, slide, glide, progress, loose, dependent, stream, flux, run, course, move, shifting, restless, nomadic, (still, fixed, stationary, quiet, calm, anchor, still, restful)

flower-n produce, create, construct, form, fabricate, manufacture, build, erect, edify, organize, establish, achieve, evolve, develop, grow, genesis, bear, generate, impregnate, (destroy, destruct, waste, dissolve, consume, ruin, crash, smash, extinction, subversive, suicidal, squash, squelch)

flush-v flat, plane, flounder, jet, spurt, squirt, spout, splash, rush, gush, deluge, inundation, stream, flux. flow, brook, torrent, (gust, blast, breeze, squall, gale, storm, tempest)

fly-v flit, elapse, lapse, flow, run, proceed, advance, slide, glide, pass, transient, fleeting, shifting, spasmodic, wild, abrupt, impetuous, turbulent, disorderly, (moderate, gentle, lenient, still, slow, smooth, tame, peaceful, standing, perpetual)

fold-*v* halve, divide, split, cleave, bisect, enclose, envelope, (circumvent, skirt, twine)

follow-*v* succeed, next, ensue, conform, observe, obey, comply, supervene, consecutive, continue, sequel, behind, attend, pursue, beset, tread, example, (precede, forerun, lead, advance, prior, former, foregoing, before, advance, start, preliminary)

foot-*n* bottom, nadir, sole, toe, hoof, fundamental, founded, based, ground, broad, support, foundation, base, basis, bearing, hold, landing, aid, prop, stand, shore, truss, beam, rafter, (suspend, hang, pendulum, swing, dangle, swag, flap, loose, flowing)

forbid-*v* prohibit, disallow, bar, forefend, withhold, limit, circumscribe, restrict, taboo, interdict, exclude, dissent, negative, unconsenting, unavowed, discontented, (assent, admission, agreement, affirm, recognition, acknowledge, permit, indulgent, allow)

force-*v* power, potency, might, energy, ascend, control, authority, ability, ableness, competency, efficiency, enablement, influence, capability, almighty, adequate, efficacious, valid, able, (powerless, impotent, unable, incapable, incompetent, harmless, weaponless, null, void, nugatory, ineffectual, failing, inadequate)

forefathers-*n* paternal, parental, maternal, family, ancestral, linear, patriarchal, descendant, heir, generation, (succeed, ensue, alternate, after, latter, follow)

foreign-*adj* irrelative, irrespective, unrelated, arbitrary, independence, adrift, isolated, insular, extraneous, strange, alien, outlandish, exotic, intrude, emigrant, outsider, inadmissible, (implicate, integral, member, merge, constitute, relative, cognate, referable, akin, family, allied, affiliated, fraternal)

forfeit-*v* fail, evasion, unobservance, omission, neglect, informality, infringement, infraction, violation, transgression, break, retraction, repudiation, nullification, protest, lapse, deprivation, loss, (fulfillment, satisfaction, faithful, profit, earnings, proceeds, acquire, advantageous, gainful, remunerative, paying, lucrative)

form-*n* copy, facsimile, counterpart, effigy, likeness, similitude, semblance, cast, imitation, model, representation, orderly, regular, correct, methodical, uniform, symmetrical, unconfused, arranged, systematic, (disorderly, promiscuous, indiscriminate, chaotic, complex, intricate, complicated, perplexed, knotted, tangled, dislocated)

formula-*n* rule, routine, uniformity, constancy, standard, model, precedent, conformity, principle, steady, legal process, law, code, statute, canon, ordinance, decree, numeral, divisible, prime, fractional, (irregular, diversified, indiscriminate, desultory, difference, illegal, prohibited, unlawful, illicit, uncharted, unauthorized, unofficial)

fortune-*n* chance, indetermination, accident, hazard, haphazard, random, fate, lottery, casually, happen, destiny, foredoom, predestined, fatalism, wealthy, rich, affluent, opulent, moneyed, capital, afford, (poor, indigent, poverty, needy, necessary, distressed, bereft, bereaved, reduced)

forward-*adj* early, prime,

timely, punctual, prompt, summary, discourteous, disrespect, impudent, ill-breed, vulgar, unpolished, rude, saucy, harsh, austere, sarcastic, biting, caustic, snarling, surly, (courteous, polite, civil, mannerly, urbane, well-behaved, polished, cultivated, refined, gallant, late, tardy, slow, behind, behind, backward)

foundation-*n* stability, constancy, immobile, sound, vital, stable, established, fixture, tower, pillar, fixed, durable, tethered, anchored, moored, (unstable, fluctuation, movable, vicissitude, shake, totter, flitter, flutter, flounder, mobile, transient)

fracture-*n* separation, parting, detachment, segregation, divorce, supposition, divide, sunder, sever, cut, saw, carve, dissect, mangle, gash, hash, slice, whittle, disperse, apportion, (attach, fix, join, unite, embody, affix, fasten, bind, secure, tie, pinion, string, strap, link, marry)

free-*adj* sunder, divide, sever, abscind, splinter, chip crack, divorce, part, detach, separate, cutoff, adrift, loose, disentangle, isolate, liberate, apart, rupture, breach, split, divulge, section, rift, incision, fission, (attach, fix, affix, fasten, pinion, string, gird, tether, moor, harness, chain, fetter, join, twine, twist, incorporate, close, secure, leash, couple, nail, bolt)

frequent-*adj* repeat, again, often, anew, over again, once more, ditto, many, iterate, harping, recurrence, succession, monotony, rhythm, imitate, incessant, perpetual, continual, constant, habitual, commonly, (seldom, rarely, scarcely, hardly, infrequently, few, never, inconstant)

fresh-*adj* new, novelty, recent, immaturity, youth, innovation, renovation, modern, mushroom, renew, green, evergreen, raw, virgin, neoteric, newborn, (old, antiquity, maturity, decline, decay, senility, seniority, archaism, ancient, venerable, prime, obsolete)

fret-*v* suffer, pain, dolor, ache, twinge, twitch, gripe, headache, hurt, cut, sore, discomfort, malaise, spasm, cramp, nightmare, sharp, piercing, throbbing, gnawing, anguish, experience, writhe, (enjoy, luxurious, sensual, comfortable, cozy, snug, agreeable, grateful, refreshing, cordial, genial, palatable, fragrant,

melodious, lovely, beautiful)

fringe-*n* closure, obstruction, plug, block, stop, button, shut, bar, bolt, stop, seal, plumb, choke, border, (vent, vomiter, orifice, mouth, throat, portal)

front-*n* cover, guise, outfit, envelop, involve, sheathe, swathe, swaddle, circumvent, fore, foreground, face, advance, outpost, countenance, pioneer, insolence, (rear, back, posteriority, guard, nape, stern, rump, breech, dorsal, after, aft, astern, behind, divest, bare, dishabille)

frugal-*adj* economical, saving, thriftiness, retrenchment, prevention, sparing, careful, parsimony, abstinence, moderation, temperance, forbearance, self-denial, restraint, (pleasurable, indulgence, self-indulgence, effeminacy, excess, dissipation, generous, bountiful, liberal, free, unsparing, carte blanche)

fuel-*n* firing, combustible, coal, anthracite, coke, carbon, charcoal, turf, peat, firewood, bobbing, match, light, incense, brand, torch, fuse, (non-combustible, non-flammable)

fugitive-*n* temporarily,

awhile, short, briefly, transient, evanescence, impermanence, fly, gallop, vanish, evaporate, refugee, emigrant, vagabond, nomad, wanderer, adventurer, rover, straggler, rambler, (durable, lasting, permanent, survive, long-standing, persistent, perpetual)

full-*adj* much, great, might, importance, considerable, fair, huge, big, abundant, intense, strong, sound, heavy, plenary, complete, entirety, perfection, altogether, effectual, wholly, totally, (incomplete, imperfect, fault, short, meager, lame, sketchy, small, minimum, little, diminutive, minute)

fumble-*v* jumble, muddle, toss, hustle, derange, misarrange, misplace, mislay, decompose, disorder, disorganize, embroil, unsettle, disturb, touch, feel, handle, thumb, paw, grope, grabble, twiddle, (arrange, distribute, sort, assort, allotment, apportionment, analyze, classify, digest)

fumigate-*v* vaporize, gasify, evaporate, exhale, volatile, smoke, transpire, emit, clean, purify, defecate, purge, launder, (rot, fester, putrefy, reek, stink, mold, dirty, filthy, grimy, soiled, contaminate, taint, corrupt,

liquefied, soluble)

function-*n* numeral, symbol, divisible, prime, fractional, decimal, arithmetic, analysis, algebra, integral, calculus, useful, serviceable, subservient, conducive, efficient, effective, applicable, advantageous, expedient, (uselessness, inefficacy, futility, inadequate, inefficient, unskillful)

furbish-*v* improve, betterment, melioration, mend, amend, advance, elevate, increase, reform, correct, refine, prepare, provide, forthcoming, adornment, embellishment, japanning, varnish, cosmetic, (pitted, discolored, imperfect, impairment, injury, damage, loss, detriment, decline, decay, dilapidation, atrophy, collapse)

G

gag-*n* render mute, constrained, imprisoned, pent up, stiff, control repress, smother, suppress, rein, hold, enchain, shackle, bridle, muzzle, pinion, handcuff, secure, (liberate, disengage, release, emancipate, discharge, dismiss, deliver, acquittal)

gain-*v* benefit, improvement, advantage, interest, service, behalf, satisfactory, commend, useful, good, blessing, fortune, treasure, happiness, profit, earnings, income, proceeds, fruition, harvest, (lose, forfeit, lapse, privation, bereavement, deprivation, riddance, incur, mislay, minus)

gall-*n* torment, torture, rack, discomfort, malaise, twinge, twitch, pained, ache, unsavory, unpalatable, bitter, acrid, rough, offensive, repulsive, nauseous, loath, unpleasant, (palatable, nice, dainty, delectable, gusty, appetizing, exquisite, luscious, pleasurable, gratification)

game-*n* beast, brute, animal, fleshy, zoological, pursuit, enterprise, undertaking, adventure, quest, business, hobby, chase, hunt, sporting, follow, prosecute, fun, frolic, amusement, entertain, diversion, relaxation, solace, pastime, pleasure, merriment, laughter, regatta, (weary, disgusting, tiresome, irksome, uninteresting, dry, monotonous, dull, arid, humdrum)

gang-*n* assemblage, gathering, collection, compilation, levy, muster, crown, throng, flood, rush, deluge, horde, body, tribe, crew, band, squad, party, go, moving, mobile, mercurial, restless, shifting, nomadic, unquiet, erratic, (quiet, tranquility, calm, repose, peace, stagnate, unassembled, disperse, sparse, sporadic, adrift, disheveled, streaming)

garrison-*n* occupied, indigenous, native, domestic, domiciled, naturalized, vernacular, domesticated, domiciliary, safe, utility, efficacy, serviceable, adequate, efficient, prolific, shelter, concealment, fortification, munition, ditch, entrenchment, barrier, fence, (aggressive, attacking, offensive, obsidianus, incursion, invasion, encampment, bivouac)

gasp-*v* blow, sneeze, sternutation, hiccup, cough, waft, respire, puff, wheeze, snuff, fan, ventilate, tempestuous, droop, broken-winded, fatigue, weariness, lassitude, yawning, exhaustion, (refreshed, recuperative, respire, breathe, reinvigorate, flow, profluent, effluence)

gather-*v* assemble, collect, locate, compile, lever, muster, concourse, verge,

hoard, meet, flock,
cumulative, populous,
gainful, profitable, acquire,
advantageous,
remunerative, lucrative,
(loss, forfeit, privation,
riddance, bereaved,
dispossessed, quit)

gauge-*n* measure, weigh,
survey, appraise, assess,
estimate, reckon, gauging,
standard, rule, caliper,
meter, rod, check,
compass, rate

gay-*adj* colorful, hue, tint,
dye, shade, pigment,
chromatic, bright, vivid,
intense, deep, fresh,
unfaded, rich, gorgeous,
gaudy, florid, showy,
flaunting, flashy, glaring,
flaring, discordant,
(mellow, harmonious,
sweet, delicate, tender,
refined, dismal, somber,
melancholy, dark, gloomy)

gazette-*n* publication,
current, notorious, flagrant,
circulated, propagation,
edition, newspaper,
journal, imprinted, edition,
diary, log, book, record,
note, almanac, ledger,
archive, scroll, chronicle,
portfolio, (obliterate,
erasure, cancel, out of
print, unregistered,
unwritten, efface)

general-*adj* universal,
miscellany, catholic, every,
all, generic, common,
transcendental, prevalent,
prevailing, always,
prescription, usage, rule,

standing order, precedent,
routine, rut, groove,
habitual, conformable,
military authority, marshal,
potentate, sovereign,
tyrant, (servant, subject,
retainer, squire, vassal,
slave, unusual,
uncommon, special,
disusage, unconformity,
unaccustomed)

genius-*n* intellect,
understanding, reason,
mental, rational,
subjective, faculties,
senses, consciousness,
observation, percipience,
instinct, conception,
capacity, wit, ability,
skillful, dexterous, adroit,
expert, proficient, masterly,
clever, (foolish, inept,
inexperienced,
incompetent, stupid,
unqualified, vacant,
thoughtless, diverted,
narrow-minded, dull)

gentle-*adj* moderate,
temperate, sober,
calmness, relaxed,
tranquil, mitigate, pacify,
sedative, lessen, slow,
smooth, unexciting,
hypnotic, soft, bland,
lenient, reasonable,
peaceful, mild, demure,
imperturbable, enduring,
(vehement, demonstrative,
violent, wild, furious, fierce,
fiery, hot-headed, madcap,
over-zealous, enthusiastic,
impetuous, passionate,
fanatical)

gestation-*n* production,

creation, construction, formation, fabrication, manufacture, building, erection, flowering, fructify, birth, delivery, confinement, travail, labor, midwife, obstetrics, gender, propagation, impregnation, (destroy, waste, disruption, consumption, ruin, smash, sacrifice, demolish, dispel, smash, quell, shatter)

ghastly-*adj* pale, uncolored, achromatic, hueless, pallid, faint, dull, muddy, dead, dingy, ashy, cadaverous, ashen, misshapen, plain, homely, ugly, deformed, disfigurement, distorted, graceless, uncouth, rugged, rough, gross, rude, awkward, (beautiful, elegant, graceful, adorned, brilliant, radiance, splendor, gorgeous, magnificent, pretty, handsome, dapper, jaunty, shiny)

gild-*v* cover, canopy, bandage, cutaneous, armor-plated, iron-clad, sheath, wrap, veneer, face, coating, paint, anoint, incrustation, whitewash, envelop, deceive, falseness, untruth, fraud, deceit, guild, misrepresent, trick, cheat, juggle, collusion, (line, stuff, incrust, wad, pad, truth, open)

gird-*v* bind, firm, fast, close, tight, taut, secure, set, nail, bolt, hasp, clasp, rivet, solder, wedge, miter, attach, affix, secure, engage, strengthen, vigor, force, might, robust, sturdy, hardy, powerful, potent, dynamic, (weak, feeble, debilitate, impotent, relaxed, unnerved, unstrung, flaccid, soft, effeminate, frail, flimsy)

glance-*v* view, look, espial, ken, glimpse, peep, gaze, stare, leer, contemplation, visual, ocular, behold, perceive, ophthalmic, sight, examine cursorily, skim, watchful, (inattentive, unobservant, blind, close, dismiss, discard, discharge, oversight, disregard, heedlessness, overlook)

glare-*v* garish, blazing, ablaze, rutilant, meteoric, phosphorescent, aglow, shining, luminous, bright, vivid, splendent, lustrous, flash, sparkle, scintillate, coruscate, reflection, refraction, dispersion, gleam, twinkle, shimmer, radiate, (dark, dim, dull, dingy, fade, grimey, shade, obscure, eclipse, gloom, extinguish)

glass-*n* transparent, pellucid, lucid, diaphanous, limpid, clear, serene, crystalline, vitreous, hyaline, smooth, polish, gloss, even, flat, sleek, brittle, fragile, break, frail, lacerate, (tenacious, tough, strong, opaque, film, thick, cloudy, hazy,smoky,murky, dirty, rough, rugged)

glide-*v* motion, movement, move, going, flow, flux, run course, stir, evolution, kinematics, step, rate, pace, tread, stride, gait, port, cadence, carriage, transitional, motive, shifting, mobile, mercurial, unquiet, (still, fixed, stationary, sedentary, stay, pause, lull, tranquil, deliberate, slow, gradual)

glimmer-*n* light, ray, beam stream, gleam, streak, moon, glow, flush, halo, glory, luminous, lucid, bright, vivid, lustrous, shimmer, sparkle, scintillate, radiate, (dark, obscurity, gloom, eclipse, shade, sunless, somber, dim, dingy, gloomy, overcast)

glorify-*v* dedication, consecration, enthronement, canonization, celebration, enshrinement, hero, worthy, notability, rank, great, eminence, importance, elevation, ascent, super, exaltation, dignify, aggrandizement, (discredit, disrepute, bad, disapprobation, dishonor, disgrace, shame, humiliation, tarnish, taint, defilement, pollute)

gloss-*n* smooth, lubricity, velvet, silk, satin, slide, glass, ice, plane, file, mow,

shave, level, roll, macadamize, polish, glabrous, slippery, lubricious, oily, soft, (render rough, uneven, knotted, aspergillus, crisp, gnarled, unpolished, rough-hewed, gnarled, crumble, corrugate)

glut-*v* satiety, satisfaction, saturation, repletion, surfeit, weariness, spoiled, child, cloy, quench, slake, pall, gorge, surfeit, swallow, enough, bolt, devour, gobble up, gulp, raven, greedy, adequacy, omnivorous, over-fed, (fast, starve, clam, famish, perish, unfed, hungry)

go-*v* exist, null, void, perish, extinct, annihilate, render, destroy, neat, exhausted, gone, lost, departed, defunct, negative, elapse, lapse, flow, run, duration, proceed, advance, pass, expire, progress, (stop, admit, absorb, swallow, enter, introduce, receive, import, insert)

good-*adj* savory, well-tasted, tasty, palatable, nice, dainty, delectable, gusty, appetizing, delicate, delicious, exquisite, rich, luscious, ambrosial, relish, zest, virtue, virtuousness, moral, ethic, merit, worth, (scandal, laxity, looseness, demoralizing, depravity, pollution, profligacy, atrocity, infirmity, error, defect, deficiency)

gorgeous-*adj* beauty, form, elegance, grace, unadorned, symmetry, comeliness, fairness, polish, gloss, good looks, bloom, brilliancy, radiance, splendor, magnificence, handsome, pretty, lovely, refined, shapely, colored, bright, vivid, (achromatic, hueless, pale ,ugly, plain, homely, ordinary, unsightly, deformed, eyesore, frightful, ghastly, graceless, gross)

grace-*n* style, elegance, purity, ease, readiness, polished, classical correct, artistic, chaste, pure, academical, easy, fluent, flowing, tripping, unaffected, natural, unlabored, mellifluous, (stiffness, barbaric, euphuism, graceless, harsh, abrupt, dry, cramped, formal, forced, artificial, mannered)

gradation-*n* degree, extent, measure, amount, ratio, stint, standard, height, pitch, reach, amplitude, range, scope, caliber, shade, tenor, compass, station, rank, order, uniformity, correct, methodical, systematic, (confusion, disorder, jumble, huddle, wrong, fortuitous, perplexed, quantitative, some, more, less, any)

gram-*n* essence, small, little, tenuity, paucity, few,

insignificance, mediocre, moderate, atom, particle, molecule, diminutive, minute, paltry, faint, slender, slight, scanty, meager, sparing, modest, mere, low, infinitesimal, stark, bare, (vast, immense, enormous, extreme, excessive, extravagant, exorbitant, outrageous, preposterous)

grand-*adj* important, momentous, serious, earnest, noble, solemn, impressive, commanding, imposing, urgent, pressing, critical, prominent, grave, superior, instant, essential, vital, absorbing, considerable, significant, telling, (poor, paltry, trifling, trivial, slight, slender, light, flimsy, frothy, idle, foolish, powerless, petty, pitiful)

grant-*v* admit, acknowledge, avowal, reveal, divulge, allow, concede, confess, disclose, transpire, permission, empower, license, authorize, absolve, entrust, sanction, license, privilege, favor, (prohibit, forbid, disallow, hinder, restrict, exclude, withhold, bar, veto, limit, ambush, conceal, stalk, cover, recess)

grasp-*v* comprehend, understand, catch, follow, collect, master, lucid, luminous, transparent, plain, distinct, explicit, positive, definite, take hold, retain, detain, detention, custody, tenacity, firm hold, grip, secure, (relinquish, abandon, renounce, derelict, surrender, dispense, resign, eliminate)

gravity-*n* force, power, pressure, elasticity, electricity, magnetism, galvanism, capability, voltaism, attraction, dynamic, energy, friction, suction, capacity, weight, heaviness, ponderous, load, burden, (levity, lightness, buoyancy, leaven, subtle, airy, weightless, floating, portable, powerless, impotent, valid, effective, influential, productive)

greed-*n* desire, avidity, covetous, ravenous, craving, voracity, gluttony, hunger, longing, hankering, solicitude, impatient, impetuous, over-anxiety, gorge, gormandize, devour, gobble-up, gulp, raven, guzzle, cram, fill, (fast, starve, perish, Lenten, unfed, famish, indifferent, cold, neutrality, unconcern)

gregarious-*adj* social, companion, comradeship, conviviality, good fellowship, festivity, hospitality, heartiness, cheer, welcome, greetings, receptive, fraternize, (seclusion, exclusion, privacy, retirement, reclusion, recess, solitude, isolation, loneliness, estrangement, voluntary exile)

grind-*v* reduce, contract, decrease, lessen, shrink, collapse, emaciation, consumption, atrophy, condensation, compression, compact, smaller, squeeze, lessen, narrow, constrict, crush, dwarf, (expand, increase, enlarge, extend, augment, amplify, spread, increment, growth, develop)

grip-*n* power, retention, retain, detention, custody, tenacity, firm hold, grasp, forfeit, secure, clutch, swoop, wrench, take, catch, hook, nab, (return, restore, reparation, release, replevin, redemption, recovery, recuperate, surrender, yield, forego, renounce, abandon, expropriate)

ground-*n* land, earth, ground, dry land, continent, mainland, peninsula, delta, coast, shore, soil, clay, loam, acres, real estate, cause, origin, source, principle, element, reason, rationale, occasion derivation, (consequently, necessarily, eventually, derivative, sea, ocean, water, waves, billows)

grow-*v* increase, enlarge, extension, accession,

augment, gain, strengthen, intensify, enhance, magnify, redouble, dilate, exaggerate, expansibility, germination, growth, swollen, develop, amplify, widen, (reduce, scrape, compress, lessen, shrink, collapse, emaciate, atrophy)

H

habit-n essence, temper, spirit, humor, capacity, principle, nature, constitution, character, type, quality, garment, garb, palliative, apparel, wardrobe, wearing apparel, clothes, array, outfit, morning dress, uniform, (divestment, nudity, bareness, undress, uncover, denude, disrobe, dismantle, extraneousness, accident, derived from without)

hack-v cut, sunder, divide, subdivide, sever, abscind, saw, snip, nib, nip, cleave, rend, slit, split, splinter, carve, cut up, dissect, disintegrate, disperse, separate, discrete, ass, donkey, jackass, mule, horse, (join, attach, unite, fasten, bind, fix, affix, buckle, gird, close)

haggard-adj fatigue, weariness, yawning, drowsiness, lassitude, tiredness, exhaustion, faintness, collapse, prostration, (refreshed, recover, revival, repair, refection, renew)

hail-n welcome, arrive, advent, landing, hither, good day, reach, advent, reception, home, goal, port, haven, sleet, ice, snow, flake, crystal, drift, frost, icicle, (heat, caloric, fire, spark, flash, flame, blaze, bonfire, fireworks, depart, decampment, leave, outward, whence, hence, farewell, adieu, good bye)

half-n bisect, halving, divide, split, cut in two, cleave, dimidiate, separate, fork, bifurcate, cleft, bipartite, fork, prong, gradual, degree, retard, relax, slacken, moderate, rein, curb, leisurely, at half speed, slow, (hurry, accelerate, quicken, haste, rapid, scuttle, scud, gallop, amble, troll, hasten, duplicate, twice, once more, over again, renewal, double)

hammer-n repeat, iterate, reiterate, recurrence, succession, monotony, rhythm, recur, revert, reappear, often, blow, dint, stroke, sledge, mall, maul, mallet, flail, batter, pile-driving, punch, bat, axe, (recoil, react, spring, revulsion, rebound, reflex, reverberate, rebuff)

hand-n organ of touch, touch, feel, handle, finger,

thumb, feel, palpation, tingle, tangible, dextral, right-handed, ambidextrous, right and left, flank, quarter, (numb, intangible, impalpable, insensibility to touch)

handsome-adj liberal, free, beautiful, pretty, lovely, graceful, elegant, delicate, dainty, refined, fair, personable, comely, good-looking, dapper, jaunty, natty, quaint, (ugly, deformed, inelegance, disfigurement, squalor, monster)

handy-adj near, proximity, propinquity, vicinity, nigh, elongation, background, spread, neighboring, adjacent, adjoining, proximate, intimate, (distant, remote, far, extend, stretch, away, apart, asunder)

hang-v dependent, suspending, swing, dangle, swag, draggle, flap, trail, flow, sling, hook up, hitch, fasten, append, strangle, garrote, throttle, choke, stifle, suffocate, smother, asphyxiate, (support, bear, carry, sustain, bolster, hold, shoulder)

hard-adj strong, strength, power, vigor, force, brute force, mighty, adamantine, stout, robust, sturdy, powerful, potent, puissant, valid, reinforce, stamina, nerve, muscle, sinew, steel, energy, grip, bone,

dynamite, rigid, renitency, inflexible, stubborn, stiff, firm, (soft, pliable, flexible, plasticity, tender, supple, lithe, limber, limp, frail, fragile, flimsy, unsubstantial, rickety, drooping, withered, shattered)

hark-v hear, audible, acoustic, listen, catch a sound, attentive, mindful, observant, alive, awakened, behold, breathless, heed, cognizant, recognize, (absent, abstract, disregard, heedless, indifference)

hateful-adj bad, hurtful, evil, maltreat, abuse, injurious, deleterious, detrimental, noxious, pernicious, mischievous, malignant, vile, mean, wrong, depraved, shocking, reprehensible, disapprove, abominable, detestable, execrable, cursed, damned, infernal, diabolic, (admirable, estimable, praiseworthy, pleasing, tolerable, best, choice, select, goodness, beneficial valuable, serviceable, advantageous, edifying, favorable)

have-v possess, own, hold, tenure, occupy, depend, monopoly, heritage, inheritance, heir, engross, recreate, acquire, get, gain, win, earn, obtain, procure, gather, collect, assemble, pick, find, reap, secure, draw, confute, (lose, bereft, dispossess, rid, minus, deprive, lapse, forfeit, mislay, exempt)

hearty-*adj* healthy, well, sound, hale, fresh, green, whole, florid, flush, staunch, brave, robust, vigorous, weather-proof, willing, voluntary, propend, inclined, geniality, cordiality, goodwill, readiness, earnestness, forward, eager, (grudgingly, unwillingly, adverse, reluctant, backward, repugnant, delicate, loss of health, invalidate, atrophy, decay, decline, consumption, fatal)

heave-*v* raise, heighten, elevate, raise, lift, erect, stick, perch, tilt, upheave, exalt, hoist, cast, uplift, remain, stay, stand, lie, bring, draw-up, hold, halt, stop, rest, pause, anchor, (move, motion, shifting, mobile, restless, nomadic, lower, depress, dip, reduce, fall, sink, trample, duck)

heaven-*n* god like, kingdom, throne, paradise, eden, celestial, resurrection, supernal, unearthly, beatific, eternal home, bliss, happiness, felicity, beatitude, enchantment, transport, rapture, ecstasy,

Elysium, (grieve, mourn, yearn, repine, droop, languish, sink, despair, afflicted, demoniacal, haunted, supernatural, weird, uncanny, evil)

hedge-*n* compensate, equate, indemnification, compromise, counter, retaliate, counter-balance, hinder, impede, prevent, forefend, retard, slacken, preclude, inhibit, shackle, obstruct, stop, block, barricade, (aid, assist, help, support, lift, advance, further, promote, relief, advocate, reinforcement)

heir-*n* benefactor, grantee, trustee, holder, generative, descendant, heredity, descent, lineage

hell-*n* abyss, hollow, pit, shaft, well, crater, bottomless pit, unfortunate, unblest, unhappy, unlucky, poor, speculate, venture, stake, random shot, adversity, evil, failure, disaster, gamble, adventure, risk, hazard, stake, (intention, purpose, project, design, ambition, undertake, aim)

helm-*n* handle, hilt, haft, shaft, heft, shank, blade, trigger, tiller, treadle, key, turn screw, screwdriver, direct, manage, govern, conduct, order, prescribe, head, lead, regulate, guide, steer, pilot, drive, throne, chair, dais, (anarchy, relaxation, misrule, subordinate, dethronement, deposition, abdication)

heritage-n heirs, posterity, future, next, near, eventual, ulterior, prospective, tomorrow, eventual, ultimately, possess, own, occupy, hold, tenure, depend, retain, inheritance, revert, engross, (exemption, absence, devoid, unobtained, past, gone by, ancient, former, antiquity, immemorial, bygone, forgotten, irrecoverable obsolete)

hermitage-n abode, dwelling, lodging, domicile, residence, address, habitation, berth, seat, lap, housing, quarters, headquarters, tabernacle, throne, ark, home, fatherland, country, homestead, stall, fireside, hearth, stone, household

hesitate-v uncertain, suspense, perplexity, embarrassment, doubt, dubiety, vague, haze, fog, obscurity, contingency, puzzle, bewilder, bother, indecisive, ambiguous, questionable, precarious, disputable, (certain, necessary, assured, reliable, gospel, positive, solid, authoritative, authentic, official, evident, infallible)

hiss-n sound, hoot, gibe, flout, jeer, scoff, taunt,

sneer, quip, fling, wipe, slap in the face, disrespect, disregard, slight, trifle, discourteous, dishonor, desecrate, insult, affront, outrage, (respect, regard, consideration, courtesy, attention, reverence, honor, esteem, admiration, homage)

hit-v blow, dint, stroke, knock, tap, rap, slap, smack, pat, dab, slam, bang, whack, squash, dowse, whop, swap, probability, possibility, contingency, odds, long odds, run of luck, hammer, mall, knock, strike, (duck, recoil, rebound, revulsion, repercussion)

hobble-v creep, craw, lag, slug, draw, linger, loiter, saunter, plod, trudge, stump along, move-slowly, slouch, stagger, mince, slacken, moderate, easy, leisurely, deliberate, gradual, slow-paced, (trip, speed, hasten, move quickly, scuttle, scud, scamper, race, run, shoot, tear, whisk, sweep, brush, accelerate)

hobby-n pursuit, purse, prosecute, enterprise, adventure, quest, game, desire, wish, whim, devotee, aspirant, solicitant, avid, (indifferent, neutral, of no interest, have no desire, cold, frigid, lukewarm, avoid, shun, steer clear, deny)

hollow-*adj* vanish, unsubstantial, incomplete, deficiency, short measure, shortcoming, insufficient, imperfect, concave, dip, indentation, cavity, pit, follicle, depressed, excavate, furrow, trough, basin, valley, (convex, project, sell, bilge, bulge, protrude, tumor, hump, hunch, bulb, node, nodule)

holocaust-*n* kill, put to death, slay, shed blood, murder, assassinate, butcher, slaughter, suffocate, sacrifice, destroy, ravage, (creation, produce, generate, establish, give life to, complete)

homely-*adj* plain, disfigured, blemished, pitted, freckled, discolored, imperfect, injured, simple, ordinary, chaste, severe, (polished, festoon, garland, adorned, decorated, embellished, detailed, fleur-de-lis)

honor-*n* glory, distinction, reputation, notability, notoriety, dedication, consecration, enthronement, canonization, celebration, enshrinement, glorification, immortalize, exalt, glitter, distinguished, great, eminence, height, important, (disrepute, discredit, repute, dishonor, disgrace, shame, humiliation, scandal, vile, turpitude, tarnish, disgrace, degrade, vile, stain, shameful, degrading)

hook-*n* attach, fix, affix, saddle on, fasten, bind, secure, clinch, twist, tie, fast, close, tight, taut, inseparable, entangle, parting, (sunder, divide, disengage, subdivide, sever, cut, snip, split, carve, hack, lacerate, mangle, rupture, shatter, shiver, crunch, chop)

hop-*v* leap, jump, spring, bound, vault, station, dance, caper, curvet, caracole, skip, frisky, fun, frolic, merriment, pleasure, amusement, sport, laughter, reel, festivity, play, game, (wearisome, tediousness, drag, tiresome, hum-drum, slow, plunge, douse, sink, engulf, wallow)

hope-*v* desire, expectation, trust, confidence, reliance, faith, belief, assurance, reassurance, promise, optimism, enthusiasm, encouraging, cheering, bright, rose-colored, prosperity, welfare, well-being, affluence, blessings, thrive, flourish, (adverse, disastrous, calamitous, ruinous, dire, deplorable, unfortunate, unhappy, unlucky, hapless, despair, despondence, abandonment)

horn-*n* receptacle, recipient, receiver, reservoir,

compartment, vessel, vase, utensil, sharp, keen, pyramidal, spindle, needle-shaped, spiked, thorny, bristling, barbed, copious, abundant, abounding, enough, rich, sufficient

hostile-adj disagreeing, discordant, discrepant, unharmonious, inapt, opposed, antagonistic, counteractive, clashing, conflicting, against, disfavor, (cooperation, complicity, participation, collusion, association, alliance, combined)

I

idea-n notion, conception, thought, apprehension, impression, perception, image, sentiment, reflection, observation, consideration, abstract idea, point of view, theory, fancy, imagination, topic, thesis, text, business, affair, matter, argument, motion, inkling, (indifference, incurious, impassive, ignorance, remote)

identification-n identity, sameness, coincidence, exactness, similar, copy, recognize, equality, comparable, deduce, derived, gather, collect, draw an inference, make a deduction, whet, ween, estimate, appreciate, (discover, find, determine,

evolve, contrary, oppose, differ, invert, reverse, turn the tables, contradict, antagonize, oppose)

idle-adj shallow, imbecility, incapacity, vacancy of mind, poverty of intellect, weak, wanting, dull, powerless, frivolous, petty, inane, ridiculous, worthless, (paramount, essential, vial, all-absorbing, serious, earnest, grand, impressive, commanding, imposing)

idol-n favorite, pet, spoiled, desire, devotee, aspirant, solicitant, heretic, antichrist, pagan, heathen, bigot, (orthodox, sound, strict, faithful, evangelical)

ignore-v neglect, carelessness, trifling, omission, default, inactivity, inattention, nonchalance, insensibility, imprudence, recklessness, inconsiderate, heedless, thoughtless, uninformed, ignored, (knowledge, cognizance, acquaintance, insight, familiarity, intuition, perception, enlightenment)

Illegitimate-adj illegal, unlawful, smuggling, poaching, prohibited, illicit, contraband, despotic, deceitful, delusive, insidious, untrue, feigned, fraudulent, artificial, unsound, (legal, legitimacy, rule, regulation, equity, enact, vested, constitutional, permitted)

Illuminate-*v* light, ray, beam, stream, gleam, streak, sun, aurora, shining, luminous, lucid, bright, vivid, reflection, refraction, lighten, irradiate, color, hue, tint, intense, unfaded, gay, (pale, faded, colorless, decolorize, bleached, tarnished, blanch, dull, muddy, dingy)

Illustrate-*v* exemplify, cite, quote, exemplary, example, uniformly, in point, interpretation, definition, explicit, decipher, expound, unravel, disentangle, resolve, (misrepresent, pervert, garble, distort, travesty, stretch, aberration, irregularity, exemption)

imitation-*n* duplication, repetition, mirror, reflect, mimic, reproduce, repeat, echo, parody, travesty, caricature, burlesque, imitative, verbatim, duplicate, transcript, impersonate, (original, prototype, model, pattern, precedent, standard)

immaculate-*adj* perfect, best, pure, good, paragon, unparalleled, supreme, superhuman, divine, approbation, faultless, spotless, impeccable, unblemished, ripen, mature, scathless, intact, harmless, purity, clean, purify, (decay, corrupt,

mold, must, rot, putrefy, fester, rank, reek, stink, dirty, soil, smoke, tarnish, spot, dirty, filthy, grimy)

immature-*adj* new, novelty, recent, youth, innovation, modernism, recent, fresh, neoteric, new-born, young, vernal, renovated, brewing, hatching, forthcoming, (old, ancient, antique, venerable, elder, archaic, classic, seniority, mature, decline, senility)

immortal-*adj* perpetual, eternal, everlasting, perpetuity, continual, endless, unending, ceaseless, incessant, unfading, evergreen, never-ending, enthrone, signalize, consecrate, dedicate, enshrine, (discredit, disrepute, dishonor, disgrace, sudden, instant, abrupt, hasty, quick)

impartial-*adj* intelligent, keen acute, alive, discerning, wise, straightforward, conscientious, scrupulous, (undignified, partial, disloyal, thoughtless, want of intelligence, week, feeble minded)

impeach-*v* condemnation, reflection, disparage, ostracism, dispraise, censure, detract, depreciate, exception, rebuke, reprehension, reprobation, admonition, reproach, reprimand,

castigate, lecture,
disapprove, blame, frown
upon, (approbation,
approval, sanction,
advocacy, esteem, good
opinion, praise, applaud,
commend, compliment,
laudatory)

imperative-*adj* required,
need, necessary,
essential, indispensability,
urgency, prerequisite,
uncompromising, inflexible,
relentless, peremptory,
absolute, unsparing,
ironhanded, oppressive,
ruthless, (moderate,
lenient, moderation,
tolerant, mildness,
forbearing, compassion)

impossible-*adj*
impracticable,
unachievable, infeasible,
insurmountable,
incompatible, inaccessible,
impassible, unobtainable,
refuse, rejection, declining,
repulse, rebuff, reject,
deny, decline, protest,
disclaimer, (offer, present,
tender, move, start, invite,
possibility, potentiality,
agree, compatibility,
feasibility, practicability,
perhaps, perchance,
surmountable, accessible,
achievable, within reach)

impressive-*adj* sensational,
eloquent, vigorous,
nervous, powerful,
command of words, bold,
racy, slashing, pungent,
(feeble, tame, meager,
vapid, dull, dry, languid,

monotonous)

imprint-*v* propagate,
spread, advertise, affix,
type, figure, emblem,
cipher, device, represent,
motto, circumscribe,
enclose, imbedded

improper-*adj* inapt, unapt,
inappropriate, discordant,
hostile, incompatible,
irreconcilable, inconsistent,
unconformable,
exceptional, unjust, unfair,
wrong, encroach,
inequitable, unequal,
partial, unfit, (right, fit,
justice, equity, propriety,
impartiality, reasonable,
legitimate, justifiable)

impudent-*adj* insolence,
haughtiness, arrogance,
airs, overbearance,
sauciness, flippancy,
swagger, presumption,
usurpation, assurance,
audacity, hardihood, front,
shamelessness, effrontery,
assumption of infallibility,
(servile, cringing, fawning,
groveling, sniveling, mealy-
mouthed, precocious)

inane-*adj* nothing, naught,
nil, nullity, zero, cipher, no
one, nobody, never, no
such thing, insubstantiality,
nonsense, senseless,
inexpressible, undefinable,
trivial, quibbling,
(intelligent, clearness,
explicitness, lucidity,
perspicuity, legibility, plain
speaking, luminous,
transparent)

inaugural-*adj* precursor,

precedent, forerunner, pioneer, prelude, preamble, preface, prologue, preliminary, introductory, (sequel, suffix, successor, trail, rear, appendix, postscript, codicil, epilogue)

Incapable-*adj* impotence, disability, impiousness, helplessness, prostration, paralysis, palsy, apoplexy, exhaustion, collapse, (capability, capacity, faculty, quality, attribute, endowment, virtue, gift, property, qualification, susceptibility, puissance, might, force)

Incase-*v* cover, superpose, overlay, wrap, face, veneer, pave, bind, cap, coat, paint, incrust, limit, bound, encystment, imprisoned, enshrined, (lining, inner coating, covering, filling, stuffing, padding)

Incendiary-*adj* destructive, subversive, ruinous, deleterious, suicidal, deadly, with a crushing effect, demolish, dispel, dissipate, consume, squelch, exterminate, devastate, extinguish, burn, inflame, roast, toast, fry, grill, singe, parch, scorch, cauterize, sear, char, incinerate, (cool, fan, refrigerate, refresh, ice, congeal, freeze, glaciate, solidification, produce, establish, constitute)

Incessant-*adj* monotonous, harping, iterative, mocking, chiming, repeatedly, often again, over again, once more, ditto, encore, everlasting, continual, endless, ceaseless, (instantaneous, momentary, sudden, instant, abrupt)

Incidental-*adj* casual, fortuitous, accidental, adventitious, causeless, contingent, undetermined, indeterminate, possible, unintentional, hap-hazard, random probability, possibility, (attribution, theory, ascribe, impute, explanation, ascription, reference, to, rationale, imputation)

Inclusive-*adj* addition, annexation, adjection, supplement, subjunctive, annex, affix, superpose, including, inclusive, component, integral, ingredient, element, constituent, contents, appurtenance, (extraneousness, foreign, alien, intruder, ulterior, excluded, exceptional, deduction, retrenchment)

Incomparable-*adj* superior, greater, major, higher, exceeding, great, distinguished, vaulting, ultra, supreme, utmost, paramount, preeminent, foremost, crowning, first-rate, important, excellent, paragon, unparalleled, unequaled, unapproached, unsurpassed, superlative, (inferior, minority, subordinate, shortcoming, deficiency, minimum, smallness, diminished, subordinate)

Inconsistent-*adj* illogical unreasonable, false, unsound, invalid, unwarranted, unproved, contrary, opposite, counter, opposed, contrasted, conflicting, negative, differing, (similar, identical, facsimile, exact. identical, equal)

Increase-*v* enlargement, augmentation, extension, increment, accretion, accession, development, growth, ascent, acerbate, sprout, raise, exalt, magnify, many, several, manifold, multiplied, multiple, populous, (few, paucity, rarity, handful, abate, decline, shrink, wane, reflux)

Incurable-*adj* hopeless, despair, despondency, forlorn, inconsolable, cureless, remediless, incorrigible, irreparable, irrecoverable, ruined, undone, immitigable, (hope, trust, confident, presumptuous, feed, foster, nourish, healthy, sound, hearty, fresh)

Indebted-*v* owing, debt, obligation, liability, arrears, deficit, default, insolvency, grateful,

thankfulness, acknowledgement, allegiance, dueness, propriety, fitness, sense of duty, recognition, binding, imperative, behooving, (ungrateful, credit, trust, tick, score, tally, account)

Indemnity-*n* compensation, counteract, balance, hedge, square, give and take, compromise, excuse, exoneration, quitting, release, acquittal, conciliation, propitiation, reprieve, reward, remuneration, (penalty, retribution, confiscation, forfeit, revenge, vengeance, retaliation)

Indicate-*v* examine, scan, scrutinize, consider, inspect, review, rivet, direct, observe, mean, signify, express, convey, imply, bespeak, suggest, allusive, significant, symbolism, feature, diagnostic, recognize, (without meaning, senseless, nonsensical, void, vacant, insignificant)

Individual-*n* human being, person, creature, mortal, body, somebody, earthling, party, head, personal, individuality, special, particular, realize, designate, determine, private, characteristic, originality, (general, universal, miscellaneous, generic, broad, collective, every, all, unspecified)

indomitable-*adj* strong, might, vigorous, forcible, hard, adamantine, stout, robust, sturdy, hardy, powerful, potent, puissant, valid, resistless, irresistible, invincible, impregnable, unconquerable, determined, resolute, (vacillating, unsteady, changeable, cowardly, facile, pliant, reversible)

indulge-*v* lenient, mild, gentle, soft, tolerant, easy going, clement, compassionate, forbearing, permission, allow, leave, sufferance, tolerance, liberty, law, license, concession grace, favor, dispensation, exemption, connivance, (prohibit, disallow, veto, embargo, taboo, restrictive, forbid)

inert-*adj* dull, inactivity, torpor, languor, latency, sloth, irresolution, obstinacy, passive, sluggish, heavy, tame, slow, blunt, lifeless, dead, uninfluential, latent, dormant, smoldering, insensibility, apathy, lethargic, neutrality, vegetation, (sensitive, impressionable, enthusiastic, spirited)

inexorable-*adj* unavoidable, necessity, obligation, compulsive, subjection, imperious, iron, adverse, fate, compel, inevitable, irrevocable, impulsive,

(volition, voluntary, willful, intended, voluntary, spontaneity, original, optional, discretionary)

inexperience-*n* ignorance, incomprehensive, simplicity, unexplored, uncertainty, incapable, unknown, bungling, awkward, clumsy, maladroit, incompetent, rusty, without former knowledge, unskillful, disqualification, (skill, dexterity, experience, accomplish, competence, talent, capacity)

infernal-*adj* bad, hurtful, virulence, wrong, arrant, rank, foul, vile, abominable, detestable, cursed, confounded, damned, diabolic, malevolent, grudge, annoy, malicious, rancorous, spiteful, caustic, bitter, envenomed, acrimonious, grinding, galling, (benevolent, benignity, brotherly love, charity, sympathy, tenderness, goodness, excellence, value, merit, virtue)

infidelity-*n* dishonor, dishonest, disgrace, fraudulent, faithlessness, betrayal, degrade, derogate, stoop, grovel, sneak, unscrupulous, contemptible, abject, untrustworthy, (upright, honest, virtuous, honorable, fair, right, just, equitable, impartial, even

handed, square,
straightforward, honest)

Infiltrate-v intervene,
interference, introduce,
import, throw, insinuate,
dovetailing, permeation,
passage, transmission,
transudation, ingress,
instill, mix, join, combine,
infect, (eliminate,
purification, simple,
uniform, disentangle,
encompass, beset)

Influence-n change,
alteration, mutation,
permutation, variation,
modification, modulation,
mood, qualification,
innovation, deviation, turn,
transfiguration, pressure,
dominance, reign,
authority, capability,
interest, power, carry
weight, leverage,
(impotence, inertness,
powerless, irrelevant,
permanence, stability,
persistence, endurance)

Infringe-v transgression,
trespass, encroach,
transcendence, surpass,
go beyond, redundance,
strain, disobey, violate,
shirk, defiance,
uncomplying, (obedient,
complying, loyal, faithful,
devoted, restrainable,
resigned, passive,
submissive, henpecked)

Infuse-v mix, alloy, junction,
combination, impregnation,
infiltration, seasoning,
springing, interlard, instill,
imbue, infiltrate, dash,

tinge, tincture, season
sprinkle, attempter
medicate, blend, (pure,
eliminate, sift, uniform,
homogeneous, single,
neat, clear, sheer)

Injury-n impairment,
damage, loss, detriment,
laceration, outrage, havoc,
contamination, canker,
corruption, adulteration,
alloy, decay, dilapidation,
deteriorate, weaken, hurt,
harm, scathe, injurious,
deleterious, malignant,
nocuous, evil, wrong,
(beneficial, valuable,
advantageous, profitable,
edifying, improve,
betterment, mend,
amendment, refine)

Inkling-n supposition,
assumption, postulation,
condition, hypothesis,
postulate, theory, proposal,
suggestion, conceit, rough
guess, conjecture,
surmise, suspicion, hint,
insinuate, allude, desire,
wish, fantasy, leaning,
(indifferent, neutral,
unconcern, nonchalance,
earnestness, anorexia)

Insinuate-v cast reflection,
reproach, disapprove,
disparage, condemnatory,
damnify, denunciate,
abusive, objurgatory,
clamorous, vituperative,
defamatory, satirical,
severe, withering,
trenchant, sarcastic,
hypercritical, fastidious,
critical, hint, suggestion,

innuendo, (manifest, apparent, salient, striking, demonstrative, prominent, flagrant, notorious, approbation, approval, sanctioned, advocate)

Insipid-*adj* savorless, flat, stale, fade, mild, gutless, ingestible, mawkish, indifferent, cold, frigid, unconcerned, phlegmatic, easy-going, (avidity, greediness, covetous, grasping, craving, voracity, taste, savor, smack, gusto)

insist-*v* argue, reason, discuss, debate, dispute, wrangle, bandy, controvert, canvass, rational, argumentative, claim, warrant, controversial, dialectic, command, order, ordinance, act, instruct, dispatch, demand, imposition, require, charge, prescribe, (unreasonable, illogical, false, unsound, invalid, unwarranted, inconsequential)

Insolvent-*adj* destitute, indigence, penury, pauperism, want, need, necessity, privation, distress, difficulties, needy, poor, poverty-stricken, debt, obligation, liability, impecuniosity, mendicant, nonpayment, (credit, trust, tally, account, accredited, wealth, riches, fortune, opulence, affluence)

inspire-*v* encourage, infuse, give, reassure, embolden, inspirit, cheer, nerve, put,

enliven, elate, exhilarate, gladden, animate, raise the spirits, perk up, give pleasure, (depress, discourage, dishearten, dispirit, damp, dull, deject, lower, sink, dash)

instance-*n* example, specimen, sample, quotation, exemplification, illustration, accommodate, conformity, illustrate, accordance, cite, quote, inducement, consideration, attraction, enticement, allurement, (disincline, indispose, shake, dissuade, remonstrate, without rhyme or reason)

instant-*n* moment, second, minute, twinkling, flash, breath, crack, jiffy, burst, hasty, quick, flash of lightning, present, actual, current, important, consequence, prominence, consideration, (whenever, occasion, upon, sooner or later, perpetual, eternal, everlasting, immortal)

Instinct-*n* intellect, mind, understanding, thinking, principle, rationality, faculties, senses, observation, percipience, association of ideas, conception, judgment, wit, capacity, ability, instinctive, impulsive, gratuitous, hazarded, unconnected, (absence of intellect, imbecility, argumentative, controversial, debatable)

institution-*n* school,

academy, university,
college, seminary, alma
mater, party, faction, side,
denomination, communion,
set, crew, band, society,
association, alliance,
league, legal, legitimate,
link, banded, bonded,
unite, join, associate,
corporation, syndicate

Instruct-v teach, edification,
education, tuition,
guidance, qualification,
preparation, discipline,
exercise, direct, guide,
impress upon, convince,
expound, command,
message, direction,
requirement, order,
(misinform, mislead,
misrepresent, lie, bewilder,
deceive, mystify)

Integrate-v consolidate,
whole, totality, integrity,
totality, entirety,
collectiveness, unity,
completeness, integration,
aggregate, gross amount,
altogether, substantially,
(incomplete, deficient,
shortcoming, insufficiency,
imperfect, defective,
unfinished, fractional,
fragmentary, sectional)

Intensify-v increase,
enlargement, extension,
dilatation, expansion,
increment, develop,
magnify, enhance,
aggravate, exasperate,
stimulate, activity,
agitation, effervescence,
stir, bustle, perturbation,
exert, (inertness, inactive,

passive, torpid, sluggish,
dull, heavy, uninfluential,
decrease, diminish, lessen,
shrink, wane)

Intercede-v mediate,
intercessor, peacemaker,
negotiator, diplomat,
arbitrate, deprecate,
expostulate, protest,
negative request, (request,
motion, overture, demand,
canvass, address, appeal)

Interest-n influential,
important, weight,
prevailing, rampant,
dominance, predominant,
curious, inquisitive, stare,
gape, lionize, pry,
paramount, essential, vital,
all-absorbing, radical,
cardinal, prime,
(indifferent, passive,
irrelevancy, uninfluential)

Intermit-adj interrupt,
interrupted sequence,
discontinue, break,
fracture, flaw, fault,
suspend, interplay, cease,
desist, break off, hold,
stop, stick, pause, rest,
halt, (continue,
persistence, repetition,
sustain, unvarying,
unreversed, unrevoked)

Interrupt-v discontinue,
disjunction, break, fault,
pause, disconnect,
unsuccessful, spasmodic,
intermittent, few and far
between, alternation,
patchwork, episode,
cessation, resistance,
suspension, stop, rest, lull,
(continue, persist,

repetition, sustain, uphold, hold up, perpetuate, maintain, preserve)

Intervene-*v* mediate, peacemaker, negotiator, diplomat, moderate, time, duration, period, term, last, endure, remain, persist, elapse, while, interim, interval, intermission, interlude, (circumvent, around, about, without, skirt, twine round, lap)

Interview-*n* conference, interlocution, converse, confabulation, talk, discourse, verbal intercourse, oral communication, chatty, colloquial, parley, gossip, tattle, visit, call, assignation, appointment, (seclusion, privacy, retirement, reclusion, sequestered, private, snug, domestic)

Intricate-*adj* disorder, derangement, irregularity, unconformity, confusion, confusedness, disarray, jumble, huddle, litter, complexity, implication, intricacy, perplexity, network, involved, raveled, entangled, disarrange, (order, regularity, uniformity, symmetry, progression, series, systematically, gradation)

Introduce-*v* prefix, place before, premise, prelude, preface, preceding, prior, before, former, foregoing, aforementioned, prefatory,

introductory, preamble, prologue, precession, leading, heading, precedence, (sequence, coming after, follower, attend, beset, succeeding)

Intrude-*v* disagree, discordant, discrepant, hostile, repugnant, incompatible, irreconcilable, inconsistent, interfere, clash, intervention, partition, midriff, interpenetrate, permeate, introduce, import, interpose, (surround, beset, compass, encompass, environ, enclose, encircle)

Inundate-*v* irrigate, deluge, syringe, inject, gargle, drench, douse, dilute, dip, immerse, merge, submerge, redundance, many, super abundance, saturation, transcendency, exuberance, profuseness, accumulation, (dry, flatulent, effervescent, atmospheric, meteorological)

Invalid-*n* powerless, impotence, disability, disablement, imbecility, incapacity, indocility, inefficiency, incompetence, disqualification, helplessness, prostration, palsy, exhaustion, inefficacy, failure, (power, potency, might, force, energy, ability, capability, faculty, quality, attribute)

Invasion-*n* attack, assault,

assail, charge, impugn,
aggression, offense,
incursion, inroad, irruption,
outbreak, investment,
obsession, bombardment,
fire, volley, platoon, beset,
besiege, beleaguer,
(defense, protection,
guard, ward, shielding,
preservation, guardianship,
resistance, safeguard)

Inversion-*n* derangement,
disorder, eviction,
disturbance, dislocation,
perturbation, interruption,
corrugation, complicate,
involve, perplex, confound,
tangle, litter, scatter, mix,
(classify, divide, file, string,
together, thread, register,
catalog, tabulate, index,
graduate, digest)

Invest-*v* purchasing, buying,
procure, rent, expenditure,
expend, disburse,
circulate, remuneration,
fee, contingent, quota,
(premium, bonus, pension,
annuity, jointure, alimony,
pittance, proceeds)

Invoke-*v* address,
allocution, speech,
appeal, invocation,
salutation, request,
entreat, beseech, plead,
supplicate, implore,
conjure, adjure, obtest,
evoke, impetrate,
imprecate, (deprecation,
expostulation, intercession,
mediation, protest)

Irregular-*adj* diverse,
unevenness, multiformity,
unconformity, varied,

rough, disorder, anomaly,
disunion, discord,
confusion, disarray,
jumble, complexity,
perplexity, turmoil, ferment,
disturbance, convulsion,
riot, unsymmetrical,
intricate, complicated,
(order, uniformity,
methodical, symmetrical,
uniform, arranged)

Irrevocable-*adj* compulsory,
uncontrollable, inevitable,
unavoidable, inexorable,
involuntary, instinctive,
automatic, blind, stable,
unchangeable, constancy,
established, permanence,
fixed, steadfast, firm, valid,
irremovable, riveted,
(changeable, mutable,
variable, vagrant)

J

jabber-*v* loquacity,
talkativeness, garrulity,
jaw, gabble, chatter,
linguistic, declamatory,
open-mouthed, fluency,
flippancy, flowing, tongue,
verbosity, stammer,
hesitation, impediment,
stutter, falter, mumble,
(oratory, elocution,
rhetoric, declamation)

jail-*n* bolt, bar, lock,
padlock, rail, prison, gaol,
cage, coop, den, cell,
stronghold, fortress, keep,
dungeon, Bastille,
bridewell, house of
correction, hulks, toll-
booth, penitentiary, guard-

room, (liberate,
disengagement, release,
emancipate, dismiss)
jam-v squeeze, push,
reduce, extricate, express,
pulp, paste, dough, curd,
pudding, poultice, grume,
sugar, syrup, treacle,
molasses, honey, manna,
confection, nectar, pastry,
pie, (sour, vinegar, styptic)
jar-v clash, disagree,
interfere, intrude, discord,
capsule, vesicle, vessel,
pod, bottle, decanter,
ewer, cruise, carafe, crock,
kit, canteen, flagon,
demijohn, jug, pitcher,
mug, kettle, chalice,
tumbler, glass, rummer,
horn, saucepan
jargon-n paradox, riddle,
incomprehensible,
inconceivable, vagueness,
loose, beyond
comprehension, gibberish,
macaronic, confusion of
tongues, (verbal, literal,
titular, conjugate,
derivative, exact,
concordance, clear, plain
speaking, lucidity,
perspicuity, legibility)
jaundice-n yellow,
gamboge, cadmium,
aureate, golden, citron,
fallow, sallow, luteous,
tawny, bias, warped,
twisted, hobby, fad, quirk,
one sided, superficial,
partial, narrow, confined,
(deduce, derive, gather,
collect, judge, umpire,
assessor, discover)

jealousy-n envious, covet,
invidious, rival, suspicion,
scruple, qualm, unbeliever,
discredit, dissent, (believe,
credit, indifference)
jerk-v agitate, stir, tremor,
shake, ripple, jolt,
trepidation, quiver, quaver,
dance, disquiet, twitter,
flicker, flutter, traction,
draw, draught, pull, haul,
rake, drag, tug, tow, trail,
train, wrench, twitch,
tousle, propel, project,
throw, fling, cast, pitch,
chuck, toss, heave, hurl,
flirt, flip, (repulse, repel,
abduct, repellent,
repulsive, diverge,
divaricate, radiate, ramify
jilt-v disappoint,
disconcerted, aghast, trick
of fortune, deception,
falseness, untruth,
imposition, fraud, deceit,
guile, knavery,
misrepresentation,
delusion, trick, cheat,
deceiver, dissembler,
hypocrite, shuffler, wolf in
sheep's clothing, (dupe,
gull, gudgeon, cull, victim,
greenhorn, fool)
jog-v push, walk, march,
step, tread, pace, plod,
wend, promenade, trudge,
tramp, stalk, stride,
straddle, strut, foot it,
stump, bundle, bowl along
toddle, paddle, roving,
vagrancy, marching and
countermarching, nomad,
vagabondism, migration
join-v connect, union,

attachment, attach, fix, affix, fasten, bind, secure, clinch, twist, pinion, string, strap, sew, lace, stitch, tack, knit, gird, tether, moor, harness, chain, fetter, firm, fast, close, tight, taut, group, cluster, accumulation, assemble, compile, associate, (disperse, dissipate, distribute, apportionment, spread, cut, scatter, sow, disseminate, diffuse, separate, parting, detach)

jolt-*v* impulse, impetus, momentum, push, pulsing, thrust, shove, jog, brunt, booming, throw, strike, knock, tap, rap, slap, flap, dab, pat, thump, beat, bang, slam, dash, punch, thwack, whack, hit, agitate, shake, convulse, toss, tumble, (recoil, revulsion, rebound, reflection, reflex, reflux, reverberation, rebuff, repulse, return)

judgment-*n* instinct, conception, wits, capacity, intellect, understanding, reason, rationality, cogitative, faculties, senses, observation, intuition, discrimination, distinction, differentiation, (indiscrimination, uncertainty, indistinctness, imbecility, without reason)

judicial-*adj* judge, tribunal, municipality, bailiwick, officer, bailiff, sit in judgment, magistrate,

authority, prefiguration, auspices, forecast, omen, prognostication, premonition, (weak, feeble minded, fatuous, idiotic, imbecile, blatant, babbling, bewildered)

jump-*v* sudden change, transilience, leap, plunge, jerk, start, explosion, spasm, convulsion, throe, revulsion, cataclysm, hop, spring, bound, vault, saltation, frisky, skip, dance, caper, curvet, flounce, start, agitation, (submerge, douse, sink, engulf, send to the bottom, plunge, dip, souse, duck, dive)

jury-*n* judge, justice, chancellor, recorder, magistrate, jurat, assessor, arbiter, arbitrator, umpire, referee, archon, tribune, scapegoat, stop-gap

K

keen-*adj* strong, energetic, forcible, active, intense, severe, vivid, sharp, acute, incisive, trenchant, brisk, rousing, irritating, poignant, virulent, caustic, mordant, harsh, stringent, double-edged, (inertness, dull, inert, inactivity, torpor, languor, inaction, lithe, passive, heavy, flat)

keep-*v* retain, retention, custody, tenacity, firm hold, grasp, grip, clutches, tongs, forceps, pincers, undisposed, tenacious, preserve, safe keeping, conserve, maintain, support, sustentation, salvation, hygienic, (relinquish, abandonment, renunciation, expropriation, dereliction, surrender, dispensation, resignation, riddance, jettison, discard)

kick-v assault, thrust, lunge, pass, push, cut, fire, volley, assail, strike, impulse, whip, attack, aggressive, strike out, fling, insolent, flippant, pert, forward, impertinent, (defense, protect, guard, ward, shield, self-defense, preservation, resistance, safeguard, repel, stand one's ground)

kill-v destroy, violent death, homicide, manslaughter, murder, assassination, massacre, mortal, fatal, lethal, dead, deathly, suicidal, strangle, smother, kill with kindness, consume, burn, idle, trifle, (life, vivacity, spirit, dash, energy, animation)

king-n potentate, sovereign, monarch, despot, tyrant, crowned head, emperor, majesty, protector, president, judge, empire, royalty, regal, dominant, paramount, supreme, influential, imperial, stringent, (absence of authority, anarchy, relaxation, loosening, remission, misrule,

insubordination, depravation of power, remiss, unwarranted)

kiss-v endearment, caress, embrace, salute, smack, buss, osculation, courtship, wooing, suit, philander, flirt, obeisance, bow, courtesy, curtsy, scrape, loving, love token, (repulsive, noncomplacent, accommodating, gallant, ungentle, rough, rugged, bluff, blunt, gruff, tar)

knavery-n deception, falseness, untruth, imposition, fraud, guile, misrepresentation, delusion, gullible, conjuring, cunning, craftiness, subtlety, chicanery, juggler, concealment, sharp practice, (natural, pure, native, simple, plain, inartificial, untutored, unsophisticated, unaffected, sincere, frank, open)

knee-n angular, bent, crooked, aduncous, uncinate, aquiline, jagged, serrated, furcate, forked, dovetailed, knock-kneed, crinkled, obeisance, homage, genuflection, courtesy, curtsy, prostration, beg, request, ask, kneel to, (deprecation, expostulation, intercession, unasked)

know-v knowledge, cognizance, acquaintance, privily, insight, familiarity, appreciation, intuition, consciousness, conceive, comprehend, take, realize, understand, aware, ascertained, (ignorance, shallow, superficial, green, rude, empty, half-learned, illiterate, unread, uninformed, empty-headed)

kowtow-v bow, depress, lower, take-down, subvert, prostrate, level, fell, cast, genuflection, obeisance, surrender, succumb, submit, yield, bend, resign, (elevate, raise, lift, sublimation, exaltation, prominence, heighten, erect)

L

labor-n work, action, performance, perpetration, movement, operation, evolution, procedure, execution, handicraft, business, deed, act, transaction, job, doings, dealings, proceeding, measure, achieve, inflict, (indolent, lazy, slothful, idle, lust, slothful, idle, lust, remiss, slack, inert, torpid, sluggish, languid, supine, heavy, dull leaden, lumpish, listless, dilatory, laggard)

ladle-n receptacle, shovel, trowel, spoon, spatula, watch-glass, thimble, receiver, cup, goblet, chalice, soup, decant, draft off, transfuse, spoon, hod,

paddle, hoe, spade, spud

lag-v linger, slow, retard, relax, slacken, check, moderate, slack, tardy, dilatory, inactive, gentle, easy, leisurely, deliberate, gradual, insensible, imperceptible, languid, sluggish, slow-paced, tardigrade, snail-like, creeping, follow, attendant, shadow, dangler, get behind, (lead, in advance, before, ahead, precede, forerun, introduce)

lame-adj incomplete, imperfect, defective, deficient, wanting, failing, meager, half and half, perfunctory, sketch, crude, mutilated, garbled, lopped, truncated, helplessness, prostration, paralysis, palsy, apoplexy, syncope, collapse, exhaustion, emasculation, (ability, ableness, togetherness, faculty, quality, attribute, endowment, virtue, gift, property, qualification, susceptibility, valid, effective)

land-n arrive, reach, attain, get to, come to, overtake, light, alight, dismount, debark, disembark, here, hither, detrain, welcome, converge, meet, completion, earth, ground, continent, coast, shore, mainland, peninsula, delta, soil, globe, clay, loam, acres, real estate, (ocean, brine, water, waves, departure, cessation, decampment, embarkation, outset, start, exit, egress, exodus, farewell)

landscape-*n* agriculture, management of plants, cultivation, husbandry, farming, gardening, horticulture, floriculture, ornamental, flower garden, vineyard, till, scenery, dress the ground, undeformed, undefaced, unspotted, (deformed, defaced, ugly, uninviting)

languid-*adj* weak, poor, infirm, fantasia, sickly, dull, slack, spent, short-winded, effete, weatherbeaten, decayed, rotten, worn, seedy, wasted, washy, laid low, pulled down, frail, fragile, shatter, decrepit, feeble, debilitate, impotent, soft, effeminate, femininity, womanly, colorless, (strength, power, stoutness, strong, might, vigorous, forcible, hard, adamantine, stout, robust, sturdy, hardy)

lap-*n* abode, dwelling, lodging, domicile, residence, address, habitation, berth, seat, sojourn, housing, quarters, head-quarters, residence, tabernacle, throne, ark, supporter, aid, prop, stand, anvil, stay, shore, skid, rib, truss, bandage, sleeper, stirrup, stilts, shoe, heel, splint, bar, rod, (suspend,

loose, flowing, hang, slip, hitch, fasten to, append)

lapse-*n* elapse, course, progress, process, succession, flow, flux, stream, tract, current, tide, march, run, expire, duration, past, gone, gone by, over, passed away, bygone, foregone, expired, exploded, forgotten, former, pristine, (future, hereafter, approaching, prospectively, hereafter, tomorrow, eventually, ultimately)

large-*adj* quantity, vast, immense, enormous, extreme, inordinate, excessive, extravagant, exorbitant, outrageous, preposterous, unconscionable, swinging, monstrous, big, great, considerable, bulky, voluminous, ample, massive, mass, capacious, comprehensive, spacious, might, towering, fine, magnificent, (dwarf, pygmy, chit, minute, diminutive, microscopic, inconsiderable, exiguous, puny)

last-*n* final, end, close, termination, dissonance, conclusion, period, term, extreme, verge, consummation, finish, conclude, expire, definitive, ending, durable, lasting, standing, permanent, chronic, long-standing, macrobiotic, perpetual, lingering, (transient, impermanence, temporary, brief, quick, brisk, extemporaneous, summary, sudden, momentary)

laugh-*v* ridicule, derision, sardonic, smile, grin, scoffing, mockery, quiz, banter, irony, squib, satire, skit, quip, quibble, grin, parody, burlesque, satirize, caricature, travesty, giggle, titter, snigger, cheer, chuckle, shout, (lament, wail, complaint, plaint, murmur, mutter, grumble, groan, moan, whine, whimper, sob, sigh, suspiration, mourning, condolence, deplore, grieve)

launch-*v* beginning, commencement, opening, outset, incipience, inception, introduction, initial, inauguration, embarkation, outbreak, fresh start, origin, source, rise, bud, germ, egg, genesis, birth, nativity, cradle, start, (end, close, termination, dissonance, conclusion, period, term, extreme, consummation, finish)

lavish-*adj* profuseness, redundance, too much, super abundance, inordinate, excessive, replete, prodigal, overweening, extravagant, overcharged, supersaturated, drenched, overflowing, superfluous, (receive, take, catch, miser, waste, scrubby, touch, acquire, reception, susceptibility, release)

lax-*adj* slackness, loose, toleration, anarchy, interregnums, loosening, remission, dead, letter, misrule, dethrone, depose, abdicate, careless, weak, free rein, unbridled, unauthorized, (authority, influence, patronage, hold, rasp, grip, reach, clutch, talons, power, preponderance, credit, jurisdiction)

lazy-*adj* inactive, inertness, obstinacy, idle, remiss, sloth, indolence, indulgence, dawdling, languor, sluggishness, procrastination, torpidity, somnolence, drowsiness, drone, droll, nothingness, slow, slack, moderate, linger, loiter, tortoise, (active, brisk, liveliness, animation, life, vivacity, spirit, dash, energy, nimbleness)

leak-*n* crack, interval, interspace, separation, break, gap, opening, hole, chasm, interruption, cleft, mesh, crevice, chink, creek, cranny, chap, slit, fissure, scissure, rift, flaw, breach, gorge, defile, transude, run out, strain, distill, perspire, sweat, filter, filtrate, dribble, gush, spout, flow, (excretion, discharge, emanation, exhalation, exudation, extrusion, contiguity, contact, proximity, apposition, join, adjoin, graze, meet, osculate, coincide, adhere, touching)

lean-*adj* thin, narrowness, closeness, exiled, exiguity, tenuity, emaciation, shaving, slip, skeleton, shadow, anatomy, spindle, meager, gaunt, tendency, aptness, proneness, proclivity, bent, turn, tone, bias, set, (breadth, width, latitude, amplitude, diameter, bore, caliber, radius, superficial, thickness, corpulence, dilation, wide, broad, ample, extended, thick)

leave-*v* fissure, breach, rent, split, rift, crack, slit, incision, fission, dissection, anatomy, disjoin, disconnect, disengage, sunder, divide, sever, abscind, relinquish, abandon, defection, secession, withdrawal, discontinuance, renunciation, abrogation, resignation, (arrive, reunion, remain, confinement, restrict, forbid, hindrance, taboo, embargo, ban)

leaven-*n* component, integral, element, constituent, ingredient, part and parcel, contents, appurtenance, feature, member, to be implicated in, cause, origin, source, principle, element, agent, groundwork, foundation, (effect, consequence, result, upshot, issue, produce, work, handiwork, fabric, performance, creature)

ledge-*n* shelf, support, ground, foundation, base, basis, bearing, fulcrum, footing, prop, stand, anvil, shore, skid, rib, truss, bandage, stirrup, stilts, tower, pillar, column, obelisk, monument, steeple, spire, escarpment, edge, brae, height, (lowness, neap, debased, nether, flat, level with the ground)

left-*adj* residuary, remaining, remainder, residue, remnant, rest, relic, leavings, heel-tap, odds and ends, surplus, overplus, excess, complement, sinistrality, left-handed, port, (dextral, right-handed, ambidextrous, adjunct, affix, appendage, reinforcement, accompaniment, adjective)

leg-*n* support, travel, wayfaring, journey, excursion, expedition, tour, trip, grand tour, circuit, peregrination, discursion, ramble, pilgrimage, course, ambulation, march, step, tread, pace, plod, wend, promenade

legion-*n* multitude,

numerousness, multiplicity, profusion, host, enormous number, array, sight, army, sea, galaxy, scores, peck, bushel, shoal, armed force, troops, soldiery, military, standing army, volunteers, (few, paucity, small number, small quantity, rarity, infrequency, handful, minority, thin)

leisure-*n* spare time, slow, deliberate, quiet, calm, undisturbed, slack, tardy, dilatory, gentle, easy, gradual, insensible, imperceptible, languid, sluggish, slow-paced, tardigrade, creeping, (speed, velocity, celerity, swiftness, rapidity, expedition, eagle speed, haste, spurt, dash, race, lively)

lend-*n* loan, advance, accommodation, federation, mortgage, investment, pawnbroker, money lender, usurer, advance, intrust, invest, let, lease, demise, aid, assistance, help, support, lift, patronage, countenance, favor, interest, advocacy, (prevention, preclusion, obstruction, stoppage, interruption, restriction, borrow, pledge, hire, rent, farm brace, touch, hold up)

lenient-*adj* moderate, temperateness, gentleness, sobriety, quiet, mental calmness,

relaxation, remission, mitigation, tranquilization, assuagement, contemplation, pacification, measure, (violence, inclemency, vehemence, might, impetuosity, boisterousness, uproar, riot, severity)

lessen-*v* decrease, subtraction, reduction, abatement, declination, shrinking, abridgment, diminish, abridge, shrink, fall away, waste, wear, wane, ebb, decline, subside, compression, compactness, collapse, emaciation, atrophy, (expansion, enlargement, extension, augmentation, growth, development, increase, additional, undiminished, exaggerate, exasperate)

let-*v* permit, leave, allow, tolerance, liberty, law, license, concession, grace, indulgence, favor, dispensation, exemption, release, connivance, vouchsafement, authorization, warranty, lend, advance, accomodate, (prohibition, disallowance, borrow, interdict, injunction, embargo, ban, taboo, restriction, release, hindrance, exclusive)

letter-*n* mark, character, hieroglyphic, writing, printing, abc's, consonant, vowel, diphthong, mute, liquid, labial, dental, guttural, spelling, orthography

liberty-*n* freedom, independence, immunity, exemption, emancipation, franchise, liberalism, permission, leave, allow, sufferance, tolerance, law, concession, grace, indulgence, favor, dispensation, release, (prohibit, disallowance, interdict, unlicensed, contraband, subjection)

lick-*v* eat, feed, fare, devour, swallow, take, gulp, bolt, snap, dispatch, pick, peck, crunch, chew, masticate, nibble, gnaw, mumble, strike, deal a blow to, smite, slap, face, smack, (discharge, emanation, exhalation, exudation, extrusion, secretion, effusion, saliva, outpour)

limbo-*n* purgatory, hell, bottomless pit, place of torment, everlasting fire, torment, Gehenna, abyss, inferno, mental suffering, pain, ache, smart, displeasure, vexation of spirit, (pleasure, gratification, enjoyment, fruition, relish, zest, satisfaction, heavenly, paradise, eden, celestial)

limit-*n* restrain, hindrance, restraint, coercion, constraint, repression, discipline, control, confinement, durance,

duress, imprisonment, end, close, termination, conclusion, finish, (begin, commence, originate, conceive, initiate, open, dawn, liberation, disengagement, free, deliverance)

linear-*adj* continuity, consecutive, progressive, gradual, serial, successive, immediate, unbroken, entire, uninterrupted, unremitting, perennial, paternity, parentage, consanguinity, maternal, family, ancestral, patriarchal, (discontinue, pause, interrupt, intervene, break, disconnect, break, fracture)

link-*n* pin, nail, bolt, hasp, clasp, clamp, screw, rivet, impact, solder, set, weld, fuse-together, wedge, rabbet, mortise, mire, jam, dovetail, encase, graft, ingraft, inosculate, close, tight, taut, (sunder, divide, subdivide, sever, dissever, abscind, saw, snip, nib, nip, cleave, rive, rend, slit, split)

lion-*n* courage, hero, demigod, tiger, panther, bull-dog, prowess, heroism, chivalry, manliness, nerve, pluck, mettle, game, spunk, face, virtue, prodigy, phenomenon, potent, (coward, timidity, effeminacy, poltroonery, baseness, dastardliness, sneak, recreant, shy)

liquid-*n* fluid, inelastic, liquor, humor, juice, sap, serum, blood, serosal, succulent, sappy, flowing, soluble, lymph, (atmospheric, airy, aerial, meteorological weather-wise, ventilate) climate)

list-*n* catalog, inventory, schedule, register, account, file, index, book, ledger, synopsis, bill of lading, prospectus, statistics, directory, score, census

listless-*adj* inattentive, inconsiderateness, absent, abstracted, lost, preoccupied, engrossed, napping, dreamy, disconcerted, (attention, mindfulness, observance, consideration, notice, regard)

literary-*adj* lingual, dialectic, vernacular, polyglot, book, writing, work, volume, publication, portfolio, periodical, style, diction, phraseology, wording, manner, strain, literary power

litigation-*n* citation, arraignment, prosecution, impeachment, accusation, apprehension, arrest, committal, writ, summons, subpoena, strife, warfare, outbreak, disagreement, variance, difference, (concord, accord, harmony, symphony, agreement, sympathy,

response, union, unison)

litter-*n* disorder, irregularity, anomaly, unconformity, anarchy, confusion, disarray, jumble, huddle, lumber, mess, mash, muddle, hash, hodgepodge, (order, regularity, uniformity, symmetry, gradation, progression, series, subordination, routine, method, disposition, arrangement)

little-*adj* small, quantity, vanishing,diminutive, minute, inconsiderable paltry, faint, unimportant, weak, slender, light, slight, scanty, scant, limited, mere, simple, sheer, stark, bare, dwarf, pygmy, chit, (corpulent, stout, fat, plump, squab, full, lusty, strapping, bouncing, portly, burly, huge, immense)

live-*v* exist, being, entity, subsistence, reality, actuality, positiveness, fact, matter of fact, real, actual, absolute, true, permanence, persistence, endurance, standing, maintenance, present, occupying, inhabiting, dwell, reside, stay, sojourn, abide, lodge, (absence, inexistent, empty, void, vacant, inexistent, extinction, annihilate, nullify, abrogate, destroy, negative, blank, missing, omitted)

load-*n* cargo, contents,

lading, freight, shipment, bale, shipload, stuff, oppress, care, anxiety, solicitude, trouble, trial, fiery ordeal, shock, blow, dole, fret, burden, (pleasure, gratification, enjoyment, fruition, relish, zest, gusto, satisfaction, complacency, well-being, good)

loadstar-n motion toward, attraction, pulling toward, adduction, magnetism, gravity, siderite, beacon, cairn, seamark, lighthouse, guide, address, direction, heliograph

loathe-v dislike, repugnance, disgust, queasiness, turn, nausea, averseness, antipathy, abhorrence, horror, hatred, detestation, animosity, hydrophobia, insulting, irritating, provoking, abomination, aversion, (love, fondness, liking, inclination, affection, sympathy, tenderness)

local-adj location, lodgement, reposition, stow, package, settlement, installation, fixation, insertion, anchorage, mooring, encampment, plantation, colony, place, situate, locate, localize, station, house, (displacement, transposition, eject, exile, removal, dislocation, unload, empty)

lock-v fasten, attach, fix, affix, bind, secure, clinch, twist, string, strap, firm, close, knot, shackle, rein, padlock, rivet, stake, hook, latchet, resistance, stand, front, oppugnant, opposition, reluctant, (separate, parting, detachment, segregation, divorce, divide, unlock, detach, isolate)

locomotion-n moving, stream, flow, flux, run, course, evolution, kinematics, step, transitory, shifting, movable, mobile, mercurial, restless, nomadic, erratic, cadence, (quiet, tranquility, calm, repose, peace, dead calm, immobility, fixed, stay, stagnate, rest, pause, lull)

log-n fuel, firing, combustible, coal, anthracite, culm, coke, carbon, charcoal, turf, peat, firewood, bobbing, faggot, cinder, record, note, minute, register, roll, list, entry, memorandum, document, deposition, affidavit, certificate, (efface, obliterate, erase, expunge, cancel, blot, scratch)

long-adj durable, lasting, permanent, chronic, long-standing, protracted, prolonged, lengthy, drawn out, profuse, verbose, copious, exuberant, rambling, broad, wide, ample, extended, thick,

dumpy, streak,
outstretched, elongate,
extend, stretch, (short,
little, abbreviated, brief,
curt, compact, stubby,
temporary, cursory, short-
lived, deciduous, mortal,
summary, concise, terse)

longevity-*n* age, oldness,
senility, anility, climacteric,
declining years,
decrepitude, caducity,
seniority, eldership,
matronly, anile, ripe,
mellow, wrinkled, (youth,
juvenility, cradle, nursery,
green, budding)

longitude-*n* situation,
position, locality, status,
footing, standing,
standpoint, post, stage,
aspect, attitude, posture,
place, site station, seat,
length, span, linear,
measure of length,
(shortness, brevity,
littleness, shortening,
abbreviation, abridgment,
concision, retrenchment,
curtailment)

look-*v* see, vision, sight,
view, glance, glimpse,
peep, gaze, stare, leer,
contemplation, squint,
visual, ocular, optic,
appear, aspect, phase,
guise, complexion, color,
image, apparent, seeming,
ostensible, (invisible,
imperceptible, conceal,
blind, sightless)

loose-*adj* detach, sunder,
divide, subdivide, sever,
dissever, abscind, saw,

snip, nib, nip, cleave,
rupture, shatter, shiver,
lacerate, scramble,
mangle, gash, hash, slice,
whittle, carve, dissect,
liberate, disengagement,
release, enlargement,
emancipation,
enfranchisement,
discharge, dismissal,
(restraint, hindrance,
coercion, compulsion,
constraint, repression,
discipline, control)

love-*v* desire, wish, fancy,
fantasy, want, need,
exigency, longing,
hankering, inkling,
solicitude, anxiety,
yearning, coveting,
aspiration, liking, fondness,
relish, passion, rage,
mania, ambition,
eagerness, zeal, ardor,
breathless, impatience,
impetuosity, (indifferent,
cold, frigid, lukewarm, cool,
careless, listless,
lackadaisical, half-hearted,
apathy, insensibility)

luxury-*n* enjoyment,
pleasure, gratification,
relish, complacency,
comfort, ease, cushion,
joy, gladness, delight, glee,
cheer, sunshine,
happiness, felicity, bliss,
paradise, ecstasy,
Elysium, indulgence, high
living, excess, sensuality,
(temperance, moderation,
forbearance, self-denial,
frugality, total abstinence,
sufficient, care, anxiety,

solitude, concern)

M

maceration-n saturation, water, serum, serosal, lymph, rheumy, delude, dilution, dip, immerse, submerge, plunge, souse, duck, drown, soak, steep, pickle, sprinkle, atonement, reparation, compromise, composition, compensation, quitting, expiation, redemption, (atmospheric, airy)

mad-adj insane, disordered, lunacy, madness, mania, mental alienation, aberration, demented, frenzy, raving, incoherence, wandering, delirium calenture of the brain, delusion, hallucination, vertigo, dizziness, fanaticism, (sanity, soundness, rationality, sobriety, lucidity, senses, sound mind)

madcap-n buffoon, humorist, wag, with, repartee, life of the party, wit-snapper, joker, jester, farceur, tumbler, acrobat, harlequin, clown, motley, motley fool, zany, dandy, caricaturist, lunatic, maniac, dreamer, excitable, impetuosity, boisterousness, impatience, (passive, coolness, calmness, serene)

magnetism-n power, potency, puissance, might, force, energy, almightiness, omnipotence, authority, strength, ability, ableness, competency, efficiency, validity, cogency, enablement, pressure, elasticity, gravity, electricity, galvanism, (impotence, disability, disablement, impiousness, imbecility, incapacity)

magnify-v increase, augment, enlargement, extension, expansion, increment, accretion, accession, development, intensify, enhance, redouble, exaggerate, exasperate, heighten, overestimate, oversensitive, vanity, over-rate, (underestimate, depreciate, detraction, undervalue, modesty)

magnitude-n size, quantity, dimension, amplitude, mass, amount, quantum, measure, substance, strength, more or less, greatness, multitude, immense, enormity, infinity, might, volume, heap, (minimum, particle, molecule, corpuscle, small, diminutive, minute, inconsiderable)

main-adj important, consequence, moment, prominence, consideration, mark, materialistic, import, significance, concern, emphasis, interest, gravity, seriousness, solemnity, conduit, channel, duct, (unimportant, insignificant, nothingness, immaterial, triviality, levity, frivolity, minor detail, nonsense)

maintain-v sustain, act upon, perform, play, support, strain, take effect, quicken, strike, preservation, safe keeping, conservation, keep, prophylactic, unimpaired, unbroken, continue, persist, perpetuate, undying, unvaried, (discontinue, cease, desist, stop, slacken, decay, deteriorate, suspend, interrupt)

major-adj greater, supreme, higher, exceeding, distinguished, vaulting, utmost, paramount, foremost, crowning, first-rate, excellent, transcendent, sovereign, superlative, inimitable, incomparable, potentate, lord, sovereign, monarch, autocrat, despot, tyrant, (servant, subject, flunky)

make-v constitute, composition, combination, inclusion, admission, comprehension, reception, form, compose, contain, embrace, embody, involve, implicate, produce, create, fabricate, manufacture, establish, perform, achievement, (destruction, waste, dissolution, ruin, annihilation)

makeshift-n substitute, supplanting, supersession, stop-gap, jury-mast, dummy, scapegoat, double, alternative, representative, supersede, replace, ostensible motive, ground, plea, pretext, pretense, lame, excuse, (interchanged, reciprocal, mutual, communicative, intercurrent)

malaise-n pain, suffering, bodily, physical pain, dolor, ache, smart, twinge, twitch, ripe, headache, hurt, cut, sore, discomfort, spasm, mental suffering, annoyance, irritation, infliction, plague, (happy, blest, blessed, blissful, beatified, comfortable, overjoyed, entranced, enchanted)

malaria-n contagious, infectious, catching, taking, epidemic, insalubrious, noxious, deleterious, pestilent, poisonous, bane, curse, evil scourge, leaven, virus, mephitis, (remedy, help, restorative, corrective, tonic, therapeutic, sedative)

man-n adult male, he, manhood, gentlemen, sir, master, yeoman, swain, fellow, blade, beau, chap, gaffer, good man, husband, masculine, manly, hero, demigod, bully, courageous, lion-hearted

manager-*n* director, manager, governor, rector, comptroller, superintendent, over-seer, inspector, surveyor, moderator, monitor, taskmaster, leader, conductor, property man, machinist, prompter, call-boy, (unmanaged, abandoned, without direction)

mangle-*v* separate, part, detachment, segregation, divorce, fissure, breach, split, rift, crack, slit, incision, sunder, divide, haggle, lacerate, gash, hash, slice, scramble, whittle, impairment, injury, damage, infect, (improve, mend, revise, refine, rectify, enrich, mellow, elaborate, fatten)

mania-*n* disordered, abnormal, unsound, derangement, insanity, lunacy, madness, mental alienation, aberration, demented, frenzy, raving, incoherence, wandering, hallucination, dizziness, kleptomania, dipsomania, hypochondriasis, hysteria, (sane, rational, reasonable)

manner-*n* description, denomination, designation, character, stamp, predicament, sort, genus, species, variety, family, race, tribe, clan, type, kit, sect, assortment, feather, kidney, suit, range, style, mode of expression, method, way, manner, wise, gait, form, mode, fashion, tone, guise

many-*adj* frequent, repetition, many times, incessant, perpetual, continual, constant, numerous, multiplicity, profusion, plenty, majority, huge numbers, several, sundry, various, manifold, multiplied, thick, studded, (fewness, reduction, weeding, elimination, decimation, scanty, thin)

marble-*n* hard, rigid, stubborn, stiff, firm, starched, stark, unbending, unlimber, unyielding, inflexible, tense, indurate, adamantine, concrete, stony, granitic, vitreous, (soft, tender, supple, pliant, lithe)

march-*v* advance, precession, leading, heading, precedence, priority, forerun, proceed, progress, roving, vagrancy, countermarching, nomad, vagabondism, (regression, withdrawal, retirement, recession, follow, pursue, shadow, trail, lag)

margin-*n* edge, verge, brink, brow, brim, border, skirt, rim, flange, side, space extension, extent, expanse, room, field, way, expansion, compass, sweep, play, swing, spread, capacity, stretch, range, latitude, scope,

(center, interior, surface, climate, zone, meridian)

mark-*n* indication, sign, symbol, type, figure, emblem, cipher, representation, epigraph, motto, characteristic, pointer, note, token, line, stroke, dash, score, witness, voucher, position, place, period, pitch, stand, (insignificant, disregard, non-representative, without affirmation)

market-*n* purchase, buying, shopping, bribery, patron, client, customer, invest in, procure, rent, spend, mart, place, bazaar, staple, exchange, hall, stall, booth, wharf, office, chambers, warehouse, establishment, (sale, seller, vendor, dispose of, dispense, merchant, vent)

martial-*adj* warfare, fighting, hostilities, war, arms, battle array, campaign, crusade, expedition, mobilization, battle, campaigning, service, havoc, tribunal, court, board, bench, law, arbitration, inquisition, (pacification, conciliation, reconciliation, accommodation, terms, compromise, amnesty)

marvelous-*adj* great, wonderful, admire, surprise, astonish, amaze, astound, dumbfound, dazzle, wondrous, overwhelming, stupendous, indescribable,

inexpressible, awesome, aghast, agape, spellbound, (common, ordinary, expected, foreseen, astonished at nothing)

mash-*v* mix, blend, tincture, sprinkle, cross, alloy, amalgamate, compound, adulterate, infect, instill, infiltrate, confusion, disorder, disarray, jumble, huddle, litter, lumber, mess, muddle, hash, hodgepodge, (uniformity, symmetry, orderly, neat, tidy, well regulated, correct, methodical, uniform)

mask-*v* conceal, hide, mystification, seal of secrecy, screen, disguise, masquerade, stealthiness, reticence, reserve, evasion, suppression, white lie, cover, blind, gauze, veil, mantle, cloud, mist, shade, shadow, (inform, acquaint, announce, tell, impart, mention, make known, enlighten, specify)

master-*v* understand, comprehend, take in, catch, grasp, follow, collect, make out, easily understood, clearness, simplify, explain, plain, distinct, explicit, positive, precise, graphic, expressive, conceive, accomplished, profound, book-learned, (shallow, superficial, rude, empty, illiterate, uninformed)

mate-*n* similar, resemblance, likeness, affinity, approximation, parallelism, sameness, fellow, analog, pair, twin, double, counterpart, likeness, wife, espouse, marry, join, spousal, bridal, helper, auxiliary, recruit, assistant, associate, midwife, colleague, (opposition, enemy, adversary, dissimilar, unlike, unmatched, unlikeness, diversity, dissemblance, difference, original)

mature-*adj* old, age, antiquity, decline, decay, seniority, eldership, tradition, custom, venerable, time-honored, prime, adolescent, pubescent, of age, grown up, virile, adult, (new, novel, recent, fresh, young, green, immature, virgin, modern, late, neoteric, renovated)

maze-*n* convolution, winding, circumvolution, wave, undulation, tortuosity, coil, roll, curl, buckle, spiral, helix, corkscrew, worm, volute, tendril, dilemma, embarrassment, perplexity, intricacy, entanglement, awkwardness, mesh, (ease, feasibility, flexibility, smoothness, round, rounded, oval)

meager-*adj* small, little, tenuity, paucity, few,

mediocrity, moderation, minute, slight, limited, sparing, incomplete, insufficient, immature, deficit, omission, lack, hollow, (complete, large, entirety, full, sufficiency, replenish, whole, quantity, volume, unlimited, vast, immense, enormous, extreme)

mean-*adj* contemptible, wretched, vile, scrubby, pitiful, sorry, trashy, worthless, medium, intermediate, average, balance, mediocrity, generality, commonplace, neutrality, compromise, (gravity, seriousness, solemnity, pressure, urgency, stress, matter of life and death)

measure-*n* compute, survey, valuation, appraisement, assessment, estimate, reckoning, gauging, standard, rule, compass, calipers, gage, meter, scale, coordinates, degree, extent, amount, ratio, intensity, strength, quantity, mass, comparative, gradual

medley-*n* alloy, mixture, jumble, sauce, mash, instill, infiltrate, blend, cross, amalgamate, compound, infect, complex, intricacy, perplexity, disarrange, entangled, deranged, haphazard, random, luck,

(orderly, regularity, subordination, methodical, unconfused, arranged)

meet-*v* assemble, crowd, throng, flood, rush, deluge, rabble, mob, horde, body, tribe, crew, gang, group, cluster, muster, convene, gather, converge, concur, come together, unite, concentrate, expedite, convenient, due, proper, eligible, seemly, (exit, emergence, burst, evacuation, diverge, repel, push, dispel, leave, depart, disperse, dismember)

mellow-*adj* ascend, increase, fructify, ripen, pick up, come about, rally, better, improved, enrich, cultivate, enhance, render, elaborate, season, bring to maturity, mature, nurture, (crude, raw, virgin, unprepared, improvise, coarse, deteriorate, degenerate, impair, weaken)

melt-*v* convert, pervert, render, mold, form, merge, liquefy, dissolve, solvent, boil, heat, calcination, ignite, inflammation, adust, incendiary, caustic, smelt, digest, stew, cook, seethe, simmer, (cool, fan, refrigerate, refresh, congeal, freeze, glaciate, benumb, starve, quench, extinguish)

mental-*adj* intellect, understanding reason, rationality, cogitative, faculties, senses, consciousness, observation, percipience, under consideration, thought, reflect, consider, deliberate, (unendowed with reason, imbecility, vacant, thoughtless, diverted, irrational)

mercy-*n* leniency, moderation, tolerance, mildness, gentleness, favor, clemency, forbearance, compassion, tolerance, pity, commiseration, sympathy, ruthful, humane, exorable, melt, thaw, relent, unhardened, (severity, strictness, harshness, rigor, stringency, austerity, inclemency, relentless)

merge-*v* combine, mixture union, unification, synthesis, incorporation, amalgamation, embodiment, coalescence, fusion, blending, absorption, centralization, impregnate, ingrained, (decompose, analysis, dissect, catalysis, dissolution, corruption, unravel, disperse)

merit-*n* goodness, excellence, virtue, value, worth, price, perfection, prime, flower, cream, champion, beneficial, profitable, advantageous, salutary, favorable, good, superior, fine, genuine, admirable, praiseworthy, (vile, oppressive, burdensome, malign, corrupting, corrosive, destructive, destroy)

merriment-*n* cheerful, geniality, gaiety, cheer, good humor, high spirits, liveliness, vivacity, animation, joviality, jollity, jocularity, mirth, hilarity, exhilaration, laughter, rejoicing, elate, exhilarate, gladden, inspire, perk up, delight, (dejection, depression, lowness, heaviness, melancholy, sadness, dismal)

mess-*n* mixture, combine, intermix, mingle, shuffle, knead, brew, impregnate with, instill, imbue, infiltrate, compound, infect, among, amongst, amid, amidst, miscellaneous, dilemma, embarrassment, perplexity, intricacy, entanglement, awkwardness, delicacy, maze, vexed, quandary, (ease, facilitate, smooth, emancipate, free, manageable, light, simple, eliminate, single, pure, clear)

meteor-*n* heavenly body, cosmically, mundane, terrestrial, solar, heliacal, lunar, celestial, sphere, starry, stellar, luminary, light, flame, spark, phosphorescence, star, blazing, (shade, sunshade, gauze, veil, mantle, mask, cloud, mist, umbrageous)

mettle-*n* sensible, impressionable, susceptive, impassion, gushing, warm-tender, soft-hearted, romantic, enthusiastic, highflying, spirited, vivacious, lively, expressive, mobile, trembling, excitable, fastidious, (insensible, inertness, apathy, dull, frigid, cold-hearted, indifferent, lukewarm, careless)

middle-*n* midst, half-way, navel, equidistance, bisection, half-distance, equator, diaphragm, midriff, intermediate, equatorial, midship, compromise, compensation, middle term, meet one half way, give and take, arrange, adjust, agree, moderate, average, mediocrity

midst-*n* centrality, center, core, kernel, nucleus, heart, pole, axis, navel, backbone, marrow, symmetry, center of gravity, bring to focus, intermediate, intervention, introduce, (surround, beset, encompass)

mild-*adj* moderate, temperate, relaxation, remission, mitigation, tranquilization, pacification, gentleness, sobriety, quiet, contemplation, appease, soothe, lull, swag, calm, cool, hush, quell, tame, (violent, fury, storm, rough, vehement, warm, acute, sharp, rude, impetuous, rampant)

mill-*v* reduce, grind,

pulverize, comminute, granulate, triturate, levigate, scrape, file, abrade, rub down, grate, rasp, pound, bray, bruise, contuse, beat, crush, crunch, crumble, disintegrate, (lubricate, oil, glycerine, lather, grease, lather, smooth)

mind-*n* intellect, understanding, reason, thinking, rationality, cogitative, faculties, senses, consciousness, observation, percipience, intuition, association of ideas, instinct, conception, judgment, wits, capacity, genius, ability, thoughtful, reflect, speculate, contemplate, consider

mine-*n* sap, destroy, waste, dissolution, breaking up, disruption, consumption, disorganization, fall, downfall, ruin, perdition, annihilation, demolition, overthrow, subversion, suppress, abolish, ruinous, incendiary, deleterious, (produce, perform, operate, form, construct, fabricate, frame, contrive, forge)

minister-*n* subserve, mediate, intervene, instrumental, useful, give, bestow, donation, presentation, accordance, delivery, consignment, dispensation, communication, endowment, award, generosity, liberality, offering, bequest, legacy, devise, deliver, present, (receive, acquire, accept, assign, admit)

minor-*adj* inferior, shortcoming, deficiency, minimum, smallness, less, lesser, minus, lower, subordinate, second-rate, least, lowest, diminished, decrease, infant, babe, youth, youngster, master, (veteran, old, seer, patriarch, superior, supreme, major, great, noble, higher, exceeding)

minute-*adj* small, little, diminutive, inconsiderable, paltry, faint, slender, light, slight, scanty, limited, sparing, inappreciable, infinitesimal, mere, simple, sheer, stark, bare, period of time, duration of, moment, instant, second, twinkling, flash, breath, burst, sudden, instantaneous, hasty, quick, lightning, (perpetuity, eternity, ever, everlasting, great, magnitude, considerable, ample)

mirror-*n* imitate, copy, repetition, duplication, quotation, reproduction, mimicry, simulation, reflector, speculum, looking glass, pier, model, standard, pattern, best, inimitable, paragon, unparalleled, supreme, perfect, (imperfect, faulty,

unsound, deficient,
unimitated, original,
unmatched)

misbehave-v coarse,
indecorous, ribald, gross,
unseemly, unpresentable,
ungraceful, ill-mannered,
underbred, ungentlemanly,
unladylike, unpolished,
uncouth, heavy, rude,
awkward, (good taste,
cultivated, delicacy,
refinement, gust, finesse,
nicety, polish, elegance,
grace, connoisseur)

mischief-n evil, harm hurt,
nuisance, disaster,
accident, casualty, mishap,
calamity, bale, mental
suffering, outrage, wrong,
injury, foul play, grievance,
disastrous, bad, aggrieve,
oppress, persecute, inflict,
maltreat, abuse,
(goodness, admirable,
estimable, praise-worthy,
satisfactory, favorable)

misconduct-n mismanage,
misapplication, absence of
rule, bungling, blunder,
unskillful, quackery,
mistake, misguided,
foolish, inconsistent,
ignorant, (accomplished,
expert, skillful, competent)

misfortune-n adversity, evil,
failure, bad fortune,
trouble, hardship, curse,
blight, blast, load,
pressure, mishap, disaster,
calamity, catastrophe,
accident, casualty, ruin,
failure, affliction,
(prosperity, welfare, well-

being, affluence, wealth,
success, thrift, roaring,
prosper, thrive)

mishap-n source of
irritation, annoyance,
grievance, nuisance,
vexation, mortification,
bore, bother, plague, pest,
infestation, molestation,
(pleasant, inviting,
attractive, lovely,
enchantment, seduction)

misjudgment-n bias, warp,
twist, hasty conclusion,
preconceived,
partisanship, partial,
narrow, blind side,
confined, error, fallacy,
laxity, mistake, fault,
blunder, (accuracy,
exactness, honest,
precise)

mismatch-v different,
diverse, varied, modified,
various, dissimilarity,
disagreement, disparity,
discord, unconformity,
conflict, unfitness,
inaptitude, impropriety,
inconsistency, disjoining,
(conformity, uniformity,
concert, relevancy,
admissibility, compatibility,
relation)

misrepresent-v lie,
falsehood, deception,
untruth, guile, mendacity,
perjury, forgery, invention,
fabrication, suppression of
truth, perversion,
distortion, exaggeration,
prevarication,
misinterpretation,
misconstrue, mistake,

parody, equivocation, evasion, fraud, (veracity, truthfulness, frankness, sincerity, honesty)

miss-v girl, lass, wench, damsel, maiden, virgin, fail, unsuccessful, labor, toil in vane, miscarry, omission, oversight, slip, trip, stumble, mess, mishap, misfortune, collapse, (success, advance, lucky, fortunate, prosperity, triumph, gain, advantage, conquest, victory)

mist-n cloud, bubble, foam, froth, head, spume, lather, spray, surf, yeast, barm, vapor, fog, haze, stream, effervescence, fermentation, nebulous, (semi-fluid, stickiness, viscidity, adhesiveness)

mitigate-v abate, moderate, soften, temper, mollify, leniency, dull, take off the edge, blunt, obtund, sheathe, subdue, chasten sober, tone, smooth down, lessen, palliate, tranquilize, assuage, appease, (violent, sharpen, quicken, excite, explode, convulse, infuriate, madden, lash)

mix-v combine, instill, imbue, transfuse, join, intermix, mingle, shuffle, knead, brew, impregnate, infiltrate, dash, stir-up, together, compound, adulterate, (simple, purity, homogeneity, eliminate)

mob-n crowd, assemblage,

throng, flood, rush, press, crush, horde, body, tribe, crew, gang, knot, squad, band, party, swarm, school, covey, flock, herd, drove, array, bevy, galaxy, company, troop, group, cluster, clump, (disperse, scatter, sow, disseminate, diffuse, shed, spread, disembody)

mobile-adj motion, movement, going, unrest, stream, flow, run, coarse, stir, evolution, kinematics, step, transitional, motor, motive, shifting, mercurial, unquiet, restless, nomadic, inconstancy, versatility, mobility, unstable, restlessness, fidget, disquiet, agitation, (stable, constant, immobility, stand, established, fixture, foundation, permanence, durable)

model-n represent, imitation, illustration, delineation, depiction, imagery, portraiture, design, art, personation, impersonation, image, likeness, (misrepresent, distort, exaggerate, daub)

moderate-adj small, allay, slow, sufficient, cheap, temperate, low, reasonable, inexpensive, depreciated, nominal, bargain, sufficient, adequate, enough, satisfactory, competent, mediocrity, fill, (scarcity, want, need, lack, poverty, insufficient, inadequate)

modesty-n humility, timidity, diffidence, bashfulness, blushing, self-knowledge, shy, nervous, skittish, coy, sheepish, shamefaced, unpretending, reserved, constrained, demure, private, without ceremony, (vanity, conceit, self-confidence, airs, pretension, egotism, gaudery, elation, ostentation)

mold-n frame, fabric, constitute, habitude, stamp, set, fit, mode, form, shape, tone, tenor, prototype, original, model, pattern, precedent, standard, type, rush, weed, fungus, mushroom, toadstool, lichen, moss, conferva, growth, (result copy, facsimile, duplicate)

monotonous-adj uniform, consistent, even, invariable, always, without exception, regularity, routine, conformity, equal, even, match, symmetrical, (uneven, countervail, varied, diversified, irregular)

monstrous-adj huge, giant, gargantuan, mammoth, corpulent, stout, fat, plump, immense, enormous, might, vast, stupendous, monstrous, gigantic, (small, dwarf, pygmy, inconsiderable, puny, atom)

monument-n memorial,

cenotaph, shrine, grave, tombstone, hatchment, slab, tablet, trophy, achievement, obelisk, pillar, column, monolith, commemoration, celebration, (obliterate, erasure, cancellation, deletion)

mood-n affection, character, disposition, nature, spirit, tone, temper, idiosyncrasy, propensity, humor, grain, mettle, sympathy, passion, temperament, vein, tendency, aptness, prone

more-adj added, addition, annex, affix, extra, plus, likewise, furthermore, further, including, inclusive, besides, to boot, et cetera, supplement, accessory, appendage, reinforce, (subtract, deduct, retrench, minus, without, except, diminish)

mortal-adj fatal, kill, assassination, massacre, butcher, slayer, lethal, dead, deathly, suicidal, internecine, transient, impermanence, fugacity, caducity, mortality, temporary, (durable, lasting, permanent, long-standing, chronic, perennial)

mortar-n cement, glue, gum, paste, size, wafer, solder, lute, putty, bird-lime, stucco, plaster, grout, arms, weapon, missile, bolt, projectile, shot, ball, canister, cannon, grenade, shell, bomb, rocket

motion-*n* movement, going, stream, flow, flux, run, course, stir, evolution, kinematics, progress, offer, proffer, presentation, tender, bid, overture, proposal, invitation, advances, (refusal, rejection, projection, disclaimer, dissent, revocation, remain, stay, stop, stagnate, halt)

mount-*v* ascend, rising, ascension, upgrowth, leap, acclivity, ladder, arise, apprise, climb, escalade, soar, display, show, flourish, parade, magnificence, splendor, mountain, hill, elevate, high, (low, neap, debased, flat, under, descent, declination, fall, drop, lapse, downfall, slip, tilt)

mournful-*adj* melancholy, sadness, depression, dejection, prostration, despondency, dismal, spiritless, unhappy, somber, dark, gloomy, lamenting, dreadful, (cheerfulness, geniality, gaiety, good humor, glee, light, liveliness, vivacity, merriment, hilarity, exhilaration, animation, jovial)

mouth-*n* entrance, beginning, opening, outset, incipience, inception, inchoation, introduction, initial, origin, source, receptacle, recipient,

receiver, reservoir, gizzard, ventricle, bread-basket, (end, close, termination, dissonance, conclusion, consummation, finish, terminate, conclude)

muddy-*adj* moist, damp, watery, undried, humid, wet, dank, muggy, dewy, swampy, soft, sodden, swashy, soggy, dabbled, reeking, dripping, soaking, (dry, anhydrous, arid, dried, undamped)

multitude-*n* numerous, multiplicity, profusion, legion, host, great, enormous, quantity, number, array, army, sea, galaxy, scores, peck, bushel, shoal, swarm, many, several, sundry, various, (few, small quantity, rarity, infrequency, handful, maniple, minority, reduction)

musical-*adj* melody, rhythm, measure, rhyme, pitch, tone, modulation, temperament, syncopation, song, glee, madrigal, compose, perform strains, (discord, harshness, tuneless, unmusical, dissonance)

mute-*adj* silent, stillness, peace, hush, lull, solemn, dead, render, hold one's tongue, stifle, muffle, muzzle, inaudible, faint, suppress, smother, dumb, (vocal, cry, utter, exclaim, pronounce)

mysterious-*adj* obscure, dark, muddy, dim, nebulous, undiscernible, invisible, indefinite, perplexed, confused, undetermined, vague, loose, ambiguous, mystic, transcendental, occult, recondite, undefinable, (intelligent, clear, explicit, lucid, perspicuity, legibility, plain speaking, understandable)

N

name-*n* imprint, label, indicate, symbolize, mark, note, stamp, earmark, ticket, docket, score, dash, trace, print, appoint, nominate, return, charter, ordinate, install, inaugurate, investiture, accession, coronation, enthronement, (countermand, disclaim, abolish, dissolve, dismiss, nullify, annul, cancel)

napping-*v* dull, unentertaining, depress, humdrum, monotonous, inactive, heaviness, absent, bemused, dreaming, unreflective, (attentive, observant, absorption of mind)

native-*adj* inhabitant, resident, dweller, occupier, householder, lodger, inmate, tenant, incumbent, sojourner, settler, squatter, indigent, aborigines, free, plain, outspoken, blunt, downright, (cunning, craft, artful, skillful, subtle, alien, foreign)

near-*adv* loom, impending, destined, about to happen, coming, eventually, prospective, approaching, future, precipitation, anticipation, premature, soon, shortly, (now, occurring, happening, immediate)

necessity-*n* requirement, need, want, have occasion for, needful, essential, indispensable, prerequisite, demanding, urgent, obligatory, involuntary, compulsive, inevitable, (willing, volition, free-will, voluntary, optional, discretionary, intentional, spontaneous)

neglect-*v* abandon, negligent, careless, omit, default, thoughtless, remiss, perfunctory, inconsiderate, reckless, (care, watchful, vigilant, survey, alert, regardful, cautious, considerate, prepared)

negotiate-*v* mediate, intervene, peacemaker, diplomat, moderate, arbitrate, intercede, bargain, agree, promise, stipulate, barter, compromise, settle, conclude, come to an understanding

net-*n* remainder, residue, remains, remnant, rest, relic, leavings, result, left, unconsumed, sedimentary, surviving, exceeding, over and above, outlying, superfluous, (adjunct, addition, addendum, affix, appendage, augment)

neutralize-*v* counteract, opposition, contrariety, antagonism, polarity, clashing, compensation, cross, interfere, conflict with, jostle, antagonize, withstand, counterpoise, retroactive, reactionary, contrary, (concur, conspire, cooperate, agree, consent)

nice-*adj* pleasing), savory, good, fastidious, agreeable, delectable, lovely, beatify, satisfy, refreshing, comfortable, genial, glad, sweet, luxurious, voluptuous, sensual, attractive, enticing, appetizing, charming, (annoying, painful, grievance, vexation, mortification, bother, displeasing, disturbing)

nightmare-*n* fright, affright, alarm, dread, awe, terror, horror, dismay, consternation, panic, scare, stampede, intimidation, terrorism, reign of terror, demonic, scarecrow

nil-*n* inexistent, negative, annihilation, extinction, destruction, abrogate, destroy, take away, perish, blank, missing, omitted,

absent, exhausted, gone, lost, departed, defunct, dead, (subsist, presence, positive, realty, actuality, live, breathe, real, actual, positive, substantial)

nip-*v* cut, destroy, shorten, sunder, divide, subdivide, sever, dissever, abscind, saw, snip, nib, cleave, rive, rend, slit, split, splinter, crack, snap, carve, dissect, hinder, impede, obstruct, stop, (attach, join, hinge, seam, suture, stitch, link, miter, close, combine, fix, affix, fasten)

noble-*adj* great, virtuousness, morality, ethical, rectitude, integrity, cardinal virtues, merit, worth, desert, excellence, credit, self-control, resolution, self-denial, exemplary, saintly, seraphic, godlike, commendable, praiseworthy, (wicked, immoral, impropriety, weak, fault, deficient, vicious, sinful)

nomination-*n* commission, delegation, assignment, procuration, deputation, legation, mission, embassy, agency, appointment, return, charter, ordination, installation, inauguration, investiture, accession, coronation, enthronement, (dismiss, abolish, dissolve, cancel, repeal, revocation, annul)

nonsense-*n* absurdity, vagary, tomfoolery, mummery, imbecility, blunder, muddle, farce, absence of meaning, meaningless, empty, jargon, gibberish, balderdash, insanity, (significant, expression, substantial, literal, plain, simple, suggestive, convey, imply, indicate, interpret)

nook-*n* limited space, lieu, spot, pint, dot, niche, hole, compartment, premises, station, abode, angle, cusp, bend, fold, notch, for, corner, recess, oriel

noose-*n* snare, trap, pitfall, decoy, bait, cobweb, net, meshes, mouse-trap, mine, scaffold, block, axe, guillotine, stake, cross, gallows, gibbet, drop, rope, halter, bowstring

normal-*adj* regular, intrinsic, fundamental, implanted, inherent, essential, natural, innate, inborn, inbred, radical, incarnate, thoroughbred, immanent, instinctive, (extraneousness, incidental, accidental)

note-*n* remark, examine, scan, scrutinize, consider, revise, pour over, inspect, review, indication, observe, look, see, view, notice, regard, give, heed, contemplate, attentive, mindful, watchful, (inattentive, blind, deaf,

inconsiderate, absent, abstracted, lost, overlook, disregard, dismiss)

noteworthy-*adj* exceptional, non-conformity, unconventional, unusual, uncommon, extraordinary, unparalleled, fantastic, exceptional, (conventional, usual, common, ordinary, natural)

notorious-*adj* famous, notability, notoriety, vogue, celebrity, renown, popular, glory, honor, illustriousness, regard, respect, reputable, respectable, dignity, stateliness, solemnity, grandeur, splendor, noble, majesty, sublime, (shameful, disgrace, tarnish, blot, taint, discredit, degrade, vilify)

null-*adj* powerless, impotent, disable, impiousness, invalidity, inefficiency, incompetence, disqualification, helplessness, prostration, paralysis, palsy, apoplexy, exhaustion, emasculation, (power, potency, ability, ableness, energy, force, control, authority, strength, influence, magnetism)

nurture-*n* feed, food, nourishment, nutriment, sustenance, fodder, provision, ration, keep, commons, board, commissariats, pasture, dietary, eatable, edible, culinary, succulent, potable, (starve, excrete, deject, perspire, sweat, diarrhea, salivation, discharge)

O

oak-*n* strong, mighty, vigorous, forcible, hard, adamantine, stout, robust, sturdy, hardy, powerful, potent, puissant, valid, courage, brave, valor, resolute, bold, gallant, intrepid, defiant, (coward, timid, poltroonery, baseness, dastard, sneak, weak, relaxed, frail, fragile, shatter, flimsy)

oar-*n* paddle, navigate, fin, flipper, natation, handle, hilt, haft, shaft, heft, shank, blade, trigger, tiller, helm, treadle, key, turn screw, screwdriver

oasis-*n* separation, parting, detachment, segregation, divorce, supposition, deduction, discerptible, unconformable, exceptional, abnormal, continent, mainland, peninsula, delta, isthmus, (attach, fix, affix, fasten, bind, secure, clinch, twist, pinion)

obdurate-*adj* obstinate, tenacious, stubborn, case-hardened, inflexible, immovable, inert, unchangeable, severe, strictness, harshness, rigor, stringency, austerity, inclemency, (lenitive,

moderation, tolerance, mildness, gentleness, favor, indulgence, clemency, mercy)

obey-*v* rules, observance, compliance, submission, subjection, resignation, allegiance, loyalty, fealty, homage, deference, devotion, complying, (violate, infringe, shirk, insubordination, disobedient)

object-*n* thing, matter, body, substance, stuff, element, principle, material, article, something, still life, decision, determination, resolve, purpose, ultimatum, resolution, motive, intention, advise, (speculation, venture, stake, game of chance, risk, hazard, fortuitous, indiscriminate)

obscure-*adj* dark, murky, gloomy, extinguish, cloudy, confused, indistinct, shadowy, indefinite, ill-defined, opaque, (visible, conspicuousness, distinct, exposure, discernible, apparent, perceptible)

obstruct-*v* hinder, prevent, preclude, stoppage, interruption, retard, embarrassment, restriction, impede, obstacle, drag, stay, stop, shut, blockage, bar, bolt, seal, choke, occlusion, (open, vent, vomiter, perforate, pierce, puncture, support, lift, advance, assist, promote, favor, relief, rescue)

obtain-*v* get, acquisition, gaining, procuration, purchase, descent, inheritance, gift, recover, retrieval, redemption, salvage, gain, remuneration, proceeds, harvest, benefit, (deprived, loss, lapse, bereft)

obtrude-*v* interfere, intervention, introduce, import, insinuate, smuggle, infiltrate, ingrain, partition, interpenetrate, permeate, insert, implantation, inoculation, immersion, imbed, (removal, elimination, extrication, eradication, evolution, wrench, evulsion)

occasion-*n* opportunity, opening, room, suitable, proper, tempestuous, crisis, turn, juncture, conjuncture, turning point, given time, timely, providential, lucky, fortunate, happy, favorable, propitious, auspicious, critical, (unsuitable, ill timed, intrude, premature, intrusion)

occult-*adj* concealed, hidden, secret, recondite, mystic, cabalistic, dark, cryptic, private, privy, auricular, clandestine, close,inviolate, stealthy, skulking, surreptitious, (informant, enlightenment, case, specification,

communicative, advice, monition, statement, affirmation)

occupation-*n* business, employment, pursuit, affair, concern, matter, case, task, work, job, errand, commission, mission, charge, care, duty, vocation, calling, profession, industry, trade, officiate, serve, capacity, handicraft

occupy-*v* presence, attendance, where, permeation, pervasion,diffusion, dispersion, omnipresence, inhabit, dwell, reside, stay, sojourn, live, abide, lodge, nestle, roost, perch, locate, fill, domiciled, (truant, absent, absence, inexistent, emptiness, void, vacant, deserted, devoid)

occur-*v* eventuality, event, occurrence, incident, affair, transaction, proceeding, phenomenon, advent, concern, circumstance, casualty, accident, adventure, passage, crisis, pass, emergency, contingency, consequence, (impending, threaten, loom, await, approach, destined, approaching)

odd-*adj* individuality, idiosyncrasy, originality, mannerism, exception, peculiarity, infraction, violation, infringement, eccentricity, bizarre, monstrosity, rarity, freak, remainder, residue, remains, relic, (supplement, continuation, rider, off-shoot, conformity, symmetry, conventionality, pattern, specimen)

offensive-adj unsavory, repulsive, nasty, acrid, acrimonious, rough, sickening, nauseous, loathsome, unpleasant, displease, annoy, discompose, trouble, disquiet, disturb, cross, perplex, molest, (refreshing, comfortable, cordial, genial, glad, sweet, delectable, good, palatable, nice, dainty)

offer-v proposal, presentation, tender, bid, overture, motion, invitation, candidature, move, start, gift, donation, present, fairing, favor, benefaction, grant, oblation, sacrifice, (receive, acquire, reception, acceptance, release, admission, refusal, rejection, denial, decline, repulse, rebuff, discountenance)

official-adj authoritative, influence, patronage, power, preponderance, absolute, command, empire, rule, dominion, sovereign, hold, grasp, certain, necessity, surety, unerring, infallible, reliability, (uncertainty, doubt, dubiety, hesitation, precariousness, unfortunate, fallible, adverse, disastrous)

offset-n compensate, equate, commutation, indemnification, compromise, neutralization, nullification, counteraction, counterpoise, equivalent, consideration, offshoot, ramification, descendant, heir, presumptive

often-adv repetition, iteration, reiteration, harping, recurrence, succession, monotony, rhythm, repeat, echo, frequent, many times, repeatedly, perpetually, continually, constantly, incessantly, (sometimes, occasionally, at times, rarity, fewness, seldom, scarcely)

oil-n lubricate, anointment, glycerine, grease, lather, grease, soap, wax, ointment, unctuous, slippery, oleaginous, adipose, sebaceous, fatty, (pulpy, paste, dough, curd, jam, poultice, watery)

old-adj age, ancient, antique, long standing, time-honored, venerable, elder, prime, primitive, igneous, primordial, seniority, maturity, decline, decay, senility, ripe, mellow, longevity, decrepitude, (young, youthful, juvenile, green, callow, budding, new, novel, recent, fresh, modern, recent, immature)

omission-n exclusion, exception, rejection, repudiation, exile, seclusion, separation, segregation, supposition, elimination, bar, leave, shut, reject, repudiate, blackball, banish, (include, admit, consist of, embrace, embody, involve, implicate, contain, constitute, complete, entire, supplement)

one-adj whole, total, integrity, collectiveness, unity, complete, indivisibility, integration, aggregate, main, essential, identity, sameness, monotony, identical, (inversion, contrariety, contrast, part, portion, division, segment, fraction, parcel, piece, morsel)

oneself-n identity, sameness, coincidence, facsimile, similar, alter ego, identification, self, monotony, exactness, identical (opposite, reverse, inverse, converse, contrary)

only-adj small, unity, individual, sole, single, solitary, apart, alone, unaccompanied, isolation, seclusion, lone, lonely, desolate, dreary, simple, purity, homogeneity, uniform, neat, (mixture, tinge, tincture, compound, infusion, combination, matrimony, accompany,

coexist, attend, part)

open-adj divulge, reveal, break, split, disclose, resection, unveiling, deterred, revelation, exposition, acknowledgement, avowal, confession, disclose, allow, concede, grant, admit, (ambush, screen, cover, shade, blinker, veil, curtain, blind, cloak, cloud, mask, visor, disguise, masquerade, dress)

operate-v cause, groundwork, foundation, support, spring, genesis, descent, produce, perform, fabricate, frame, construct, manufacture, contrive, forge, coin, carve, build, raise, edify, rear, erect, constitute, (extinction, annihilation, destroy, ruin, demolish, over-turn, sacrifice, subvert)

operator-n agent, doer, actor, agent, performer, perpetrator, executor, practitioner, worker, stager, bee, ant, artisan, handicrafts, workman, artisan, craftsman, mechanic, operative, maker, journeyman, pursuit, pursuing, prosecution, (abstain, refrain, spare, eschew, maintain, spare)

opinion-n persuasion, conviction, convince, self-conviction, certainty, mind, view, conception, impression, surmise,

conclusion, judgment,
tenet, dogma, principle,
popular belief, (misbelief,
discredit, miscreant,
infidelity, dissent,
retraction, doubt,
skepticism, misgiving,
demur, mistrust)

opponent-n antagonist,
adversary, adverse party,
opposition, enemy,
assailant, obstructive,
brawler, wrangler,
disputant, malcontent,
demagogue, reactionary,
rival, competitor, (helper,
recruit, assistant, midwife,
colleague, partner, mate,
collaborator, ally, friend,
confidant)

opportunity-n occasion,
opening, room, suitable
time, proper time, crisis,
turn, juncture, turning
point, timely, lucky,
fortunate, happy,
providential, favorable,
propitious, auspicious,
suitable, (untimely,
intrusive, inopportune,
unlucky, inauspicious)

oppressor-n tyrant, severe,
strictness, harshness,
rigor, stringency, austerity,
inclemency, arrogance,
arbitrary power, despotism,
dictatorship, autocracy,
tyranny, domineering,
assumption, usurpation,
inquisition, reign of terror,
disciplinarian, despot,
inquisitor, extortioner,
(lenient, mild, gentle,
clement, tolerant,

indulgent, easy-going,
forbearing)

oral-adj voice, vocal, organ,
lungs, bellows, cry,
utterance, breathe,
ejaculate, rap out,
articulate, distinct,
stertorous, melodious,
enunciate, pronounce,
accentuate, aspirate,
deliver, (stammer,
hesitation, impediment,
titubation, whisper, lisp,
drawl, twang, accent,
stutter, mumble, mutter,
whisper)

oratory-n speaking, speech,
locution, talk, parlance,
verbal intercourse, oral
communication, oration,
recitation, delivery, lecture,
harangue, sermon, formal
speech, rhetoric,
declamation

orbit-n world, creation,
nature, universe, earth,
globe, wide world, cosmos,
sphere, heavens, sky,
firmament, celestial
spaces, stars, asteroids,
nebulae, galaxy, milky
way, path, way, manner,
method, gait, form, mode,
fashion, tone, guise,
procedure

orchestra-n music, concert,
strain, tune, air, melody,
instrumental music, full
score, minstrels, band,
concerted, piece, stringed
instruments, wind
instruments, vibrating
surfaces

ordain-v appointment,

nomination, return, charter, installation, inauguration, investiture, accession, coronation, enthronement, vicegerency, regency, regentship, viceroy, consignee, commission, accredit, (abrogate, annul, cancel, destroy, abolish, revoke, repeal, rescind, reverse, retract, recall)

ordeal-*n* concern, grief, sorrow, distress, affliction, woe, bitterness, heartache, broken hearted, anxiety, solicitude, trouble, fiery ordeal, shock, blow, dole, fret, burden, load, (happiness, felicity, bliss, beatitude, enchantment, transport, rapture, ravishment, ecstasy, paradise, pleasing)

order-*n* regular, uniformity, symmetry, gradation, progression, routine, method, disposition, arrangement, array, system, economy, discipline, orderliness, rank, place, methodically, systematically, periodically, (disorder, derangement, irregularity, confusion, complexity, perplexity)

ordinary-*adj* indifferent, middling, mediocre, average, tolerable, fair, passable, decent, admissible, bearable, secondary, inferior, second-rate, second-best, typical, normal, orthodox, regular, steady, (irregular,

abnormal, unconventional, unusual, perfect, impeccability, model, paragon)

organize-*v* arrange, plan, preparation, distribution, allocation, sorting, assortment, allotment, apportionment, taxis, graduation, organization, analysis, classification, division, digestion, atlas, (disorder, disturbance, dislocation, perturbation, interruption, shuffling, inversion, misplace, mislay)

original-*n* prototype, model, pattern, precedent, standard, scanting, type, protoplasm, module, exemplar, example, ensample, text, (imitation, copy, transcription, repetition, duplication, mimicry)

oscillation-*n* motion, vibration, liberation, motion of a pendulum, nutation, undulation, pulsation, pulse, alternate, wave, rock, swing, pulsate, beat, waggle, fluctuate, dance, curvet, reel, change, inconstancy, vicissitude, (stable, constant, established, fixture, permanence, solidity, firm, steadfast)

ostensible-*adj* probable, likely, hopeful, to be expected, in a fair way, plausible, specious, colorable, well-founded, reasonable, credible, presumable, presumptive, apparent, apparently, seemingly, (improbability, unlikelihood, unfavorable, possibility, incredibility, rare, infrequent, inconceivable)

oust-*v* eject, emit, exit, dispatch, exhale, excerpt, excrete, secrete, secern, extravagate, shed, void, evacuate, effuse, spend, expend, pour forth, squirt, spurt, spill, slop, perspire, exude, (admit, receive, import, introduce, ingest, absorb, suction, sucking, insertion)

outburst-*n* violence, inclemency, vehemence, might, impetuosity, effervescence, turbulence, ferocity, rage, fury, exacerbation, (moderation, lenitive, gentleness, sobriety)

outcome-*n* profit, earnings, winnings, innings, pickings, net profit, proceeds, return, harvest, benefit, get back, recover, regain, retrieve

outlandish-*adj* ridiculous, ludicrous, comic, droll, funny, laughable, grotesque, farcical, odd, whimsical, fanciful, fantastic, queer, eccentric, strange, awkward, (tasteful, unaffected, cultivated, refined)

outline-*n* origin, source, rise, but, germ, egg, rudiment, genesis, birth, title page, heading, rudiments, elements, grammar, alphabet, begin, commence, inchoate, arise, originate, conceive, initiate, open, (end, close, finish, terminate, conclude, expire, consummation, definitive)

outrage-*n* bad turn, affront, disrespect, atrocity, ill usage, intolerance, persecution, malevolent, grudge, abolish, malign, molest, worry, harass, haunt, wreck, impair, wane, (benevolent, kind, well meaning, amiable)

outrageous-*adj* violent, vehement, warm, acute, sharp, rough, rude, ungentle, bluff, boisterous, wild, brusque, abrupt, impetuous, excite, incite, urge, lash, stimulate, irritate, inflame, kindle, (tranquilize, assuage, appease, swag, lull, soothe, compose, still, calm, cool, quiet, hush, quell)

outset-*n* beginning, commencement, opening, incipience, inception, inchoation, introduction, alpha, initial, inauguration, embarkation, outbreak, onset, brunt, initiative, fresh start, (end, close, finish, terminate, conclude, be all over with, expire, final, crowning, complete, hinder)

outside-*n* exterior, surface, eccentricity, face, superficial, skin-deep, frontal, external, outward, covering, extramural, (interior, inside, interspace, innermost, indoor, inward, enclosed)

outstanding-*adj* remainder, residue, remains, remnant, rest, relic, leavings, heel-tap, odds and ends, left, unconsumed, sedimentary, surviving, exceeding, outlying, (adjunct, addition, affix, appendage, augment, increment, reinforcement, supernumerary, accessory, item, garnish, sauce)

ovation-*n* celebration, solemnization, jubilee, commemoration, triumph, jubilation, keep, signalize, rejoice, (nonobservance, evasion, failure, omission, neglect, laxity, informality)

overburden-*adj* redundant, luxury, excess, surplus, margin, remainder, duplicate, surplusage, extravagance, lavishness, superfluous, unnecessary, needless

P

pack-*v* arrange, dispose, place, form, collocate, marshal, size, rank, group, parcel out, allot, distribute, dispose of, assign, assort, classify, divide, file, string, assembled, closely

packed, dense, swarming, (dispersion, divergence, scattering, dissemination, misplace, mislay, disorder)

paddle-*v* walk, march, step, tread, pace, plod, wend, promenade, trudge, tramp, stalk, stride, straddle, strut, stump, bundle, handle, hilt, haft, shaft, heft, shank, blade, trigger, tiller, helm, treadle, key

padlock-*n* fasten, bolt, latch, latchet, tag, tooth, hook, holdfast, rivet, anchor, grappling, stake, post, tie, strap, tackle, rigging, brace, girder

page-*n* numeration, numbering, pagination, tale, recension, enumeration, summation, reckoning, computation, check, prove, demonstrate, balance, audit, part, issue, number, album, portfolio, periodical, serial, magazine, circular, paper, bill, sheet, broadsheet

pair-*n* couple, duality, duplicity, two, deuce, brace, cheeks, twins, duplex, analog, the like, match, similarity, resemblance, likeness, affinity, pendant, fellow, mate, double, counterpart, (dissimilar, unlike, disparate, of a different kind, unmatched, nothing of the kind)

palatable-*adj* savoriness, zest, dainty, delicacy, ambrosia, nectar, appetite,

relish, like, smack the lips,
well-tasted, good, nice,
dainty, delectable, gusty,
appetizing, lickerish,
delicate, delicious,
exquisite, rich, luscious,
(offensive, repulsive,
nasty, sickening,
nauseous, loathful,
unpleasant)

pale-*adj* dimness, darkness,
half-light, glimmer,
nebulosity, aurora, dusk,
twilight, shades, moonlight,
lackluster, dingy, dark,
pallid, tallow-faced, faint,
dull, cold, muddy, leaden,
discoloration, neutral tint,
monochrome, (pigment,
color, dye, tinge,
illuminate, emblazon,
bright, vivid, intense, deep)

pall-*n* cloak, mantle,
mantlet, mantua, shawl,
wrapper, veil, cape, tippet,
kirtle, plaid, muffler,
comforter, coffin, shell,
sarcophagus, urn, bier,
hearse, catafalque,
offensive, repulsive, nasty,
sickening, nauseous,
loathful, unpleasant,
(dainty, delicacy,
ambrosia, nectar, game,
relish, like)

palpable-*adj* material,
bodily, corporeal, physical,
somatic, sensible, tangible,
ponderable, substantial,
objective, impersonal,
neuter, unspiritual, plain,
distinct, definite, well
defined, marked, in focus,
recognizable, (invisible,

non-appearance,
concealment, dim,
confused, indistinct)

palpitate-*v* tremble,
agitation, stir, tremor,
ripple, jog, jolt, jar, jerk,
shock, succussion,
trepidation, tingle, thrill,
heave, pant, throb, quiver,
flutter, twitter, shake

panel-*n* partition, septum,
diaphragm, midriff, party-
wall, vail, between, betwixt,
sandwich, parenthesis, list,
catalog, inventory,
schedule, register,
account, bill, calendar,
index, table, contents,
(surround, beset,
compass, encompass,
environ, inclose, enclose,
encircle, embrace)

paper-*n* write, pen, copy,
engross, write out, fair,
transcribe, scribble, scrawl,
scrabble, scratch, interline,
stain paper, write down,
record, sign, compose,
indite, draw up, dictate,
inscribe

paradox-*n* absurdity,
imbecility, nonsense,
inconsistency, blunder,
muddle, bull, farce,
rhapsody, farrago,
extravagance, romance,
obscure, dark, muddy, dim,
nebulous, shrouded in
mystery, invisible, (plain,
distinct, explicit, positive,
definite, graphic,
expressive, illustrative,
lucid)

parallel-*adj* similarity,

resemblance, likeness,
similitude, semblance,
affinity, approximation,
agreement, analogy,
brotherhood, repetition,
uniformity, imitation,
copying, transcription,
duplication, quotation,
(unimitated, unmatched,
unparalleled, original,
dissimilar, unlike,
disparate)

paramount-*adj* supreme,
essential, vital, all-
absorbing, radical,
cardinal, chief, main,
prime, primary, principal,
leading, capital, foremost,
over-ruling, of vital
importance, significant,
telling, trenchant,
emphatic, pregnant,
urgent, pressing, critical,
(poor, paltry, pitiful,
contemptible, sorry, mean,
meager)

paraphrase-*n* explanatory,
expository, explicative,
exegetical, polyglot, literal,
significative, synonymous,
equivalent, interpret,
explain, define, construe,
translate, phrase,
expression, set phrase,
sentence, paragraph,
figure of speech,
periphrase, (misrepresent,
pervert, garble, falsify)

part-*n* divide, portion, dose,
item, particular, aught, any,
division, ward, subdivision,
section, chapter, verse,
article, clause, count,
paragraph, passage,

sector, segment, fraction,
fragment, parcel, (whole,
totality, integrity, entirety,
aggregate, gross amount,
sum total, bulk, mass,
lump, altogether)

particular-*adj* exact,
accurate, definite, precise,
well defined, just right,
correct, strict, close, rigid,
rigorous, punctual,
genuine, authentic,
legitimate, orthodox, pure,
natural, sound, sterling,
(error, fallacy,
misconception, mistake,
miss, fault, blunder,
oversight, misprint, slip,
blot, flaw, loose thread)

partner-*n* companion,
accompany, coexist,
attend, fellow associate,
escort, consort, spouse,
colleague, satellite,
concomitant, accessory,
spouse, mate, yokefellow,
husband, man, consort,
goodman, squaw, lady,
matron, wedded pair,
husband, wife, (separation,
divorce, unity, oneness)

pass-*v* move through,
transmission, permeation,
transudation, infiltration,
endosmose, ingress,
egress, opening, journey,
perforate, penetrate,
thread, conduit, gone, last,
latter, bygone, foregone,
elapsed, lapsed, expired,
(future, prospectively,
impending, next, stay,
eventual)

passion-*n* emotion,

character, qualities,
disposition, nature, spirit,
tone, temper, idiosyncrasy,
soul, pervading, spirit,
humor, mood, grain,
mettle, sympathy, desire,
wish, fancy, fantasy, want,
need, exigency, inclination,
leaning, (indifferent, cold,
frigid, lukewarm,
unconcerned, careless,
listless)

paste-n bond, tendon,
tendril, fiber, ribbon, rope,
cable, line, hawser, painter,
mooring, wire, chain,
fasten, tie, strap, tackle,
rigging, adhere, fuse

pat-v blow, stroke, knock,
tap, rap, slap, smack dab,
fillip, slam, bang, hit,
whack, thwack, cuff,
squash, dowse, whop,
swap, punch, thump, pelt,
kick, cut, thrust, lunge,
hammer, batter, (recoil,
retroaction, revulsion,
rebound, rebuff, reflux,
reverberation, return)

patch-n plot, enclosure,
close, arena, precincts,
tract, territory, country,
canton, county, shire,
domain, blemish,
disfigurement, deformity,
defect, flaw, injury, stain,
blot, spot, speck, freckle,
mole, blotch, disfigure,
pitted, (spacious, roomy,
extensive, expansive,
capacious, ample,
boundless)

patience-n perseverance,
resolution, determination,

desperation, devotion,
tenacity, obstinacy, self-
control, submission,
resignation, forbearance,
longanimity, fortitude,
(ruffle, hurry, fuss, stew,
ferment, fit, violence, rage,
fury, desperation,
madness, distraction,
raving, delirium, frenzy,
hysterics)

patter-v rap, snap, tap,
knock, click, clash, crack,
crash, pop, slam, bang,
clap, rustle, loquacity,
talkativeness, garrulity,
eloquent, jaw, gabble,
jabber, chatter, orate,
fluent, (silence, mute,
mum, still, reserved,
reticent, conceal, hush)

pause-v rest, lull, respite,
truce, drop, interregnums,
abeyance, cessation,
resistance, intermission,
interruption, stop, halt,
arrival, closure,
discontinue, quiet, tranquil,
calm, repose, stand still,
stagnate, quell, stationary,
anchor, (move, motion,
transitorily, restless,
changeable, nomadic)

peace-n concord, accord,
harmony, symphony,
agreement, love,
response, union, unison,
unity, assent, unanimity,
friendship, alliance,
understanding,
conciliation, fraternize,
(dissension, odds, discord,
disagreement, division,
split, quarrel, squabble,

altercation, wrangling, strife, embroilment)

peak-*n* summit, top, vertex, apex, zenith, pinnacle, acme, culmination, meridian, utmost height, pitch, maximum, climax, tip, crown, garret, ceiling, pediment, (bottom, base, basement, foundation, substructure, ground, earth, pavement, floor)

peck-*n* multitude, numerous, multiplicity, profusion, plenty, legion, host, large, enormous, array, army, sea, scores, bushel, sundry, dilemma, stumbling block, pickle, stew, hot water, (smooth, unload, emancipate, easiness, capability, fewness, paucity, small number, handful, minority, scanty)

peculiar-*adj* unusual, unexpected, monstrous, wonderful, remarkable, noteworthy, nondescript, curiosity, abnormal, exception, infraction, distinctive, specific, original, respective, (general, generic, universal, every, unspecified, impersonal, conformity, conventional)

pedigree-*adj* continuity, sequence, succession, round, suite, progression, series, train, chain, entire, linear, uninterrupted, unbroken, paternal, maternal, family, ancestral,

patriarchal, line, genealogy, descent, extraction, forefathers, (broken, discontinue, unsuccessful)

peep-*v* short sight, sharp, quick, piercing, penetrating, look, glance, glimpse, gaze, stare, leer, regard, watch, peer, pry, visible, perceptible, exposed to view, (invisible, obscure, misty, veiled)

pelt-*n* skin, covering, pellicle, fleece, fell, fur, leather, hide, cuticle, scarf, mask, concealment, shield, stone, lapidate, hurl, beset, besiege, beleaguer, cut and thrust, kick, strike, impulse, (protect, guard, safeguard, shield, preserve)

pen-*n* enclosure, envelope, case, wrapper, receptacle, paddock, pound, net, wall, rail, railing, barrier, barricade, gate, door, hatch, restraint, hindrance, coercion, confinement, imprisonment, captivity, (liberation, release, emancipation, dismissal, discharge, free, unfetter, disengage, acquit)

penalty-*n* retribution, punishment, pain, amercement, forfeit, sequestration, confiscation, damage

penchant-*n* disposition, willing, inclination, leaning, humor, mood, vein, bent, aptitude, desire, geniality, cordiality, goodwill, readiness, earnestness, forwardness, (unwilling, grudgingly, indifferent)

pensive-*adj* thoughtful, thinking, meditative, reflective, museful, wistful, contemplative, speculative, deliberate, studious, sedate, introspective, (vacancy, unintellectual, unoccupied, thoughtless)

people-*n* mankind, human race, species, nature, humanity, mortality, flesh, generation, human being, person, individual, creature, mortal, body, somebody, soul, living soul, earthling, party, persons, folk, general public, national, realm, population

pepper-*n* pungent, strong taste, twang, sharp, rough, unsavory, seasoning, palatable, spice, full-flavored, condiment, high-tasted, biting, spicy, herb, (insipid, weak, flat, vapid, tasteless, mawkish)

perch-*n* place, locate, situate, localize, put, lay, set, seat, station, lodge, quarter, post, install, house, stow, camp, root, shelve, deposit, reposit, cradle, moor, tether, picket, pack, vest, (displace, eject, set aside, remove, unload, empty, dispel, banishment, exile, vacate, cart-away)

perchance-*adv* possibility, potentiality, compatibility, agreement, practicability, feasibility, practicable, contingency, compatible, chance, feasible, (impossible, no chance whatever, hopeless)

perennial-*adj* continual, consecutive, progressive, gradual, successive, immediate, unbroken, entire, evergreen, constant, (discontinue, pause, interrupt, intervene, spasmodic, intermission, alternate)

perfect-*adj* great, faultless, immaculate, spotless, impeccable, flawless, inimitable, paragon, unparalleled, supreme, superhuman, divine, (fault, weak, imperfect, deficient, defective, cracked)

perform-*v* achieve, accomplish, completion, fulfillment, execution, dispatch, consummation, culmination, finish, conclusion, close, issue, (incomplete, shortcoming, unfulfilled, neglect)

perhaps-*adv* possibly, potentiality, feasibility, conceivable, credible, compatible, achievable, chance, contingency, practicable, within reach, accessible, surmountable, (impossible, absurd, contrary)

perish-*v* die, death, decease, demise, dissolution, departure, release, rest, loss, bereavement, end, cessation, extinction, death rattle, (life, vitality, animation, vivification, alive, respire, subsist, revive)

permeate-v pervade, fill, present, occupy, inhabiting, moored, domiciled, omnipresent, dwell, reside, diffusion, haunt, revisit, sojourn, abide, lodge, nestle, roost, (empty, vacuum, truant, absent, vacate)

perplex-v distressing, bothersome, afflicting, unlucky, uncomfortable, disheartening, depressing, distasteful, unpleasant, unpopular, thankless, (refreshing, comfortable, cordial, genial, glad, pleasant delightful, lovely, felicitous)

persecute-v oppress, wrong, aggrieve, trample, tread, overburden, weigh-down, victimize, molest, maltreat, abuse, ill-use, ill-treat, harm, injure, (goodness, merit, beneficial, valuable)

persist-v continue, last, endure, go on, remain, intervene, elapse, continue, seize an opportunity, permanent, duration, pending, interval, (never, nevermore, at no time, hesitant, doubtful)

persuade-v induce, prevail, overcome, carry, bring

round, procure, enlist, engage, invite, court, tempt, seduce, entice, allure, captivate, fascinate, (discourage, dampen, restrain, reluctance)

pertinent-adj relative, bearing, reference, connection, concern, correlative, cognate, association, nearness, interest, relevancy, comparison, correlation, (incidental, parenthetical, remote, far fetched)

pervert-n misrepresent, garble, distort, travesty, retort, stretch, strain, misinterpreted, hardening, backsliding, declination, reprobation, (elected, adopted, regenerated, inspired, consecrated, converted)

pessimism-n underestimate, depreciate, detract, undervalue, modest, under rate, disparage, minimize, (over-estimation, exaggeration, oversensitive, vanity)

petrify-v density, solidity, solidness, constipation, solidified, compact, thickset, substantial, massive, impenetrable, impermeable, (rare, subtile, thin, fine, tenuous, compressible, flimsy, slight, spongy)

phantom-n imaginary, fancy, conceive, deal, realize, create, originate, devise, invent, fabricate, improvise, fertile, unreal, ideal, legendary, whimsical, fairy-like, mythological, illusory, fallacious

photography-*n* representation, illustration, delineation, depiction, portraiture, engraving, daguerreotype, image, likeness, facsimile, (misrepresent, distort, exaggerate, daub)

physical-*adj* materialistic, substantiality, condition, matter, body, substance, stuff, element, principle, object, article, (immaterial, disembody, spiritualize, extramundane, earthy, pneumatolysis)

pick-*v* select, choice, option, discretion, volition, alternative, dilemma, adoption, decision, judgment, election, poll, ballot, exception, preference, (indifferent, neutral, abstain, refrain, indecision)

picket-*n* place, situate, locate, moor, tether, pack, tuck in, imbed, vest, make a place for, put, lay, set, seat, station, lodge, quarter, post, sentinel, watch, patrol, vedette, bivouac, scout, spy, spiel

piercing-*v* shrill, harsh sounds, acute, high note, scream, discordant, cry, roar, shout, hoop, whoop, yell, bellow, howl, scream, screech, shriek (muffled, dead silence, melodious)

pin-*v* fasten, restraint, hindrance, coercion, compulsion, constraint, repression, discipline, control, confinement, durance, duress, imprisonment, (liberate, disengagement, release, dismissal)

pinch-*v* requirement, need, want, necessities, stress, exigency, essential, indispensability, urgency, pain, suffer, ache, smart, bleed, tingle, hurt, chafe, (pleasure, bodily enjoyment, gratification, luxury)

pioneer-*n* precursor, antecedent, precedent, predecessor, forerunner, van-courier, prodrome, outrider, leader, herald, prelude, prior, groundwork, (sequel, suffix, successor, tail, train, wake, rear)

pitch-*v* degree, grade, extent, measure, amount, ratio, stint, standard, reach, amplitude, range, scope, gradation, shade, tenor, station, comparative, gradual, limit, height

place-*v* arrange, prepare, plan, disposal, distribute, sort, assort, allotment, apportionment, analysis, classification, division, digest, (disorder, misarrange, disturb, confuse, perturb, jumble, muddle)

placid-*adj* passive, tranquil, collness, calmness, composure, serenity, quiet, peace of mind

plagiarism-*n* steal, theft, thievery, borrowed, forgery, imitator, echo, transcribe, match, parallel, simulate, impersonate, represent, counterfeit, parody, travesty, caricature, burlesque

plain-*adj* simple, plain, homeliness, undress, chastity, unaffected, chaste, severe, bald, flat, dull, unvaried, monotonous, unornamented, blank, (ornate, florid, rich, flowery, elegant)

platform-*n* pulpit, desk, reading, theater, amphitheater, forum, stage, rostrum, hustings, tribune, plan, scheme, design, project, proposal, suggestion, sketch, skeleton, outline, draught, draft

plausible-*adj* probable, likelihood, hopeful, specious, ostensible, founded, reasonable, credible, presumable, presumptive, apparent, most-likely, (improbable, unlikely, long odds)

plea-*v* vindication, justification, warrant, exoneration, exculpation, acquittal, whitewashing, extenuation, softening, mitigation, reply, (accusation, charge, imputation, slur, libel, challenge)

pleasant-*adj* flatter, adulator, eulogist, euphemism, optimist, encomiast, laudatory, whitewasher, toady, sycophant, courtier, puffer, touter, amuse, entertain, diversion, relaxation, solace, fun, frolic, merriment, laughter, labor of love, (weariness, lassitude, disgust, nausea, loathing)

pledge-*v* promise, undertaking, word, troth, plight, parole, word of honor, vow, oath, affirmation, assurance, warranty, guarantee, insurance, contract, borrow, (demise, lease, advance, loan,)

plenty-*n* sufficient, adequate, enough, withal, satisfaction, ample, copious, abundant, abounding, replete, rich, luxuriant, affluent, inexhaustible, liberal, (scarcity, want, need, lack, poverty, dole)

plod-*v* slow, languor, slow-goer, linger, loiter, sluggard, snail, dawdle, creep, crawl, lag, drawl, saunter, trudge, stump along, retard, slacken, (move quickly, trip, speed, hasten, scuttle, scud)

pluck-*v* take, catch, hook, nab, bag, sack, pocket,

receive, accept, assume, possess, take possession of, ravish, seize, pounce, assault, intercept, scramble for, snatch, (return, restore, recuperate, reinvest, reparation, remit, rehabilitate)

plump-adj huge, immense, enormous, might, vast, stupendous, monstrous, colossal, gigantic, infinite, large as life, hulky, unwieldy, lumpish, whopping, (dwarf, pygmy, atom, microscopic, gaunt, molecular, thin, inconsiderable)

pocket-n receptacle, compartment, hole, corner, niche, recess, nook, crypt, stall, chest, box, coffer, caddy, case, basket, pouch, sack, wallet, scrip, poke, knit, knapsack, haversack, satchel

point-v mark, topic, food for thought, subject matter, theme, thesis, text, business, affair, argument, motion, resolution, inquiry, problem, question, (notion, conception, reflection, observation, idea)

pommel-v rotund, round, circular, cylindrical, columnar, spherical, ball, boulder, oblong, oblate, drop, vesicle, bulb, bullet, barrel, drum, rolling pin, rundle, cone

ponderous-adj judgment, result, conclusion, upshot,

deduction, inference, egotism, illation, corollary, porism, estimation, valuation, appreciation, assessment, (detection, discovery, find, determine, trace)

poor-adj poverty, indigence, penury, pauperism, destitution, want, need, lack, necessity, distress, difficulties, bad, embarrassed, reduced, circumstances, slender, stricken, (wealth, rich, fortunate, opulence, affluence, provision, livelihood, maintenance, dowry, means, resources)

pop-v abruptly, unexpectedly, plump, unaware, without notice, startle, take aback, electrify, stun, stagger, astonish, surprise, (expected, anticipating, reckoning, suspense, waiting, abeyance)

popular-adj celebrated, distinction, mark, name, figure, repute, reputation, fame, renown, approbation, notoriety, illustriousness, hero, nobility, glory, honor, (disgrace, shame, humiliation, tarnish, scandal)

portable-adj transit, transition, passage, removal, conveyance, relegation, portage, carting, shoveling, freight, convoy, bring, fetch, reach,

send, consign, deliver,
transpose, movable,
contagious

portfolio-*n* book, part,
issue, number, album,
magazine, periodical,
serial, annual, journal,
paper, bill, broadsheet

positive-*adj* certain,
necessity, certitude,
surety, assurance,
infallibleness, reliability,
gospel, scripture, absolute,
unqualified, inevitable,
infallible, unchangeable,
impeachable, conclusive,
authoritative, (uncertain,
doubtful, dubious,
indecisive, value,
ambiguous, undefined,
confused)

possess-*v* ownership,
tenure, occupancy,
holding, tenancy, heritage,
inheritance, enjoy, labor
under, come to pass,
conditional, (circumstance,
situation, phase, position)

posthumous-*adj* late, tardy,
slow, behind, belated,
unpunctual, backward,
slowly, leisurely,
deliberately, delay,
postponement,
adjournment, prorogation,
retardation, (punctual,
promptitude, prematurity)

posture-*n* form, figure,
conformation, make,
formation, feature,
lineament, turn, phase,
aspect, situation, locality,
latitude, footing, standing,
standpoint, stage, aspect

potentiality-*n* possibility,
compatibility, agreement,
practicability, feasibility,
feasible, performable,
achievable, accessible,
superable, surmountable,
obtainable, contingent,
(impossibility, absurd,
unreasonable, incredible,
inconceivable, improbable,
prodigious, impervious)

potpourri-*n* fragrant,
aromatic, redolent, spicy,
balmy, scented, sweet-
smelling, perfumed,
muscadine, ambrosial,
scent, mixture, join,
combine, intermix, mingle,
instill, compound, medicate

pout-*v* moody,
discourteous, displacency,
grim, sullen, peevish,
acrimonious, surly, rough,
blunt, gruff

poverty-*n* indigence -
penury, pauper,
destitution, want, need,
necessity, privation,
distress, needy, difficulties,
beggar, (wealth, riches,
fortune, opulence,
affluence, livelihood)

practical-*adj* operative,
efficient, efficacious,
effectual, maintaining,
practice, procedure,
practical joking, ridicule,
sarcasm, mockery,
discourtesy

praiseworthy-*adj*
commendable, praise,
laud, good work, tribute,
eulogy, homage,
benediction, blessing,

applause,complimentary, uncritical, (frown upon), reprehend, admonish, reprimand, chastise, castigate, lash out, trounce)

precedent-*n* coming before, lead, superiority, antecedent, anterior, prior, former, foregoing, prefatory, introductory, precursor, (sequence, coming after, succeed, follow, ensure, alternate)

precious-*adj* valuable, dear, extravagance, exorbitance, extortion, overcharge, bleed, fleece, extort, expensive, costly, beneficial, serviceable, advantageous, edifying, (cheap, depreciated, bargain)

precipice-*n* slope, obliquity, inclination, slant, crooked, leaning, bevel, tilt, bias, twist, swag, cant, lurch, rise, ascent, gradient, rising ground, dip, fall downhill, steepness, cliff, escarpment

pregnant-*adj* productive, fertility, luxurance, puberty, pullulating, fructify, multiplication, propagation, procreation, superfetation, generate, (sterile, waste, barren, addle, unfertile, arid)

prejudice-*adj* misjudgment, miscalculation, hasty conclusion, foregone conclusion, narrow-minded, confined, illiberal,

intolerant, besotted, infatuated, fanatical, positive, dogmatic, bias, underestimate, overestimate, (solve, resolve, render right, be near the truth, recognize, realize, verify, make certain)

prepense-*v* predetermination, premeditation, deliberation, foregone conclusion, resolve, propend, intention, project, redesigned, advised, calculated, well-laid, (impulse, sudden thought)

prerogative-*n* right, privilege, prescription, title, claim, pretension, demand, birthright, immunity, license, liberty, franchise, vested interest, sanction, authority, (impropriety, emptiness, illegality)

present-*v* bestowal, donation, delivery, consignment, dispensation, endowment, investment, almsgiving, generosity, liberality, charity, dispensation, (receive, acquire, admission, benefactor)

pretend-*v* feign, assume, make believe, false, simulate, counterfeit, sham, malign, deceitful, dishonest, evasive, hollow, insincere, forsworn, fabricate, prevaricate, (veracity, truth, frankness)

primary-*adj* important,

significant, concern, emphasis, greatness, superiority, notability, gravity, seriousness, solemnity, no laughing matter, urgent, prominence, (trivial, frivolous, paltry, small)

privacy-*n* seclusion, exclusion, retirement, reclusion, recess, snugness, solitude, solitary, isolation, loneliness, voluntary exile, aloofness, convent, exile, ostracism, (social, companionship, association, acquaintance, conversable, convivial, jovial, hospitable)

profession-*v* part, cue, province, function, look-out, department, capacity, sphere, orb, field, line, routine, career, race, vocation, calling, craft, trade, actively employed, employment

promise-*v* undertaking, work, troth, plight, pledge, parole, affirmation, vow, oath, profession, assurance, warranty, guarantee, insurance, obligation, contract, (release, liberation, absolute, free)

pronounce-*v* utter, breathe, give, ejaculate, vocalize, prolate, articulate, enunciate, accentuate, aspirate, deliver, mouth, phonetic, oral, (silence, render mute, muzzle,

muffle, suppress, smother)

prosecute-*v* accuse, charge, imputation, slur, inculpation, elation, criminative, argument, condemnation, defendant, prisoner, charge, (vindication, justification, warrant, exoneration)

provide-*v* supply, purvey, commissariats, grist, resource, caterer, furnish, find, cater, victual, prepare, anticipate, foresight, arrange, ripening, maturation, evolution, (waste, expenditure, dispersion, consumption, exhaustion)

province-*n* region, sphere, ground soil, area, realm, hemisphere, quarter, district, beat, orb, circuit, circle, domain, tract, territory, country, canton, county, shire, parish, (abyss, free space, expanse)

prune-*v* retrench, cut short, scrimp, cut, chop up, hack, hew, clip, dock, lop, shear, shave, mow, reap, crop, snub, truncate, pollard stunt, nip, curtail, (long, lengthy, outstretched, elongate)

punctual-*adj* accuracy, exact, precise, delicacy, rigor, mathematical, clockwork precision, genuine, authentic, legitimate, substantial, tangible, valid, undistorted, (laxity, indefinite, erroneous, untrue)

pure-adj innocent, spotless, clear, immaculate, clean, not guilty, irreproachable, virtuous, above suspicion, exceptional, without flaw, blameless, (guilt, atrocity, fault, sin, error, transgression)

purpose-n intent, project, predetermination, design, ambition, contemplation, mind, view, proposal, study, decision, resolve, settled, resolution, wish, motive, deliberate, (speculation, venture, chance)

pursue-v continue, persist, keep, stick to, maintain, carry on, uninterrupted, sustain, uphold, hold up, perpetuate, preserve, harp upon, repeat, (cease, discontinue, desist, pause, rest, respite)

Q

quackery-n unskillful, incompetency, inability, disqualification, folly, stupidity, indiscretion,neglect, thoughtless, absence of rule, blunder, (skill, dexterity, clever, talent, ability)

quadrant-n angular measurement, elevation, distance, velocity, sextant, miter, obtuse, salient, fusiform, wedge-shaped, cuneiform, triangular,

rectangular, multilateral, cubical, pyramidal

quagmire-n marsh, swamp, morass, moss, fen, bog, slough, sump, wash, mud, squash, slush, embarrassing, awkward, unwieldy, unmanageable, intractable, (ease, feasibility, smooth)

quake-v flutter, trepidation, fear and trembling, perturbation, tremor, quivering, shaking, trembling, throbbing, palpitation, fright, affright, quiver, quaver, twitter, twirl, writhe, toss

quantity-n magnitude, amplitude, mass, amount, quantum, measure, substance, strength, quantitative, some, any, more or less, (comparative, gradual, shading, range, scope, caliber)

quarrel-n dispute, tiff, squabble, altercation, words, big words, wrangling, jangle, babble, cross questions, strife, broil, brawl, row, racket, embroilment, (accord, peace of mind, comfort, harmony, unison, agreement)

quarter-n quadratic, quartile, tetracid, four, tetrad, quartet, abode, dwelling, lodging, domicile, residence, address, habitation, berth, seat, lap, sojourn housing, headquarters, throne

quasi-adj imitate, copy, mirror, reflect, reproduce, repeat, do like, echo, catch, transcribe, match, parallel, mock, mimic, simulate, impersonate, counterfeit, (original, unique, unimitated)

quell-v becalm, hush, lull to sleep, lay an embargo on, remain, stay, stand, resting place, bivouac, anchor, rest, cast, quiet, tranquility, repose, (motion, stream, flow, restlessness, nomadic)

quench-v dissuade, deport, cry out against, remonstrate, expostulate, warn, contraindicate, disincline, repel, damp, cool, calm, quiet, deprecate, (persuade, prevail, overcome, carry, procure)

question-n inquiry, examination, review, scrutiny, investigation, exploration, sifting, calculation, analysis, dissection, resolution, induction, (answer, respond, reply, rebut, retort, rejoin)

quibble-v sophism, solecism, paralogism, quirk, fallacy, subterfuge, subtlety, quilled, inconsistency, mockery, pervert, equivocate, mystify, evade, elude, (logical sequence, good cause, sound, valid)

quick-adj hurry, hasten, accelerate, quicken, swift, rapid, eagle speed, acceleration, spurt, rush, dash, fast, speedy, nimble, agile, expeditious, express, (slow, dawdle), retard, slacken, falter)

quiet-adj moderation, lenitive, temperate, gentle, tranquilize, assuage, appease, hush, quell, sober, soothe, compose, lull, calm, pacify, (loud, violent, ear-breaking, blast, fury)

quip-n cranks, jest, joke, conceit, quirk, merry, bright, happy, flash of wit, scintillation, witticism, work-play, riddle, smartness, retort, repartee, ridicule, (dull, uninteresting, unlively, stupid, slow, flat)

quirk-n amusement, entertainment, reaction, relaxation, solace, pastime, sport, labor of love, fun, frolic, merriment, jollity, heyday, laughter, (weariness, lassitude, fatigue, disgust, loathing)

quit-v relinquish, abandon, desertion, defection secession, withdrawal, break off, desist, stop, vacate, renounce, forego, discard, abandon, discontinue, resignation, retirement

quiz-v question, interrogate, interpolation, challenge, examination, cross-examination, inquire, investigate, seek, search, rummage, explore, (answer, respond, reply, rebut, unriddle)

quota-*n* apportionment, dividend, contingent, allotment, measure, dose, dole, meed, pittance, ration, proportion, allowance, share, portion, assign, appropriate

R

rack-*n* care, anxiety, solicitude, trouble, trial, ordeal, shock, blow, dole, fret, burden, load, vessel, vase, bushel, barrel, canister, utensil, hamper, crate, cradle (well-being, good, snugness)

racket-*n* loudness, power, loud noise, din, clang, clatter, bombination, roar, uproar, peal, swell, blast, boom, resonance, vociferation, hullabaloo, thunder, resound, (whisper, inaudible, low, dull, muffled)

radical-*adj* cause, original, primary, aboriginal, embryonic, germinal, having a common, review, improve, refine upon, rectify, enrich, mellow, elaborate, fatten, promote, cultivate, advance

rage-*n* resentment, displeasure, animosity, anger, wrath, indignation, exasperation, violence, vehemence, impetuosity, boisterousness, effervescence, row, (calm, moderate, gentle, sobriety)

raise-*v* increase, augment, enlarge, extend, expand, increment, accretion, accession, develop, aggravate, ascent, acerbate, spread, exalt, deepen, (decrease, diminution, lessen, subtraction)

rake-*v* drag, draw, pull, haul, lug, tug, tow, trail, train, take in tow, wrench, jerk, twitch, tousle, traction, rascal, scoundrel, villain, miscreant, wretch, reptile, viper, scamp, (model, paragon, good example)

rampant-*adj* influential, important, weighty, prevailing, prevalent, rife, dominant, regnant, predominant, run through, pervade, (impotence, inertness, irrelevant, uninfluential, powerless)

random-*adj* indiscriminate, aimless, promiscuous, undirected, drift, causeless, without purpose, casually, by the way, accidental, speculate, unintentional, (intentional, purpose, decision, motive)

rapture-*n* love, fondness, liking, inclination, regard, admiration, affection, sympathy, yearning, tender passion, flame, devotion, (hate, detest, abominate, abhor, loathe, revolt)

rare-*adj* unusual, extraordinary, singular, unique, curious, odd, strange, monstrous, unexpected, remarkable, noteworthy, queer, quaint, nondescript, original, (typical, normal, ordinary, conventional)

rate-*v* estimation, valuation, appreciation, judicature, result, conclusion, upshot, deduction, ponderous, assessment, deduce, derive, gather, collect, (result, discover, find, determine, evolve)

ratio-*n* degree, grade, extent, measure, amount, stint, standard, height, pitch, reach, amplitude, range, scope, caliber, gradation, shade, rate, sort, comparative, (absolute, quantity, mass)

rattle-*v* repeated noise, roll, drum, rumble, clatter, patter, clack, hum, trill, shake, chime, peal, toll, tick, beat, ding-dong, tantara, whir, rat-a-tat, rub-a-dub, racket, clutter, cuckoo, repetition, devil's tattoo

raw-*adj* immaturity, crudity, abortion, disqualification, improvisation, dismantle, extemporize, non-preparation, neglect, improvidence, (preparation, ripen, maturation, evolution, elaboration, gestation)

ready-*adj* prepare, providing, provision, anticipation, foresight, precaution, rehearsal, note of preparation, arrangement, clearance, tuning, array, ripening, (extemporize, improvise, undress)

reap-*v* acquire, get, gain, win, earn, obtain, procure, gather, collect, assemble, find, receive, replevy, redeem, advantageous, gainful, remunerative, paying, lucrative, (loss, privation, bereavement, deprivation, dispossession, riddance, deprived, bereft, irretrievable)

reason-*n* wisdom, sapience, sense, common sense, rationality, judgment, solidity, depth, profundity, caliber, enlarged views, genius, inspiration, aptitude, (shallow, wanting, weak, idiotic, vacant, blatant)

reassure-*v* hope, confident, trust, rely on, presume, optimism, enthusiasm, aspiration, secure, encouraging, cheering, inspiriting, looking up, bright, roseate, (hesitate, falter, funk, cower, crouch)

recede-*v* recession, move from, retirement, withdrawal, retreat, retrocession, departure, recoil, flight, avoidance, remove, shunt, shun, shrink, depart, (approach, approximate, near, access)

receive-v acquisition, exception, introduction, susceptibility, acceptance, admission, assignee, devisee, donor, grantee, take in, (give, gift, donation, delivery, dispensation, generosity)

recess-v regress, retreat, withdrawal, retirement, recession, refluence, ebb, return, reflection, recoil, deterioration, recede, retrograde, (progression, advance, improvement, proceed, forward, onward)

reckon-v discharge, settle, quit, acquit, account, balance, square up, disgorge, make repayment, repay, refund, reimburse, retribute, make compensation, (default, defalcation, protest, repudiation)

recognize-v see, behold, discern, perceive, have in sight, descry, sight, make out, discover, distinguish, spy, witness, contemplate, speculate, cast, (blind, hoodwink, dazzle, screen from sight)

recommend-v approval, approbation, sanction, advocacy, esteem, estimation, good opinion, admiration, appreciation, regard, account, popularity, credit, repute, (reprehension, admonition)

reconcile-v forgiveness, pardon, condonation, grace, remission, absolution, amnesty, oblivion, indulgence, reprieve, conciliation, excuse, exonerate, (revenge, ruthless, avenging, retaliation, feud)

redeem-v recover, retrieval, replevin, salvage, trove, find, foundling, compensate, equate, indemnity, compromise, neutralization, nullification, retaliation, equalize

reduce-v decrease, diminish, lessen, abridge, shorten, shrink, contract, discount, depreciate, extenuate, lower, weaken, fritter away, subtract, (increase, enlarge, extend, augment, magnify, gain)

reek-v unclean, impurity, defilement, contamination, abomination, taint, decay, corruption, mold, must, mildew, dirty, filthy, grimy, soiled, stink, rank, (clean, immaculate, spotless, neat, tidy, trim)

refinement-n improvement, betterment, melioration, amendment, mend, advancement, cultivate, reformation, correction, elaboration, purification, repair, (deterioration, impairment, injury, damage)

reflux-v recoil, refluent, react, spring, rebound, revulsion, ricochet, elasticity, reflection, reverberation, resonance, boomerang, (impulse, impetus, momentum, push, thrust, hammer, punch)

refrain-v avoidance, forbearance, inaction, abstention, neutrality, evasion, elusion, seclusion, avocation, flight, escape, retreat, recoil, departure, (pursuit, prosecution, enterprising, undertaking)

refresh-v restoration, rehabilitation, reproduce, renovation, revival, resuscitation, renaissance, second youth, rejuvenescence, new birth, regeneration, (relapse, fall back, retrograde, return)

regard-v view, look, espial, glance, point of view, see, behold, discern, perceive, descry, make out, discover, distinguish, recognize, contemplate, speculate, (blindness, undiscerning)

register-v digest, synopsis, compendium, table, analysis, classification, division, atlas, classify, methodize, regulate, systematize, coordinate, settle, fix, (litter, scatter, mix, entangle, ravel, dishevel)

regret-v self-reproach, penitence, contrition, compunction, repentance, remorse, self-accusation, be sorry for, confess, reclaimed, disclose, (induration, obduracy, impenitence, uncontrite,

shiftless)

rehearse-v repetition, iteration, reiteration, harping, recurrence, succession, monotony, rhythm, chimes, imitation, reverberation, recur, reappear, renew, repeated, often, again, over again, ditto

reinforce-v aid, assist, help, appellation, support, lift, advance, furtherance, promotion, relief, sustenance, nutrition, ministry, accommodation, supply, (prevent, preclude, obstruct, stop, block)

relax-v loose, incoherence, immiscibility, looseness, laxity, loosening, freedom, disjunction, slacken, detach, disheveled, segregated, unconsolidated

relief-n aid, assist, oblige, accommodate, humor, cheer, encourage, rescue, deliverance, refreshment, easement, softening, alleviation, mitigation, palliation, soothing, consolation, (aggravate, embitter)

relish-n desire, wish, fancy, want, need, exigency, mind, inclination, bent, longing, hankering, inkling, solicitude, anxiety, yearning, coveting, aspiration, (indifference, cold, frigid, halfhearted, neutrality)

remarkable-adj paramount,

essential, vital, all-
absorbing, radical,
cardinal, chief, main,
prime, primary, principal,
leading, foremost, vital,
significant, emphatic,
(ordinary, petty, frivolous,
insignificant)

remiss-*adj* careless,
neglect, trifling, omission,
default, supineness,
reckless, inconsiderate,
slovenly, erroneous,
nonchalant, inactive,
abandoned, disorderly,
(care, heed, watchful,
exact, attentive, vigil)

remote-*adj* distant, far,
elongation, background,
removed, telescopic,
yonder, farther, further,
beyond, apart, asunder,
wide apart, (nearness,
nigh, close, adjacent,
intimate, adjoin)

remove-*v* extract,
elimination extrication,
eradication,evolution,
extermination, ejection,
egress, extirpation, export,
evolve, squeeze out,
(insertion, introduction,
insinuation, injection,
immersion)

renovate-*v* restore,
reinstate, cure, repair,
reparation, recruit,
disinfection, redemption,
deliverance, restitution,
relief, recover, return to
original state,
(deterioration, retrogress,
fall back, relapse)

repair-*v* improve, amend,

betterment, mend,
advancement, progress,
ascent, promotion,
elevation, increase, reform,
correct, refinement,
elaborate, (deteriorate,
impair, injure, damage,
loss, detriment)

repel-*v* depart, cessation,
removal, exit, egress,
valediction, farewell,
outward bound, repulsive,
abduction, chase, dispel,
(attract, magnetism,
gravity, draw, adduce)

replace-*v* substitute,
commutation, supplant,
supersession, make-shift,
alternative, supersede, in
lieu of, redeem, change,
equivalent, shift,
(exchange, reciprocation,
transposition, shuffling,
barter, swap)

report-*v* description,
account, statement,
expose, disclosure,
specification, particulars,
abstract, narrative, history,
memoir, memorials,
annals, chronicle, relate,
recount, descriptive

repose-*v* rest, sleep,
relaxation, breathing time,
halt, pause, respite,
unbend, slacken, lie down,
recline, unstrained,
cessation, vacation,
recess, holiday, (exertion,
effort, strain, tug, pull,
stress)

represent-*v* express,
exposition, demonstration,
exhibition, production,

display, showing, indication, publicity, disclosure, indicate, manifest, proclaim, (allusive, dormant, hidden, invisible, imply, conceal)

require-v need, want, necessary, essential, indispensable, urgent, requisition, exactness, demanding, compel, force, make, drive, coerce, enforce, oblige, (depletion, vacancy, low, empty, insolvency)

rescind-v abrogation, annulment, canceling, repeal, dismiss, depose, abolish, retraction, destroy, ignore, repudiate, reconsecrate, divest, (commission, delegate, assign, ensign, entrust)

resist-v refuse, reject, denial, decline, peremptory, repulse, rebuff, discountenance, protest, dissent, revocation, disclaim, (present, bid, propose, move, advance, start, invite)

resolve-v interpret, explain, define, construe, translate, render, find out, illustrate, exemplify, unfold, expound, comment upon, annotate, popularize, disentangle, (misrepresent, garble, distort)

respect-n courtesy, good manners, behavior, breeding, politeness, gentility, polish, presence,

humor, humility, obeisance, (disrespect, rude, insult, repulsive, bitter, acrimonious, sarcastic)

restless-adj disturbance, fidget, disquiet, agitation, unstable, vacillation, fluctuate, vicissitude, alteration, oscillation, unrest, agitation, (stable, stand, keep, remain firm, establish, settled, solid)

restore-v repair, reparation, recruit, reaction, redemption, restitution, relief, reconstruct, redeem, redress, resuscitate, renovate, renew, reestablish, (deteriorate, mutilate, disfigure, blemish, deface)

result-n conclusion, upshot, deduction, inference, corollary, estimation, valuation, appreciation, estimate, deduce, derive, gather, collect, settle, (discover, detect, find, determine, evolve)

retain-v retention, keep, detention, custody, tenacity, firm hold, grasp, gripe, grip, clinch, clench, secure, withhold, detain, hold, reserve, possess, entail, settle, (relinquish, abandon, dispense)

retire-v seclusion, privacy, reclusion, recess, snugness, sequestered, delitescent, hermit, estrangement, voluntary exile, solitude, isolation, loneliness, (social, companionship, comradeship, hospitality)

retort-v retaliation, reprisal, retribution, reciprocation, recrimination, accusation, revenge, reaction, turn upon

retreat-v regress, retirement, withdrawal, recede, counter-motion, re-migration, recession, recidivation, deterioration, (progression, advance, improvement, proceed, forward, forth)

return-v succession, revolve, pulsate, alternate, intermit, steady, punctual, arrive, disembark, advent, reception, welcome, recursion, remigration, (departure, cessation, removal, exit)

revenge-n vengeance, avenged, rancor, vindictiveness, implacability, malevolence, ruthlessness, unforgiving, rankling, (forgiveness, pardon, conciliate, condone, acquit, pacify)

revolt-v resistance, stand, front, oppugnant, opposition, renitency, reluctant, repulse, rebuff, insurrection, against, strong, obstinate, stubborn, (retaliate, retort, turn upon, reciprocate)

rich-adj sufficient, adequate, enough, satisfaction, competence, ample, abundant, wealthy,

luxuriant, fertile, affluent, pregnant, inexhaustible, (insufficient, deficiency, incomplete, shortcoming)

rid-v liberate, disengage, release, free, disband, discharge, unfetter, untie, loose, relax, escape, redeem, deliver, extricate, emancipate, acquit, escape, (confine, imprison, repress, control, hinder)

ride-v chase, give chase, course, hunt, hound, tread, rush upon, run, direct, pursue, quest, follow, prosecute, prowl, engage in, endeavor, search, (retreat, recoil, depart, avoid, evade, seclude)

ridiculous-adj folly, frivolity, irrationality, trifling, ineptitude, negaters, inconsistency, conceit, giddiness, inattention, eccentricity, absurd, idiotic, imbecile, (wise, sapient, reasonable, rational, sensible)

rift-n fissure, breach, rent, split, crack, slit, incision, dissection, decomposition, cutting instrument, sharp, divorce, part, detach, separate, rescind, segregate, (attach, fix, bind, secure, join, hinge)

right-n privilege, allow, sanction, warrant, authorize, ordain, prescribe, constitute, charter, enfranchise, prescribe, presume, absolute, indefeasible,

unalienable, merit,
(infringe, encroach)

ring-*n* resonance, loud,
clang, clatter, noise, roar,
uproar, racket, sonorous,
powerful, thundering, ear-
splitting, deafening,
(inaudible, scarcely, low,
dull, faint, soft, soothing,
melodious)

riot-*n* violence, row,
rumpus, inclemency,
vehemence, impetuosity,
boisterousness, rage,
ferocity, fury, exacerbation,
turbulent, disorderly,
uproarious, frenzied,
(tranquil, mild, reasonable,
cam, still)

ripen-*v* completion,
accomplish, achieve,
fulfillment, performance,
execution, dispatch,
consummation,
culmination, conclusion,
close, final, finished,
(incomplete, neglect,
undone)

rise-*v* ascend, grow, begin,
slope, progress, stir, revolt,
rocket, climb, clamber,
mount, aspire, tower, soar,
hover, spire, excelsior, up
hill, flight, (decline, fall,
drop, lapse, tumble, dip,
descend, sink)

risk-*v* danger, chance,
speculation, venture,
stake, blind bargain,
gamble, fate, hazard,
wager, game, accidental,
indiscriminate, random,
(decision, determination,
purpose, resolution)

ritual-*n* rite, ceremony,
observance, duty,
solemnity, sacrament,
service, worship, duty,
officiate, transfiguration,
consecration, ostentation,
showy, pretentious,
pompous, palatial,
theatrical, dramatic

rival-*n* competition, contest,
opposition, strive, struggle,
scramble, wrestle, spar,
square, exchange,
belligerent, combative,
unpeaceful, quarrelsome,
pugilistic, (harmony,
peace, concord, tranquil)

rivet-*v* attach, join, close,
tight, taut, taught, secure,
set, intervolved, hinge,
unite, connect, fix, bind,
tie, string, pin, nail, bolt,
hasp, clasp, fuse-together,
jam, (separate, rupture,
shatter, carve, cut)

roast-*v* heat, calefaction,
increase of temperature,
melt, burn, combustion,
ignition, warm, chafe,
stove, kindle, toast,
inflame, stew, cook,
seethe, simmer, (cool, fan,
refrigerate, refresh,
congeal)

robust-*adj* strong, mighty,
vigorous, forcible, hard,
adamantine, stout, sturdy,
hardy, powerful, potent,
puissant, valid, resistless,
invincible, impregnable,
able-bodied, (weak,
delicate, soft, limp, feeble)

room-*n* spacious, extensive,
expansive, capacious,

ample, wide-spread, vast, world-wide, uncircumscribed, boundless, capacity, stretch, absence

root-*n* base, basement, plinth, dado, wainscot, foundation, support, substructure, substratum, ground, earth, pavement, floor, paving, flag, carpet, fundamental, built-on, (summit, apex, zenith, pinnacle)

rose-*n* fragrant, aroma, redolence, perfume, bouquet, sweet, aromatic perfume, sachet, scent, spicy, balmy, muscadine, ambrosial, fragrant as a rose, (stench, stick, unclean, offensive, rank)

rot-*v* deteriorate, debase, wane, ebb, recess, retrogradation, decrease, degenerate, impairment, injury, damage, loss, detriment, outrage, pollution, poison, (relieve, refresh, infuse, reform, enhance)

rotation-*n* periodically, intermittent, beat, oscillation, bout, round, revolution, turn, cycle, stated time, routine, succession, return, revolve, pulsate, alternate, (uncertain, capricious, flicker, ramble, spasmodic)

rough-*adj* uneven, scabrous, knotted, gnarled, unpolished, rugged, grain, texture, ripple, corrugated, ruffle, crisp, crumble, (smooth, even, plane, shave, level)

round-*adj* circle, rotund, circlet, ring, areola, hoop, roundlet, annulet, bracelet, armlet, ringlet, eye, loop, wheel, cycle, orb, orbit, ellipse, oval, necklace, collar, noose

routine-*n* custom, habit, rule, standing order, precedent, red-tape, rut, groove, usual, general accustom, naturalize, repeat, prevalent, vogue, etiquette, order of the day, (breached, spontaneous)

row-*v* discord, disagreement, jar, clash, shock, broil, brawl, racket, hubbub, embroilment, disturbance, commotion, quarrel, dispute, embroil, entangle, (harmony, agreement, conciliation, peace, accord)

rude-*adj* graceless, inelegant, harsh, abrupt, dry, stiff, cramped, formal, forced, labored, artificial, mannered, ponderous, turgid, affected, barbarous, uncouth, (graceful, easy, temperate, gentle)

ruin-*n* waste, destroy, dissolution, breaking up, consumption, fall, downfall, perdition, crash, smash, havoc, extinct, annihilation, demolish, suppress, abolish, ravage, devastate, (rectify, flower, evolve)

rumple-*v* disorder,

derangement, confusion, disarray, jumble, huddle, litter, lumber, mash, muddle, complex, intricate, unsymmetrical, unsystematic, untidy, slovenly, (order, uniform, symmetry, arranged)

rush-*v* haste, urgency, acceleration, spurt, spurt, forced, march, dash, velocity, precipitancy, impetuosity, hurry, drive, scramble, bustle, fuss, fidget, flurry, (leisurely, slow, deliberate, quiet, calm)

rusty-*adj* moldy, musty, mildewed, moth-eaten, mucid, rancid, bad, gone bad, touched, effete, rotten, corrupt, tainted, unclean, dirty, filthy, sooty, turbid, (wash, clean, pure, disinfect, neat)

S

salute-*v* respect, regard, consideration, courtesy, attention, deference, reverence, honor, esteem, estimation, veneration, admiration, homage, command, (dishonor, desecrate, insult, affront, outrage)

salvage-*v* get back, recover, regain, retrieve, replevy, redeem, come by one's own, come by, receive, inherit, succeed, realize, treasure up, clear, produce, (loss, incur, rid,

forfeit, lapse)

savage-*adj* cruel, brutal, inhuman, barbarous, fell, untamed, truculent, incendiary, bloodthirsty, murderous, atrocious, fiendish, demoniacal, diabolic, devilish, (benevolent, consideration, kind)

save-*v* economy, frugality, thrift, care, husbandry, retrenchment, prevention of waste, parsimony, sparing, invest, miserly, tightfisted, mercenary, venal, greedy, (liberal, generous, charitable, bounty)

say-*v* speech, locution, talk, parlance, verbal intercourse, oral communication, spoken, lingual, phonetic, unwritten, eloquent, talkative, mouthpiece, language, (stammer, stutter, falter, mumble)

scaffold-*n* support, foundation, base, bearing, footing, hold, place, platform, block, rest, sustentation, aid, prop, stand, truss, stilt, staff, shaft, pediment, (pendant, hanging, dependent, suspended, loose)

scatter-*v* dispersion, disjunction, divergence, dissemination, diffusion, dissipation, distribution, apportionment, spread, sow, strew, dismember, interspersion, (accumulate, heap, lump, pile, stack)

scold-v execrate, beshrew, anathematize, denounce, execration, proscribe, excommunicate, fulminate, threaten, abuse, cross, grumpy, glum, morose, (hug, cuddle, address with affection, serenade)

scratch-v mark, line, stroke, dash, score, stripe, streak, tick, dot, point, notch, nick, asterisk, red letter, jotting, print, imprint, note, annotation, maltreat, abuse, bruise, hurtful, injurious

scruple-n probity, integrity, rectitude, uprightness, honesty, faith, honor, good faith, purity, clean, fairness, fidelity, loyalty, trustworthiness, candor, dignity, (dishonesty, moral turpitude, disloyalty)

scrutiny-n attention, mindfulness, intentness, thought, observance, consideration, reflection, heed, notice, regard, circumspection, study, (abstract, absence, preoccupation, reverie)

secure-v hope, desire, sanguine expectation, trust, confidence, reliance, faith, belief, affiance, assurance, reassurance, promise, well-grounded, presumption, anticipation, (despair, lose, desperate)

see-v view, vision, sight, optics, look, espial, glance, ken, glimpse, peep, gaze,

stare, leer, point of view, demonstrate, eye, field of view, contemplation, regard, survey, (close, blind, shut, cataract)

seethe-v hot, glow, flush, sweat, swelter, bask, smoke, reek, stew, simmer, boil, burn, broil, blaze, flame, smolder, parch, fume, pant, sunny, torrid, tropical, estival, canicular, sultry, oppressive

seize-v reception, carry, bear sway, abstract, hurry off, abduct, steal, ravish, size, pounce, spring upon, swoop, assault, confiscate, sequester, despoil, strip, (restitution, return, restoration, atonement)

send-v delegate, consign, relegate, turn over to, deliver, ship, embark, waft, shunt, transpose, propel, project, throw, fling, cast, pitch, chuck, toss, jerk, heave, shy, (draw, pull, haul, lug, rake, drag, tug)

sensation-n pleasure, bodily enjoyment, animal gratification, luxuriousness, dissipation, titillation, gusto, comfort ease, refreshment, voluptuous, cozy, snug, agreeable, (torment, torture, rack, agonize)

senseless-adj absurd, imbecility, nonsense, paradox, inconsistency, blunder, muddle, bull, slip-slop, anticlimax, farce, rhapsody, farrago, jargon, fustian, twaddle, no meaning, (wise, perception, belief)

sensuous-*adj* feeling, warmth, glow, unction, gusto, fervor, heartiness, cordiality, earnestness, eagerness, ardor, zeal, passion, enthusiasm, blush, flush, penetrating, absorbing, impetuous

sequence-*n* coming after, going after, order, following, consecutive, succession, posteriority, continuation, sequential, alternate, latter, posterior, subsequently, (litter, scatter, confound, tangle)

service-*n* useful, utility, efficacy, efficiency, adequacy, use, stead, avail, help, applicability, subservience, instrumentality, function, value, worth, productive, (worthless, inefficient, unskillful)

settle-*v* pay, discharge, clearance, liquidation, satisfaction, reckoning, arrangement, reimbursement, retribution, reward, expenditure, defray, quit, acquit, (repudiate, protest, dishonor, nullify)

several-*adj* many, numerous, multitude, profusion, large, enormous, array, scores, bushel, majority, multiplication, diverse,

various, populous, crowd, manifold, (few, small, handful, paltry, minority)

shade-*n* cover, screen, cloak, veil, shroud, screen from sight, draw close, curtain, eclipse, mask, disguise, ensconce, muffle, smother, whisper, conceal, hidden, clouded, (enlighten, open, impart)

shake-*v* oscillate, vibrate, liberate, nutation, undulation, pulsation, alternation, flow, flux, wave, swing, beat, wag, dance, lurch, dodge, fluctuate, to and fro, brandish, (steady, unfurl, unfold, without motion)

shame-*n* disgrace, dishonor, tarnish, stain, discredit, degrade, debase, defile, expel, punish, stigmatize, vilify, defame, slur, reprehend, despicable, unworthy, (worthy, glorification, hero, elevate)

shape-*n* form, figure, fashion, carve, cut, chisel, hew, cast, sketch, block, hammer, frame, stamp, build, mold, contour, phase, posture, attitude, sculpt, type, (destroy, shapeless, unformed, deface, mutilate)

shield-*n* defend, protect, guard, ward, preservation, resistance, safeguard, shelter, fortification, hold, armed, screen, shroud, fence, ward off, hinder, asylum, (attack, invade, outbreak, assault, siege)

shift-v deflect, divert, shunt, wear, draw aside, crook, warp, stray, straggle, sidle, diverge, digress, drift, wander, twist, meander, veer, rove, adrift, yaw, (direct, aligned, straight, straightforward)

shock-n false expectation, disappointment, miscalculation, surprise, sudden burst, thunderclap, blow, wonder, bolt of the blue, electrify, astonish, abrupt, startling, (foresight, anticipate, reckon, waiting)

shoot-v death blow, finishing stroke, execution, gallows, fast, speedy, rapid, quick, fleet, nimble, agile, expeditious, express, active, swift, (slow, languor, drawl, retard, relax, slack, tardy)

short-adj concise, brief, terse, close, to the point, exact, neat, compact, laconic, curt, pithy, trenchant, summary, compendious, compress, summarize, (amplify, profuse, drawn out, ramble)

shudder-v cold, shiver, gooseflesh, quake, shake, tremble, diddle, quiver, chill, frigid, nipping, piercing, icy, glacial, frosty, freezing, wintry, bitter, (sunny, torrid, tropical, seethe, broil)

shut-v close, enclose, surround, imprison, enfold, buy, encase, enshrine, confine, desist, stop, give over, break, relinquish, abandon, renounce, defect, withdraw, renounce, desert, forsake

sick-adj ill, disease, ailing, infirmity, seizure, stroke, atrophy, disorder, malady, sore, fever, ulcer, corruption, abscess. consumption, eruption, rash, (healthy, sound, vigor, staunch, robust)

siege-n attack, assault, assail, aggression, offense, incursion, invasion, outbreak, storming, obsession, bombardment, fire, volley, beset, besiege, beleaguer, (defend, forefend, shield, screen)

signal-n insignia, banner, flag, colors, streamer, standard, eagle, post, rocket, important, momentous, salient, prominent, memorable, stirring, eventful, (subordinate, inferior, respectable, tolerable)

simple-adj mere, sheer, stark, bare, faint, light, slight, scanty, limited, meager, insufficient, sparing, so-so, modest, tender, subtle, inappreciable, unimportant (extraordinary, important, unsurpassed)

sincere-adj veracity, truthful, frank, candor,

honesty, fidelity, plain
dealing, genuineness,
scrupulous, honorable,
pure, unfeigned,
outspoken, undisguised,
(sham, pretense, false,
forgery, fabrication)

sink-v plunge, dip, souse,
duck, dive, plumb,
submerge, douse, engulf,
bottom, wallow, descent,
decline, fall, drop,
cadence, subsidence,
tumble, (ascent, rise,
mount, arise, aspire, climb,
clamber)

situation-n circumstance,
phase, position, posture,
attitude, place, point,
terms, regime, footing,
standing, status, occasion,
predicament, event,
juncture

skepticism-n disbelieve,
discredit, doubtful,
uncertainty, misgiving,
demur, distrust, suspicion,
jealousy, qualm, refuse to
believe, dissent, hesitate,
(believe, confide, assured,
positive, satisfied)

sketch-n picture, drawing,
draught, draft, trace, copy,
photograph, image,
likeness, icon, portrait,
representation, illustration,
delineation, depict,
personification,
(misrepresent, distort, bad
likeness)

slender-adj thin, small,
trifling, narrow, close, fine,
thread-like, finespun,
taper, slim, slight-made,

scanty, emaciated, lean,
meager, delicate, gaunt,
skinny, (thick, broad, wide,
ample, extended)

slink-v retreat, turn-tail, fly,
desert, elope, scamper,
sneak, flip, steal away,
decamp, flit, abscond,
levant, skedaddle, escape,
abandon, depart, (pursue,
follow, quest, hunt, seek)

slippery-adj dangerous,
precarious, critical, ticklish,
tumble down, threatening,
ominous, alarming,
crumbling, waterlogged,
top-heavy, unsafe,
hazardous, (safe, secure,
sure, shelter)

slow-adj idle, drone, droll,
dawdle, mope, truant,
lounge, loaf, indolent, lazy,
slothful, lust, remiss, slack,
inert, torpid, sluggish,
languid, supine, heavy,
dull, leaden, listless, (fast,
hasten, lively, agile)

smash-v failure, blunder,
mistake, fault, omission,
miss, oversight, slip, trip,
stumble, claudication,
botchery, scrape, mess,
mishap, collapse, blow,
explosion, misfortune,
(fortunate, attain, secure)

smother-v repress,
suppress, restrain, stifle,
hush, bury, sink, keep
from, withhold, reserve,
ignore, silence, hoodwink,
mystify, puzzle, deceive,
(set right, awaken,
overhear, understand)

snub-v short, brevity,

abbreviated, curtailment, retrench, cut short, scrimp, chop up, hack, hew, clip, dock, prune, shear, shave, mow, crop, compact, (long, span, streak, prolong, outstretched)

sober-*adj* moderate, wise, sane, grave, temperate, abstinent, serious, sedate, staid, solemn, demure, grim, visage, rueful, wan, long-faced, disconsolate, forlorn, (cheerful, happy, smiling, blithe)

soft-*adj* pliable, flexible, sequacity, malleability, plasticity, flaccidity, laxity, clay, wax, butter, dough, pudding, cushion, pillow, feather-bed, mollify, mellow, relax, temper, mash, (hard, rigid, durable)

solution-*n* interpretation, definition, explanation, answer, rationale, meaning, translation, rendering, key, secret, clue, illustration, literal, translate, render, define, (distort, misrepresent, question)

soothe-*v* relieve, moderation, tranquilize, assuage, appease, swag, lull, compose, still, calm, cool, quiet, hush, quell, sober, pacify, alleviate, (violent, impetuous, uproar, riot, ferocity, rage, fury, row)

sore-*adj* pain, suffering, dolor, ache, smart, shooting, twinge, twitch, gripe, headache, hurt, cut, discomfort, spasm, cramp, torture, rack, agonize, (refreshed, regale, relish, treat, comforting, cordial)

sorry-*adj* trifling, care, anxiety, solicitude, trouble, grieved, concern, distress, affliction, woe, bitterness, heartache, broken-hearted, tribulation, desolation, despair, anguish, (overjoyed, entranced, at ease)

sound-*n* stable, unchangeable, constancy, immobility, vitality, fixed, steadfast, firm, fast, steady, balanced, confirmed, valid, immovable, riveted, rooted, settled, (restless, agitated, fitful, spasmodic)

span-*n* length, from end to end, outstretched, lengthy, wiredrawn, stretch out, extend, reach, stretch, elongate, prolong, (cut, chop hack, hew, crop, shave, mow, reap, nip, foreshorten)

special-*adj* individual, particular, peculiar, specific, proper, personal, original, private, respective, definite, determinate, certain, esoteric, (general, universal, impersonal, miscellaneous)

speculate-*v* supposition, assumption, postulation, condition, hypothesis, postulate, theory, proposal,

suggestion, surmise,
chance, venture, stake,
(decision, determination,
design, ambition)

split-v divide, sunder, sever,
abscind, cut, saw, snip,
nib, nip, cleave, rend, slit,
splinter, chip, crack, snap,
break, tear, burst, rend,
rupture, lacerate, mangle,
gash, (join, unite, attach,
affix, bind, secure)

spread-v disperse, scatter,
sow, disseminate, diffuse,
shed, overspread,
dispense, disband,
disembody, dismember,
distribute, strew, straw,
cast, (assemble, collect,
locate, compile, levy)

spring-v hurry, hasten,
accelerate, leap, jump,
hop, bound, vault,
saltation, dance, caper,
curvet, caracole, capriole,
demivolt, buck, trip, bob,
bounce, flounce, start,
(plunge, dip, souse, duck)

sprout-v expand, grow,
offspring, posterity,
progeny, breed, issue,
brook, litter, seed, furrow,
spawn, family,
grandchildren, child, son,
daughter, shoot, olive
branch, spirit, descendant

squat-v place, situate,
locate, localize, put, lay,
set, perch, hive, bivouac,
burrow, encamp, establish,
reposit, cradle, moor,
tether, imbed, inhabit,
settle, abode, (displace,
eject, exile, abnegate)

staff-n director, manager,
governor, rector,
comptroller, supervisor,
intendant, attendant,
squire, usher, page,
servant, footman, flunky,
valet, orderly, messenger,
herdsman, maid

stagger-v disincline,
indispose, shake,
discourage, deter, hold,
restrain, repel, turn aside,
deviation, chill, blunt, calm,
quiet, quench, deprecate,
dissuade, (stimulate,
inspirit, arouse, animate,
incite)

stand-v exist, behave,
subsist, live, breathe,
obtain, occur, event, have
place, prevail, find oneself,
vegetate, real, actual,
positive, absolute,
substantial, (perish,
annihilated, extinct,
exhausted, gone)

stare-v take an interest,
gape, prick up the ears,
see sights, lionize, pry,
curious, inquisitive, burning
with curiosity, curiosity,
inquiring mind,
(indifference, impassive,
have no curiosity)

start-v begin,
commencement, open,
outset, incipience,
inception, introduction,
initial, inauguration, rising
of the curtain, origin,
source, rudiment, genesis,
(end, close, terminate,
conclude, finale, edge)

stay-v prolong, defer, delay,

lay over, suspend, shift, waive, retard, remand, postpone, adjourn, procrastinate, dally, protract, lengthen-out, temporize, linger, loiter, (premature, early, punctual)

steel-n strong, mighty, vigorous, forcible, hard, adamantine, stout, robust, sturdy, hardy, powerful, resistless, impregnable, sovereign, valid, potent, (frail, fragile, shatter, flimsy, unsubstantial, feeble)

step-n pace, rate, tread, stride, gait, port, cadence, carriage, velocity, angular velocity, progress, locomotion, journey, voyage, transit, nomadic, motor, erratic, (remain, stay, stand, ride, pause, rest)

stereotype-n indication, mark, note, stamp, earmark, label, ticket, docket, dot, spot, score, dash, trace, chalk, print, imprint, engrave, symbolize, typify, represent

stiff-adj rigid, hard, stubborn, firm, starched, stark, unbending, unlimber, unyielding, inflexible, tense, indurate, gritty, proof, petrify, crystallization, (soft, pliable, flexible, relax, tender, supple, pliant)

stimulate-v excite, provoke, arouse, inspirit, animate, incite, instigate, actuate, encourage, influence, sway, incline, persuade, overcome, engage, invite, procure, (discourage, dampen, hinder, repel)

stock-v accumulate, amass, hoard, fund, garner, save, reserve, keep, deposit, stow, stack, load, harvest, heap, collect, preserve, conserve, (spend, expend, use, consume, swallow up)

stoop-v low-minded, disgrace, dishonor, demean, degrade, derogate, grovel, sneak, lose caste, sell oneself, dishonest, unscrupulous, fraudulent, (scrupulous, respectful, reputable, candid)

story-n narrative, history, memoir, memorials, annals, chronicle, tradition, legend, tale, journal, life, adventures, experiences, confessions, anecdote, work of fiction

straight-adj rectilinear, direct, even, right, true, in a line, unbent, undeviating, inflexible, align, (deviating, errant, desultory, rambling, stray, curved, arch)

strange-adj exceptional, abnormal, irregular, arbitrary, informal, wandering, eccentric, unusual, uncommon, remarkable, noteworthy, monstrous, wonderful, unexpected, (typical,

streak-*n* variegated, iridescence, play of colors, spottiness, spectrum, rainbow, stripe, speckle, sprinkle, stipple, maculate, dot, tattoo, inlay, polychromatic

stress-*n* labor, work, toil, travail, manual labor, exertion, effort, strain, trouble, operoseness, drudgery, slavery, flagging, hammering, hardworking, strenuous, (repose, rest, sleep, relax, unbend)

strive-*v* endeavor, attempt, speculation, probation, experiment, tempt, attempt, venture, adventure,try hard, push, exertion, contend, contest, (tranquil, calm, peaceable)

stronghold-*n* hold, asylum, refuge, sanctuary, retreat, fastness, keep, last resort, ward, prison, covert, shelter, screen, wing, shield, umbrella, anchor, (attack, assault, charge, aggression)

style-*n* tone, tenor, state, condition, category, estate, lot, case, trim, mood, pickle, plight, fashion, light, complexion, character, structure, format, (inconsequential, unconformity, unrelated)

sublime-*adj* height, altitude, elevation, eminence, pitch, loftiness, tallness, stature, prominence, colossus, giant, tower, soar, (low, depressed, underlie, squat, prostrate)

substance-*n* matter, body, stuff, element, principle, materialistic, object, article, thing, something, tangible, substantial, unspiritual, sensible, physical, (immaterial, spiritual, disembodied, subjective)

succulent-*adj* eatable, edible, esculent, comestible, alimentary, dietetic, culinary, nutritive, potable, bibulous, tasteful, delicacy, gusto, (rank, tasteless, repulsive)

sudden-*adj* instantaneous, abrupt, moment, second, minute, momentary, instant, hasty, lightning, spur of the moment, (perpetual, eternal, everlasting, continual, endless, ceaseless)

suggest-*v* advice, council, recommendation, advocacy, persuasion, mention, acquaint, instruct, inform, authorize, inform, (conceal, suppress, evasion, silence, mystery)

summary-*n* short, brief, curt, compendious, compact, concise, curtail, squat, reduce, (long, lengthy, outstretched, prolong, extend)

T

tackle-*v* undertake, engage, embark, volunteer, promise, contract, take upon one's shoulders, begin, fasten, tie, ligament, strap, rigging, standing, trace, harness, yoke, bandage, brace, roller

tactic-*n* game, policy, execution, manipulation, treatment, campaign, career life, course, conduct, behavior, carriage, demeanor, manner, direction, transact, execute, dispatch, proceed

tale-*n* description, account, statement, report, specification, particulars, summary of facts, catalog, information, fable, parable, apologue, narrative, novel, work of fiction, journal, recital, sketch

talk-*n* speech, locution, parlance, verbal intercourse, oral communication, word of mouth, oratory, elocution, rhetoric, recitation, formal speech, (stammer, hesitation, impediment, stutter, falter)

tangible-*adj* material, bodily, corporeal, physical, somatic, sensible, ponderable, palpable, substantial, objective, impersonal, neuter, unspiritual, (personal, subjective, spiritualize, disembody)

task-*n* exercise, curriculum, explanation, teach, instruct, edify, fatigue, weariness, yawning,

drowsiness, lassitude, tiredness, exhaustion, sweat, faintness, (restore, refresh, revive, repair, relief)

tattler-*n* narrator, scandal-monger, tale-bearer, gossip, many-tongued, rumored, currently, reported, glad tidings, eavesdrop, (observe, swear, hide, close mouthed)

tear-*v* separate, destroy, over-turn, nullify, annul, demolish, crumple up, sunder, divide, cut up, carve, dissect, pull, disintegrate, nip, nib, cleave, snap, break, (join secure, inseparable)

tease-*v* annoy, displease, incommode, discompose, trouble, disquiet, disturb, perplex, molest, tire, irk, vex, mortify, harass, harry, badger, persecute, harrow, (please, agreeable, amusement, charm, delight)

technical-*adj* artistic, scientific, businesslike, talent, ability, ingenuity, cleverness, endowed, skillful, experienced, efficient, qualified, handy, capable, smart, proficient, (stupidity, inexperienced, ignorant)

tell-*v* influence, weight, pressure, preponderence, prevalence, sway, predominance, ascendancy, dominance,

reign, authority,
(impotence, inertness,
irrelevancy, uninfluential,
unconducing)

temper-*n* pervading,
penetrating, absorbing,
strong, sharp, acute,
cutting, piercing, incisive,
caustic, violent, vehement,
warm, rough, boisterous,
rampant, (moderate,
gentle, mild, cool, sober,
calm)

tempt-*v* seduce, entice,
allure, captivate, fascinate,
bewitch, carry away,
charm, conciliate, coax,
lure, tantalize, cajole,
deceive, bribe, influence,
prompt, instigate,
(dissuade, discourage,
hinder)

tender-*adj* offer, proffer,
present, bid, propose,
move, advance, start,
invite, hold out, put
forward, overture, bribe,
give, (refuse, reject,
repulse, rebuff, deny,
decline, nill, repudiate)

tenor-*n* direction, bearing,
course, set, drift, tendency,
incidence, bending,
trending, dip, tack, aim,
collimation, steer, bend,
trend, verge, incline,
(deviation, swerve,
digress, depart, aberration,
sweep)

term-*n* time, duration,
period, stage, space, span,
spell, season, era, limit,
boundary, confine, frontier,
word, vocabulary, name,

nomenclature, verbal,
literal

terrorist-*n* coward, poltroon,
dastard, sneak, recreant,
weak-minded, effeminacy,
timidity, oppressor, tyrant,
firebrand, incendiary,
anarchist, destroyer,
iconoclast, savage,
(benefactor, savior,
courage)

text-*n* copy, design, type,
matter, subject, meaning,
signify, convey, imply,
breathe, indicate, bespeak,
expressive, declaratory,
(nonsense, jargon,
gibberish, jabber, absurd,
vague, balderdash, trash)

thick-*adj* dense, solid,
impenetrable, cohesion,
constipation, consistence,
condense, substantial,
lump, massive, (rarefy,
expand, dilate, subtilize,
sponginess, thin, fine,
flimsy, slight)

thin-*adj* insufficient,
inadequate, deficiency,
imperfection, scarcity,
want, need, lack, scanty,
small, stingy, meager,
poor, spare, starve,
stricken, (sufficient, ample,
abundant, enough,
adequate, full)

thorn-*n* point, spike, spine,
needle, pin, prick, spur,
rowel, barb, spit, cusp,
horn, antler, snag, tag,
bristle, nib, tooth, tusk,
spoke, cog, ratchet,
barbed, spurred, (blunt,
obtund, dull)

thoughtless-*adj* negligent, omission, careless, inattentive, nonchalance, insensibility, heedless, remiss, perfunctory, unmindful, inconsiderate, (careful, regardful, prudent, considerate, provident, cautious)

thread-*n* pass, perforate, penetrate, permeate, enfilade, traverse, journey, worm, passage, wire, string, slip, strip, filament, line, fiber, splinter, ribbon, soft, fragile, inactivity

threaten-*v* inspiring fear, alarming, formidable, perilous, danger, portentous, fearful, dread, shocking, terrible, horrid, ghastly, revolting, awful, terrorize, startle, (hopeful, confident, secure, enthusiastic)

threshold-*n* beginning, entry, inlet, orifice, mouth, portal, portico, door, gate

throw-*v* fling, toss, discharge, shy, propel, project, cast, pitch, chuck, jerk, heave, hurl, dart, lance, tilt, ejaculate, send forth, expel, shot, (draw, drag, tug, tow, trail, train, pull together)

tickle-*v* please, cause pleasure, delight, gladden, make cheerful, captivate, fascinate, enchant, entrance, enrapture, regale, amuse, stimulate, excite, (irritate, annoy, grieve, vex, displease)

tidy-*adj* orderly, regularity, uniformity, symmetry, methodically, ship shape, routine, arrangement, array, series, neat, spruced, primp, prepared, classified, (disorderly, derange, ruffle, untidy, shapeless)

tight-*adj* firm, fast, joined, close, taut, secure, set, intervoled, drunk, tipsy, intoxicated, inebriation, mellow, groggy, (sobriety, teetotaler, water-drinker, separate, scission, loose)

tilt-*v* obliquity, incline, slope, slant, crooked, leaning, bevel, bias, list, twist, swag, cant, lurch, distorted, bend, recumbent, skew, (parallel, coextension, alongside, straight)

timid-*adj* modest, humble, diffident, timorous, bashful, shy, nervous, skittish, coy, sheepish, shamefaced, blushing, reserved, constrained, demure, quiet, private, (self-satisfied, airs, pretentious)

tinsel-*n* luster, sheen, shimmer, reflection, gloss, spangle, brightness, brilliancy, splendor, lucid, illuminate, shine, glow, glimmer, sparkle, dazzle, (dark, dim, dingy, gloomy, shady, obscure, black)

title-*n* name, style, baptism, appellation, designation, surname, description, call, term, denominate, entitle, christen, characterize, specify, distinguish, label, (anonymous, nameless, misnomer, pseudonym, alias, nickname)

tone-n state, condition, category, estate, lot, case, mood, pickle, plight, temper, aspect, appearance, tenor, turn, guise, fashion, light, complexion, style, character, (circumstantial)

tonic-n remedy, help, redress, antidote, prophylactic, antiseptic, corrective, restorative, sedative, cure, physic, medicine, potion, salve, ointment, (poison, leaven, virus, venom, arsenic, fungus, rot, canker)

tool-n instrument, organ, implement, utensil, machine, engine, lathe, gin, mill, gear, tackle, apparatus, appliance, equipment, harness, hammer, fittings

top-n supreme, superior, major, greatest, higher, exceed, distinguished, vault, important, first-rate, excellent, unparalleled, culmination, foremost, (inferior, smaller, bottom diminish, short-coming)

topple-v unbalanced, unequal, difference, uneven, countervail, disparate, over-balanced, top-heavy, lop-sided, inferior, (equal, matched, reach, balanced, equate,

adjust, accommodate, level)

torture-v punish, chastise, castigate, cruelty, brutality, savagery, ferocity, barbarity, inhumanity, vivisection, outrage, persecution, atrocity, (benevolent, kind, well-meaning, amiable, obliging)

total-n complete, integration, entirety, perfection, entire, whole, full, thorough, plenary, undivided, altogether, beginning to end, saturated, limit, sufficient, (deficient, shortcoming, omit, incomplete)

totter-v fluctuate, vary, waver, flounder, flicker, flitter, flit, flutter, shift, shuffle, shake, tremble, vacillate, wamble, sway, oscillate, changing, alternating, mobile, (fixed, steadfast, firm, immovable, tethered)

touch-v contact, abutment, osculation, meet, close, adjoin, graze, coincide, coexist, adhere, deed, act, overt act, gesture, transaction, job, maneuver, (remote, distant, far off, away, apart, asunder)

tower-n pillar, column, obelisk, monument, steeple, spire, minaret, campaniles, turret, dome, cupola, pole, pikestaff, maypole, flagstaff, mountain, height, (low, depress, concave, lowland, underlie)

train-v prepare, make ready, educate, novitiate, cultivate, mature, evolve, pioneer, instruct, edify, tutor, direct, guide, qualify, drill, practice, explain, lecture, task, school, (deceive, conceal, misrepresent)

trample-v destroy, waste, dissolve, break-up, consume, disorganize, fall, downfall, ruin, crash, smash, annihilation, demolish, ravage, devastate, (produce, perform, operate, construct, fabricate)

transport-v ship, tender, transit, remove, displace, relegation, deportation, conveyance, draft, carriage, transition, send, delegate, consign, relegate, retain, keep, preserve)

transpose-v exchange, interchange, reciprocate, shuffle, castling, barter, retaliate, commute, mutual, communicative, intercurrent, (substitute, supplant, supersede, instead of, redeem, equivalent)

trash-n useless, inefficacy, futile, inaptitude, inadequate, insufficient, unskillfulness, unproductive, litter, rubbish, lumber, refuse, rubble, (useful, value,

worth, fruitful, serviceable, prolific)

tremor-n agitation, stir, shake, ripple, jog, jolt, jar, jerk, shock, succussion, trepidation, quiver, quaver, disquiet, perturbation, commotion, turmoil, turbulence, fuss, racket, fits, (calm, quiet, disentangle)

trespass-v transgression, infringement, transcendence, redundance, surpass, go beyond, over-step, exceed, surmount, encroach, infringe, (default, collapse, extricate, eliminate)

tribute-n observe, respectful, deferential, decorous, obsequious, regard, revere, venerate, worship, duty, devotion, salute, inspire, impose, dazzle, (ridicule, disrespectful, irreverent, disparaging)

trip-n journey, excursion, expedition, tour, grand tour, circuit, peregrination, discursion, ramble, pilgrimage, course, ambulation, march, walk, promenade, constitutional, (rest, pause, lull, bivouac)

trouble-n difficulty, irksome, laborious, arduous, awkward, unwieldy, unmanageable, impossible, complicated, impracticable, hopeless, embarrassing, perplexing, (easy, facilitate, smooth)

true-adv verity, gospel, authentic, veracity, accuracy, exactness, precise, delicacy, rigor, mathematical, punctuality, plain, honest, sober, naked, real, actual, (mistake, fault, blunder, error, fallacy, untrue)

trunk-n house, stem, tree, stock, stirps, pedigree, lineage, line, family, tribe, sect, race, clan, genealogy, descent, extraction, birth, ancestry, forefathers, patriarchs

truss-n support, aid, prop, stand, anvil, stay, shore, skid, rib, bandage, sleeper, stirrup, stilts, shoe, sole, heel, splint, outrigger, (suspend, hang, sling, hook up, hitch, fasten to, append)

trust-n believe, credit, give faith, credence, esteem, confide, certain, sure, assured, positive, unhesitating, convinced, accredited, persuasive, impressive, (disputable, uncertain, unworthy)

try-v experiment, endeavor, tempt, attempt, venture, adventure, speculate, tempt fortune, assay, contend, contest, strive, struggle, scramble, wrangle

tube-n channel, passage, way, path, pipe, vessel, tubule, canal, gut, fistula, chimney, flue, tap, funnel, gully, tunnel, shaft, alley, mine, (closure, occlusion, blockade, obstruction)

tug-v effort, exertion, strain, pull, stress, throw, stretch, struggle, spell, spurt, labor, work, toil, travail, drudgery, trouble, pains, duty, exert, strive, (repose, rest, slacken, inactive, recline, halt, pause)

tumble-v trip, stumble, titubate, lurch, pitch, swag, topple, tilt, sprawl, plump, descend, dismount, alight, swoop, stoop, titubation, drop, (climb, clamber, surmount, scale, tower, soar, hover, spire)

tumultuous-adj violent, inclemency, vehemence, might, impetuosity, boisterousness, effervescence, turbulence, severity, ferocity, rage, fury, exacerbation, strain, (moderation, relaxation, tranquilize)

turbulence-n disquiet, perturbation, commotion, turmoil, tumult, hubbub, rout, bustle, fuss, racket, spasm, throe, throb, palpitation, convulsion, disturbance, disorder, restlessness

turn-v rotate, revolution, gyration, circulation, convolution, whir, vortex, whirlpool, whirligig, roll, axis, axle, spindle, pivot, mandrel, swivel, (vibration, alternation, up and down, fluctuation)

twist-v distort, contort,

warp, writhe, deform, misshape, contortion, crooked, grimace, irregular, unsymmetrical, grotesque, deformed, misbegotten, (symmetrical, shapely, uniform, classic, uniform)

twitch-*v* traction, draw, draught, pull, haul, rake, tow, haulage, lug, trail, train, take in tow, wrench, jerk, tousle, tactile, (dart, propel, project, throw, fling, cast, pitch, discharge, bolt, shoot)

type-*n* form, figure, shape, conformation, make, formation, frame, construction, cut, set, build, trim, stamp, cast, mold, fashion, contour, outline, structure, feature, lineament, posture, attitude

U

ugly-*adj* deformity, inelegance, disfigured, blemish, squalor, eyesore, frightful, hideous, odious, uncanny, forbidding, repellent, repulsive, shocking, (form, elegance, grace, beauty, gorgeous)

ulterior-*adj* extraneousness, extrinsically, foreign, alien, strange, ultramontane, excluded, inadmissible, exceptional, (component, integral, element, constituent, ingredient)

ultimatum-*n* decision,

determination, resolve, purpose, resolution, with motive, settled, intent, undertaking, predetermination, design, ambition, (speculation, venture, stake, gamble, chance)

unadorned-*adj* simple, plain, homely, ordinary, unaffected, chaste, severe, ungarnished, disarrange, untrimmed, unvarnished, bald, flat, dull, (ornamented, beautified, ornate, rich, gilt)

unassisted-*adv* encumber, stop, prevent, load, burden, lumber, pack, difficulty, dampen, obstruct, stay, bar, bolt, unaided, hinder, block, impede, (assist, aid, rescue, help, contribute, furnish, relief)

unaware-*adv* uninformed, ignore, unexplored, unknown, blind, unconsciousness, shallow, superficial, (aware, cognizant, conscious of, acquainted, versed, learned, instructed, proficient)

unborn-*adv* non-existence, absence, abeyance, nullity, negative, annihilation, extinction, destruction, abrogate, uncreated, perished, exhausted, gone, lost, departed, (real, actual, positive, absolute)

uncertain-*adv* incertitude, doubt, dubiety, hesitation,

suspense, perplexity,
embarrassment, dilemma,
bewilderment, timidity,
fear, vacillation,
indetermination, vague,
obscure, (certain, unerring,
infallible)

unclog-*adv* liberate,
disengage, release,
enlarge, emancipate,
enfranchise, discharge,
dismiss, deliver, redeem,
extricate, acquit, absolve,
set free, unfetter, untie,
(confine, restraint, hinder,
repress)

unconditional-*adj*
unrestricted, unlimited,
absolute, discretionary,
unassailed, unforced,
unbiased, spontaneous,
free, autonomous,
unclaimed, (dependence,
employ, constraint, liability)

unconscious-*adj*
insensible, impassive,
blind to, unimpressionable,
unfeeling, apathetic,
phlegmatic, dull, frigid,
cold, obtuse, inert, torpid,
sluggish, inactive, languid,
(sentimental, sensible,
romantic)

uncouth-*adj* bad taste,
vulgar, awkward, coarse,
indecorum, misbehavior,
low life, boorishness,
gaudy, unkempt,
unpolished, incondite,
rude, outlandish, (tasteful,
pure, chaste, classical,
artistic)

uncover-*v* divulge, reveal,
break, split, utter, blab,

acknowledge, allow,
concede, grant, admit,
own, avow, disclose,
transpire, confess, visible,
(ambush, hide, mask,
disguise, masquerade)

under-*v* low, underneath,
below, down, neap,
crouched, squat, prostrate,
horizontal, depress,
concave, molehill,
underlie, wallow, (high,
elevated, eminent, exalted,
tall, gigantic)

underhand-*adj* reticence,
reserve, mental,
suppression, evasion,
white lie, silence,
misprision, secretive,
seclusion, hidden, sneak,
skulk, prowl, (inform,
enlighten, acquaint,
communicate)

undermine-*v* cunning,
crafty, artful, skillful, subtle,
feline, profound, contriving,
intriguing, strategic,
diplomatic, artificial,
insidious, stealthy, hidden,
underhand, (free, plain,
outspoken, blunt, direct)

understand-*v* knowledge,
acquaintance, insight,
familiarity, apprehension,
recognition, appreciation,
intuition, perception,
enlightenment, impression,
philosophy, (ignorance,
bewilder, uncertain)

unerring-*adj* unblamed,
blameless, above
suspicion, irreproachable,
venial, harmless, pure,
virtuous, innocent, model,

paragon, perfection, impeccable, (guilt, misbehave, sinful, fault, failure, atrocity)

uneven-*adj* diverse, varied, irregular, rough, multifarious, multiform, various kinds, all sorts, not uniform, lop-sided, unequal, different, partial, over-balanced, (even, level, equal, balance, monotony)

unexplored-*v* hidden, silence, mystery, concealed, darkness, unknown, invisible, impenetrable, undisclosed, unexposed, dormant, unsuspected, (apparent, prominent, flagrant, notorious, distinct)

unfamiliar-*adj* unusual, uncommon, rare, remarkable, unexpected, unaccountable, unconventional, unparalleled, newfangled, grotesque, outlandish, (conventional, ordinary, common, usual)

unfit-*adj* objectionable, unreasonable, unallowable, unjustified, improper, illegal, immoral, wrong, inequitable, partial, unfair, injustice, (right, fit, impartial, moral, reward, recompense, good, just)

unfortunate-*adj* unsuccessful, abortive, at fault, inefficient, ineffectual, foiled, defeated, ruined, broken, unattained,

uncompleted, frustrated, disconcerted, (successful, prosperous, triumphant, victorious)

unfriendly-*adj* hostile, inimical, discord, alienation, estrangement, dislike, hate, heartburning, animosity, malevolence, disaffected, (familiarity, intimacy, fellowship, friendly, welcome, harmony)

unguided-*v* extemporaneous, impulsive, improvised, unprompted, unnatural, unguarded, spontaneous, voluntary, flash, spurt, improvisation, (predetermined, aforethought)

unhappy-*adj* mope, brood, fret, sulk, pine, yearn, repine, regret, despair, refrain from laughter, depressed, gloomy, unlively, melancholy, dismal, somber, (cheering, inspiriting, jovial, hilarious)

union-*n* combination, mixture, junction, unification, synthesis, incorporation, amalgamation, embodiment, coalescence, fusion, blending, (decompose, separate, dissect, unravel)

unique-*adj* non-conformity, unconventional, abnormal, eccentricity, rarity, freak, individual, originality, exceptional, exclusive, eccentric, irregular, (conform, typical, normal, formal, ordinary)

unite-*v* gather, assemble, collect, convene, draw, conclave, accumulate, heap, converge, pile, pyramid, conglomeration, muster, meet, join, cluster, (unassembled. broadcast, stray, disperse, sow)

V

vacant-*adj* absence, inexistent, nonresidence, absenteeism, empty, void, vacuum, truant, unoccupied, uninhabited, devoid, deserted, (present, occupied, inhabited, dwell, fill, domiciled)

vacillate-*v* unsteady, changeable, unsteadfast, fickle, capricious, volatile, frothy, light, giddy, weak, feeble-minded, fidgety, tremulous, hesitate, uncertain, (steady, sound, inflexible, hard, resolute)

vagabond-*n* bad man, wrong-doer, worker of iniquity, evil-doer, sinner, bad example, rascal, scoundrel, villain, miscreant, wretch, reptile, viper, serpent, scamp, (model, paragon, hero, saintly)

vagrant-*n* roving, vagrancy, marching, nomad, gadding, flitting, migration, travel, journey, take wing, emigrate, prowl, roam, range, patrol, traverse, wander, (stagnate, stick, pause, anchor)

vague-*adj* indefinite, indistinct, perplexed, confused, undetermined, loose, ambiguous, mysterious, mystic, transcendental, occult, recondite, abstruse, crabbed, (understand, comprehend, grasp)

value-*n* price, amount, cost, expense, prime cost, charge, figure, demand, damage, fare, hire, wage, remuneration, dues, duty, toll, tax, impose, tallage, levy, gabelle, excise, assessment, benevolence

vanish-*v* disappear, dissolve, fade, melt away, pass, go, avant, be-gone, leave, no trace, retire from sight, efface, evanescent, missing, lost, gone, (appear, view, vista, spectacle, guise, look, visible)

vary-*v* differ, diverse, heterogeneous, distinguishable, modified, other, another, unequal, not the same, unmatched, distinct, characteristic, (uniform, regular, level, always, without exception)

vast-*adj* great, immense, enormous, extreme, inordinate, excessive, extravagant, exorbitant, outrageous, preposterous, swinging, monstrous, over-grown, (small, diminutive, minute, paltry)

veer-v change, alter, vary, wax and wane, modulate, diversify, qualify, tamper with, turn, shift, tack, chop, shuffle, swerve, warp, deviate, turn aside, overt, introvert, resume, (permanent, stationary)

vehemence-adv feeling, emotion, excitability, impetuosity, boisterousness, turbulence, impatience, intolerance, non-enduring, irritability, agitation, (serene, calm, placid, composure, quiet, tranquil)

velocity-n speed, swiftness, rapidity, expedition, activity, acceleration, haste, spurt, rush, dash, race, lively, gallop, move quickly, hasten, whisk, sweep, (retard, relax, slacken, gentle, easy, linger)

vent-v divulge, reveal, break, split, tell, breathe, utter, allow, acknowledge, concede, grant, admit, own, confess, avow, disguise, transpire, come to light, (screen, cover, shade, blinker, veil, curtain)

ventilate-v gust, blast, breeze, squall, gale, storm, tempest, hurricane, whirlwind, wind, blow, fan, respire, breathe, waft, flatulent, issue, bellows, blow-pipe

venture-n trial, endeavor,

attempt, essay, adventure, speculation, probation, experiment, try, strive, tempt, gamble, bet, risk, hazard, accidental, (intend, purpose, design, propose)

verdict-n result, conclusion, upshot, deduction, inference, egotism, illation, estimation, valuation, appreciation, judicature, assessment, ponderous, judgment, (discover, find, determine, evolve)

verge-n edge, brink, brow, brim, margin, border, skirt, rim, flange, side, mouth, jaws, cops, chaps, lip, muzzle, threshold, marginal, conducive, tend, incline, affect, gravitate toward, promote

very-adv fact, reality, existence, nature, truth, gospel, authenticity, veracity, accuracy, exactness, precise, unalloyed, regularity, principal, (error, fallacy, mistake, fault, blunder, heresy, deceit)

vessel-n receptacle, enclosure, recipient, receiver, reservoir, compartment, vase, bushel, barrel, canister, jar, bottle, basket, hopper, crate, cradle, bassinet, hamper, douser, cistern

vexation-n disappointment, mortification, cold comfort, regret, repining, taking on, inquietude, soreness, heartburning, lamentation, hypercriticism, malcontent, (comfort, resignation, content)

vibrate-v fluctuation, vacillation, swing, beat, shake, wag, see-saw, lurch, dodge, oscillate, alternate, undulate, pulsate, beat, dance, curvet, reel, (fixed, steadfast, firm, fast, steady, balanced)

vicious-adj vice, evil-doing, wickedness, iniquity, demerit, sin, immorality, impropriety, indecorum, scandal, laxity, infirmity, weakness, frailty, imperfection, (virtuous, good, innocent, meritorious, deserving)

victim-n pigeon, April fool, laughing stock, flat, greenhorn, fool, dupe, gull, gudgeon, cull, deceived, swallow up, bite, credulous, mistaken, (cheat, swindler, thief, knave, rogue, decoy-duck, trickster)

view-v see, observe, watch, attend to, eye, survey, scan, inspect, glance, behold, discern, perceive, discover, distinguish, recognize, spy, contemplate, (blind, hoodwink, dazzle, dim sighted, wall-eyed)

vigor-n healthy, well, sound, hearty, hale, fresh, green, whole, florid, flush, hardy, stanch, staunch, brave, robust, unscathed, perfect,

excellent, (fever, calenture, inflammation, ailing, disease, sick)

villain-n rascal, scoundrel, miscreant, wretch, reptile, viper, serpent, urchin, delinquent, criminal, malefactor, culprit, thief, murderer, jail-bird, (good, paragon, hero, innocent, good example)

vincible-adj powerless, impotent, unable, incapable, incompetent, inefficient, inept, unfit, disqualified, harmless, defenseless, unfortified, indefensible, pregnable, (powerful, puissant, potent, capable)

vindicate-v justification, warrant, exoneration, exculpation, acquittal, whitewashing, extenuation, softening, mitigation, reply, defence, recrimination, (accusation, charge, imputation, slur, inculpation, exprobration)

vindictive-adj resentful, cantankerous, pugnacious, perverse, querulous, fiery, peppery, passionate, choleric, shrewish, quick, hot, testy, touchy, animosity, exasperation, bitterness

violate-v seduction, defloration, defilement, abuse, rape, incest, social evil, adultery, harem, intrigue, debauch, defile, rampant, lustful, carnal, erotic, voluptuous, (pure, undefiled, modest, delicate)

viper-n snake, serpent, asp, vermin, beast, poison, leaven, virus, venom, arsenic, antimony, nicotine, demon, sting, fang, (remedial, restorative, corrective, palliative, balsamic, narcotic)

virgin-n new, immaculate, immaturity, novel, recent, youth, restore, evergreen, untried, modern, neoteric, new born, (old, ancient, antique, long standing, prime, primitive)

virile-adj strength, power, energy, force, physical force, stamina, muscle, sinew, vitality, athletic, adamant, steel, iron, oak, might, stout, robust, (weak, frail, fragile, languid, poor, rickety, cranky)

virtue-n good, innocent, meritorious, reserving, worthy, correct, moral, righteous, well-intentioned, creditable, laudable, commendable, praiseworthy, admirable, (vicious, corrupt, atrocity, flagrant)

visible-adj perceptibility, conspicuousness, distinctness, appearance, exposure, manifestation, ocular, ocular evidence, demonstrate, field of view, (invisible, indistinct, conceal, hidden)

visit-n courtesy, light, alight,

dismount, debark, disembark, cast anchor, arrive, land, reception, welcome, destination, harbor, haven, port, refuge, (depart, removal, exit, egress, adieu, farewell)

vitality-n life, ability, animation, vital, spark, flame, respiration, wind, breath of live, existence, vivification, nourishment, subsist, quick, tenacious, (die, expire, meet one's death, end, pass away)

vivacious-adj cheerful, genial, gaiety, good humor, glee, light hearted, mirth, merriment, hilarity, exhilaration, amusement, winsome, pleasing, (dreary, flat, dull, mournful, dreadful, depressing)

vivid-adj strong, energetic, forcible, active, intense, deep-dyed, severe, keen, sharp, acute, incisive, trenchant, brisk, rousing, exciting, (inert, inactive, passive, torpid, sluggish, dull, heavy, flat, slack)

vocabulary-n word, term, vocable, name, phrase, root, etymon, derivative, part of speech, grammar, dictionary, lexicon, index, glossary, thesaurus, concordance, literal, verbal, titular, conjugate, exact

vocation-n calling, profession, cloth, faculty, industry, art, industrial arts, craft, mystery, handicraft, trade, commerce, perform, observe, fulfill, obligation, (exempt, free, neglect, relax, excuse, fail)

void-*n* vacant, vacuous, empty, eviscerated, blank, hollow, nominal, null, inane, vanish, evaporate, fade, dissolve, melt away, disappear, nothing, (substantial, exist, object, tangible, being, substance)

volitant-*n* aeronautics, balloon, flying, flight, voyage, sail, put to sea, navigate, warp, luff, scud, boom, drift, course, cruise, row, paddle, pull, maritime, (walk, march, step, tread, pace, plod, wend)

volley-*n* shower, storm, cloud, group, cluster, clump, repeated sounds, report, thud, burst, explosion, discharge, detonation, squib, cracker, rap, snap, (rolling, monotonous)

voluntary-*adv* willing, disposition, inclination, leaning, mood, vein, free, without reluctance, graciously, assent, spontaneous, unasked, unforced, (unwilling, grudgingly, under protest, qualm)

voluptuous-*adj* impure, concupiscent, prurient, lickerish, rampant, lustful, carnal, lewd, lascivious, lecherous, social, evil, smut, unchaste, wanton, debauched, (vestal, virgin, prude, pure, undefiled)

vouch-*v* assert, declaratory, predictor, pronunciation, affirmative, positive, certain, express, explicit, absolute, emphatic, distinct, decided, confident, dogmatic, (dispute, impugn, traverse, rebut, deny)

W

wade-*v* gather, learn, acquire, gain, receive, drink in, obtain, collect, knowledge, information, peruse, pore, industrious, studious, (teach, instruct, edify, tutor, enlighten)

wait-*v* put off, defer, delay, lay over, suspend, shift, waive, retard, remand, postpone, adjourn, procrastinate, dally, prolong, protract, knee back, (early, prime, timely, punctual, forward, prompt)

wall-*n* bar, barrier, turn-stile, gate, portcullis, barricade, defense, breakwater, bulkhead, block, buffer, stopper, dam, weir, drawback, objection, stumbling block, (relief, rescue, lift, aid)

wallop-*v* strike, punish, chastise, castigate, slap, smack, spank, thump, beat, swing, buffet, thresh, thrash pummel, drum, leather, trounce, baste, belabor, pelt, stone, lapidate, torture

want-v desire, wish, fancy, fantasy, need, exigency, mind, inclination, leaning, bent, longing, hankering, inkling, solicitude, anxiety, yearning, coveting, aspiration, (indifferent, cool, unconcerned)

warehouse-n storehouse, closet, depository, repository, stock, accumulate, hoard, stack, promontory, reservoir, receptacle, amass, collect, harvest, save, reserve, (spend, expend, use, consume, spill)

warn-v discourage, dampen, disincline, indispose, stagger, repel, quench, deprecate, induce, deter, dissuade, obstinate, restrain, keep back, (prompt, persuade, bribe, lure, stimulate)

warrant-n dictate, mandate, caveat, decree, writ, ordination, bull, edict, decretal, dispensation, citation, permit, authorize, admission, grant, empower, (prohibit, forbid, disallow, bar, withhold, shut)

wash-v lavatory, laundry, clean, pure, purification, defecation, lustration, abstersion, ablution, disinfect, fumigate, deodorize, immaculate, (mud, mire, quagmire, sludge, slime, slush)

watch-v observe, attend to,

peep, peer, pry, look, witness, contemplate, speculate, cast, discover, distinguish, recognize. spy. behold, demonstrate, (blind, hoodwink, undiscerning, dim sighted)

way-n method, manner, wise, form, mode, fashion, tone, guise, procedure, path, road, route, course, trajectory, orbit, track, beat, means of access, channel, passage, avenue, approach, artery, lane

wear-v impair, injure, damage, loss, detriment, laceration, outrage, havoc, deteriorate, degenerate, decay, dilapidation, rotten, blight, (improve, refine, rectify, enrich, mellow, elaborate)

weave-v produce, perform, operate, do, make, form, construct, fabricate, frame, contrive, manufacture, forge, twine, entwine, twist, interlace, (destroy, ruin, dilapidation, deteriorate, wreck)

wedge-n fusiform, wedge-shaped, triangular, angular, bent, crooked, firm, fast, close, tight, taut, secure, hinge, tether, pin, nail, rivet, jam, dovetail, (sunder, divide, sever, carve, dissect, detach)

ween-v think, hold, opinion, conceive, trow, fancy, apprehend, embrace, assured, positive, satisfied, confident, nurture, credence, secure, impress, (dispute, fallible, uncertain, untrue, distrust, doubt)

weigh-v influence, tell, have a hold upon, magnetize, bear upon, pervade, prevail, dominate, gain, important, rampant, regnant, reign, (irrelevant, unconducive, impotence, inert, powerless)

wheedle-v coax, persuade, prevail, bring round, tempt, seduce, entice, allure, captivate, fascinate, bewitch, carry away, charm, conciliate, lure, tantalize, (remonstrate, dissuade, discourage, averse)

where-v seek, inquire, search, look for, scan, reconnoiter, explore, sound, rummage, ransack, pry, peer, hunt, canvass, investigate, examine, probe, fathom, scrutinize, (answer, respond, reply, rebut)

whet-v sharpen, hone, strop, grind, point, aculeate, picul, set, acute, prickly, thorny, bristling, studded, spike, cutting edge, (obtuse, dull, bluff, render)

whim-n caprice, fancy, humor, crotchet, quirk, freak, maggot, fad, vagary, prank, erratic, eccentric, fitful, hysterical, frivolous, fickle, giddy, volatile, skittish, inconsistent, fanciful, fantastic,

whimsical

whine-n complain, lament, murmur, mutter, grumble, groan, whimper, sob, sigh, mourn, grieve, weep, complain without cause, frown, scowl, (smile, giggle, titter, cheer, chuckle, shout, sing, triumphant)

whisper-n inaudible, low, dull, stifled, muffled, husky, melodious, speak imperfectly, mutter, undertone, faint sound, hoarse, gentle, (blast, loud, swell, clang, holler, scream, piercing, deafening)

whittle-v sunder, divide, subdivide, sever, abscind, cut, snip, nib, nip, cleave, rend, slit, split, rupture, shatter, shiver, crunch, cop, hack, hew, slash, haggle, hackle, lacerate, scramble, mangle, slice

whole-n entire, total, integral, complete, one, individual, unbroken, wholly, altogether, sum total, gross amount, embody, (fractional, fragmentary, section, divided, break, piece, compartment)

wholesale-adj trade, commerce, market, buying and selling, bargain, traffic, business, commercial enterprise, speculation, jobbing, broker, negotiation, dealing, transaction, (retail, over the counter)

whopping-*adj* huge, enormous, giant, immense, monstrosity, corpulent, stout, fat, plump, thumping, thundering, overgrown, puffy, mighty, stupendous, infinite, (small, little, dwarf, unimportant)

wide-*adj* broad, ample, extended, expanded, breadth, latitude, amplitude, diameter, thickness, crassitude, expansion, thicken, dumpy, squab, squat, (narrow, coarctate, taper, slim, scanty)

wield-*v* agitate, shake, convulse, toss, tumble, bandy, brandish, flap, flourish, whisk, jerk, hitch, jolt, joggle, buffet, hustle, disturb, stir, hake up, churn, jounce, wallop, whip, vellicate, palpitate

will-*n* voluntary, volitional, free, optional, discretionary, freedom, spontaneity, originality, of one's own accord, by choice, purposely, deliberately, (compulsory, necessary, needful, compel, requisite)

win-*v* triumph, exultation, proficiency, skill, conquer, victor, succeed, gain, attain, secure, accomplish, master, conquest, carry, secure, effect, complete, (failure, lose, ruined, defeated, broken down)

wince-*v* pain, suffering, physical pain, aching, smart, twinge, twitch, gripe, headache, hurt, sore, discomfort, malaise, spasm, cramp, nightmare, convulsion, writhe, agonize, (sensual, sensuous, pleasure, bodily enjoyment, gratification, creature comforts)

winch-*n* lever, crane, derrick, instrument, tool, implement, utensil, handle, hilt, haft, shaft, shank, blade, trigger, helm, treadle, capstan, lift, heighten, elevate, (crouch, stoop, bend, bow, sink)

wing-*n* leave, depart, exit, egress, exodus, farewell, good-bye, quit, retire, withdraw, remove, wing one's flight, spring, fly, flit, outward bound, (arrive, welcome, here, return, overtake, join)

winsome-*adj* charming, delightful, felicitous, exquisite, lovely, beautiful, ravishing, rapturous, heart-felt, thrilling, ecstatic, beatific, seraphic, heavenly, attractive, (repel, disgust, revolt, nauseate, sicken)

wise-*adj* intelligent, keen, acute, alive, awake, bright, quick, sharp, sage, sapient, sagacious, reasonable, rational, sound, sensible, judicious, strong-minded, unprejudiced, calculating

wish-*n* desire, fantasy, want, need, grasping,

longing, hankering, anxiety, yearning, aspiration, vaulting, ambition, eagerness, zeal, ardor, impatience, (indifferent, undesired, neutral)

wistful-_adj_ thinking, thoughtful, pensive, meditative, reflective, museful, contemplative, speculative, deliberate, studious, sedate, introspective, philosophical, (vacant, unintellectual, unoccupied)

wither-_v_ decrease, dwindle, shrink, contract, narrow, shrivel, collapse, lose flesh, fall away, waste, wane, decay, deteriorate, lessen, pare, reduce, strangle, restrain, file, (expand, spread, extend develop)

withstand-_v_ resist, repugn, reluctant, stand up, strive, bear up, stand firm, refractory, oppose, strike, revolt, front, repulse, insurrection, (reprisal, retort, reaction, reciprocate)

witness-_n_ spectator, beholder, observer, on-looker, eye-witness, bystander, passer by, sight-seer, spy, sentinel, be present, contemplate, survey, curiosity, (retire from sight, disappear, vanish)

wonder-_v_ astonish, amazement, marvel, bewilder, admiration, awe, stupor, fascination, sensation, surprise, wondrous, electrify, stun, confound, dazzle, baffle, stupendous, miraculous, overwhelming

word-_n_ maxim, aphorism, saying, adage, saw, proverb, sentence, motto, axiom, reflection, conclusion, term, name, phrase, part of speech, dictionary, vocabulary, literal, concordance

workmanship-_n_ produce, perform, operate, flower, bear fruit, fructify, create, beget, generate, hatch, develop, form, prolific, labor, build, edify, pride, (destroy, perish, demolish, tear up, dispel, nullify)

worldly-_adj_ atheist, septic, unbeliever, deist, infidel, heathen, alien, gentile, freethinker, rationalist, materialistic, agnostic, disbelieve, doubt, (worship, inspire, revere, adore, bow down and worship)

worn-_v_ weak, battered, shattered, pulled down, seedy, altered, fatigued, weary, drowsy, drooping, haggard, toil, footsore, weatherbeaten, faint, exhausted, prostrate, (reinvigorate, freshen up)

worse-_adv_ deteriorate, degenerate, wane, decrease, retrograde,

decline, droop, sink, from
bad to worse, recession,
decay, decrepitude,
(improve, mend, advance,
reform, ripen, better,
correct)

worthy-*adj* virtuous, good,
innocent, meritorious,
deserving, righteous, well-
intentioned, creditable,
laudable, commendable,
praiseworthy, excellent,
admirable, sterling, pure,
noble, admirable

wrangle-*v* discord, quarrel,
dispute, tiff, squabble,
altercation, words, jangle,
babble, broil, brawl, racket,
disturbance, dissent,
dissension, (agree, accord,
harmonize, concord,
united, allied)

write-*v* record, pen, scribe,
transcribe, copy, scribble,
scrawl, scrabble, scratch,
interline, write down,
compose, print, publish,
compositor, manuscript,
shorthand, handwriting

Y

yarn-*n* exaggeration,
expansion, hyperbole,
stretch, strain, coloring,
caricature, extravagance,
nonsense, fringe,
embroidery, traveler's tale,
overestimate, wire, string,
thread, twine, cord, rope

yawn-*n* nod, get sleepy,
snooze, nap, dream,
sleepy, indolent, lazy,
slothful, idle, lust, remiss,

slack, inert, sluggish,
languid, supine, heavy,
dull, leaden, listless,
(active, quick, prompt,
alert, spry, sharp)

yearling-*n* infant, babe,
child, youth, stripling,
youngster, younker,
weanling, papoose,
bambino, seedling,
whipper-snapper, (veteran,
old man, seer, patriarch,
centenarian, old stager,
forefathers)

yeast-*n* leaven, ferment,
barm, light, subtile, airy,
imponderable, astatic,
weightless, ethereal,
sublimated,
uncompressed, volatile,
buoyant, floating, portable,
(heavy, massive, lead,
millstone)

yell-*v* cry, vociferate, raise,
shout, roar, bawl, brawl,
hop, whoop, bellow, howl,
scream, screech, screak,
shriek, squeak, squall,
whine, pule, pipe, cheer,
hoot, grumble, moan,
groan

yield-*v* succumb, submit,
bend, resign, defer,
submissive,
surrender, capitulate,
retreat, downtrodden,
pliant, undefended, permit,
relinquish, sanction,
(overpower, struggle,
unbending, forbid, refuse)

yoke-*n* lock, latch, belay,
brace, hook, grapple,
leash, couple,
accouplement, link,

bracket, bridge over, span, clamp, (sever, rupture, segregate, breach, rescind, divide)

yokel-*n* bungler, blunderer, marplot, fumbler, lubber, duffer, awkward, squad, greenhorn, clod, muff, (proficient, expert, adept, connoisseur, veteran)

yokemate-*n* spouse, consort, husband, wife, better half, mate, helpmate, match, betrothment, promise, (unmarried, bachelor, virgin, single, celibacy)

yonder-*adj* distant, far-off, remote, telescopic, distal, stretching, ulterior, transmarine, span, stride, faraway, farther, further, beyond, far and wide, (near, close, no great distance, nigh, within reach)

yore-*n* formerly, of old, last, latter, retrospective, time immemorial, olden, forgotten, extinct, gone by, ancestral, (anticipate, millennium, advent, look forward, eventual)

young-*adj* youthful, juvenile, green, callow, budding, sappy, beardless, under age, junior, infant, minor, pupilage, puberty, prime, (seniority, elder, longevity, aged, antiquated, decay)

Z

zany-*adj* fool, idiot, ninny

tomfoolery, wiseacre, simpleton, witling, donkey, (authority, luminary, wise)

zeal-*adj* quick, prompt, yare, instant, ready, alert, spry, sharp, smart, fast, swift, expeditious, awake, enterprising, industrious, diligent, (indolent, lazy, slothful, idle, remiss)

zealot-*n* bigot, intolerant, obstinate, immovability, inflexibility, prejudgement, opinionist, enthusiast, tenacious, (changeful, idle, withdraw from, relinquish)

zealous-*adj* eager, animated, resolute, steadfast, vivacious, diligent, fiery, brisk

zero-*n* nothing, naught, cipher, none, no one, unsubstantial, blank, void, immaterial, groundless, nonentity, (substantial, thing, object, something

zest-*n* pleasure, gratification, enjoyment, fruition, delectation, relish, gusto, satisfaction, content, well-being, snugness, comfort, amusement, happiness, (concern, grief, sorrow, distress, affliction, woe)

zigzag-*v* diversion, digression, departure, aberration, divergence, detour, circuit, wander, vagrant, by-paths and crooked ways, oblique motion, deviate, swerve, (toward, aim, line, path, road, range)